DISCOVERING THE
AMERICAN PAST

DISCOVERING THE AMERICAN PAST

A Look at the Evidence

FIFTH EDITION

✳ **VOLUME TWO: since 1865** ✳

William Bruce Wheeler
University of Tennessee

Susan D. Becker
University of Tennessee, Emerita

Houghton Mifflin Company   BOSTON   NEW YORK

Editor-in-Chief: Jean L. Woy
Sponsoring Editor: Colleen Shanley Kyle
Associate Editor: Leah Strauss
Project Editor: Carla Thompson
Editorial Assistant: Christian Downey
Production/Design Coordinator: Lisa Jelly Smith
Manufacturing Manager: Florence Cadran
Senior Marketing Manager: Sandra McGuire
Marketing Assistant: Jim David

Cover Design: Jonathan Wallen/National Archives
Cover Image: Documents from the San Francisco Office of Immigration and Naturalization;
photo of Angel Island

*For permission to use copyrighted material, grateful acknowledgment is made to the
copyright holders listed on pages 309–310, which are hereby considered an extension of
the copyright page.*

Printed in the U.S.A.

Library of Congress Control Number: 2001131560

ISBN: 0-618-10225-6

1 2 3 4 5 6 7 8 9-QF-05 04 03 02 01

Contents

✳ CHAPTER EIGHT ✳

Presidential Leadership, Public Opinion, and the Coming of World War II: The USS *Greer* Incident, September 4, 1941

✳ CHAPTER NINE ✳

Separate but Equal? African American Educational Opportunities and the *Brown* Decision

✳ CHAPTER TEN ✳

A Generation in War and Turmoil: The Agony of Vietnam

✳ CHAPTER ELEVEN ✳

A Nation of Immigrants:
The Fourth Wave in California

Preface

The presidential election of 2000 was an incredibly exciting, confusing, and frustrating experience for our country. But as commentator after commentator noted, the election was also "a history teacher's dream." Millions of students—and a surprising number of adult Americans—were suddenly, somewhat painfully, educated about the origins, role, and philosophy of the electoral college. The previously obscure, even unknown, disputed election of 1876 between Rutherford Hayes and Samuel Tilden took on new relevance. Both state and federal judges combed the past for precedents to help them make important decisions in the present. And finally, questions about the evidence of the votes and the methods by which they were counted simply could not be settled completely and to everyone's satisfaction.

We live in a complex world, and we strongly believe that students need help in developing the skills of critical thinking so essential for coping with life in the twenty-first century. How can we rely on statements made by a president of the United States, any other world leader, the chairman of the Federal Reserve Board, a member of Congress, a radio talk show host, a TV newscaster, or a professor unless we are able to examine and analyze the available evidence to understand how it is being used? How can we ourselves learn to use evidence intelligently when we write a report, make a public address, or participate in a debate? The subject of this volume is American history, but the important skills of examination, analysis, and proper use of evidence are important to every person in every vocation.

In *Discovering the American Past: A Look at the Evidence*, we show students the importance of acquiring and sharpening these skills. Moreover, as they acquire or hone these skills, students generally discover that they enjoy "doing history," welcome the opportunity to become active learners, retain more historical knowledge, and are eager to solve a series of historical problems themselves rather than simply being told about the past. Unlike a source reader, this book prompts students actually to *analyze* a wide variety of authentic primary-source material, make inferences, and draw conclusions based on the available evidence, much in the same way that historians do.

As in previous editions, we try to expose students to the broad scope of the American experience by providing a mixture of types of historical problems and a balance among political, social, diplomatic, economic, intellectual, and cultural history. This wide variety of historical topics and events engages students' interest and rounds out their view of American history.

✳ FORMAT OF THE BOOK ✳

Historians are fully aware that everything that is preserved from the past can be used as evidence to solve historical problems. In that spirit, we have included as many different *types* of historical evidence as we could. Almost every chapter gives students the opportunity to work with a different type of evidence: works of art, first-person accounts, trial transcripts, statistics, maps, letters, charts, biographical sketches, court decisions, music lyrics, prescriptive literature, newspaper accounts, congressional debates, speeches, diaries, proclamations and laws, political cartoons, photographs, architectural plans, advertisements, posters, film reviews, fiction, memoirs, and oral interviews. In this book, then, we have created a kind of historical sampler that we believe will help students learn the methods and skills historians use, as well as help them learn historical content.

Each type of historical evidence is combined with an introduction to the appropriate methodology in an effort to teach students a wide variety of research skills. As much as possible, we have tried to let the evidence speak for itself and have avoided leading students to one particular interpretation or another. This approach is effective in many different classroom situations, including seminars, small classes, discussion sections, and large lecture classes. Indeed, we have found that the previous editions of *Discovering the American Past* have proven themselves equally stimulating and effective in very large classes as well as in very small ones.

Each chapter is divided into six parts: The Problem, Background, The Method, The Evidence, Questions to Consider, and Epilogue. Each of the parts relates to or builds upon the others, creating a uniquely integrated chapter structure that helps guide the reader through the analytical process. "The Problem" section begins with a brief discussion of the central issues of the chapter and then states the questions students will explore. A "Background" section follows, designed to help students understand the historical context of the problem. The section called "The Method" gives students suggestions for studying and analyzing the evidence. "The Evidence" section is the heart of the chapter, providing a variety of primary source material on the particular historical event or issue described in the chapter's "Problem" section. The section called "Questions to Consider" focuses students' attention on specific evidence and on linkages among different evidence material. The "Epilogue" section gives the aftermath or the historical outcome of the evidence—what happened to the people involved, who won the election, the results of a debate, and so on.

❋ CHANGES IN THE FIFTH EDITION ❋

In response to student evaluations and faculty reviews, we have made significant alterations in the content of this edition. There are five new chapters, three in Volume I and two in Volume II.

In Volume I, we have rewritten Chapter 3 to give students a broader, more diverse view of Americans in the late colonial period. Demographic and statistical material from both the Chesapeake and New England colonies allows students to make regional comparisons as well as learn to use such data to describe people who were not famous. Chapter 9 focuses on the reintroduction of the Wilmot Proviso and the subsequent congressional debates of 1847 about the westward expansion of slavery. Chapter 11 utilizes the political cartoons of Thomas Nast and Matthew Morgan as a window into the important Reconstruction issues of the election of 1872.

Although the hard-fought battle for woman suffrage was won in 1920 with the passage of the Nineteenth Amendment, many social, economic, and political questions about women's place remained. In Volume II, Chapter 6 looks at women's issues during the crucial period of the 1920s. Chapter 11 emphasizes immigration as one of the main themes of American history, examining the "fourth wave" of immigrants in California during the latter part of the twentieth century.

❋ INSTRUCTOR'S RESOURCE MANUAL ❋

Because we value the teaching of American history and yet fully understand how difficult it is to do it well, we have written our own Instructor's Resource Manual to accompany *Discovering the American Past*. In this manual, we explain our specific content and skills objectives for each chapter, and we include an expanded discussion of the method and evidence sections. We also answer some of the questions that students often ask about the material in each problem. Our suggestions for various ways of teaching and for evaluating the students' learning draw not only upon our own experiences but also upon the experiences of those of you who have shared your classroom ideas with us. Finally, we wrote brief, updated bibliographic essays for each problem.

✳ ACKNOWLEDGMENTS ✳

We would like to thank all the students and instructors who have helped us in developing and refining our ideas for the fifth edition. In addition to our colleagues across the United States, we would like to thank especially our colleagues at the University of Tennessee who offered suggestions and read chapter drafts, along with Penny Hamilton, Kim Harrison, and Denise Barnaby who helped in preparing the manuscript. At Houghton Mifflin, we are indebted to Colleen Kyle, Leah Strauss, and Carla Thompson for their editorial assistance. Finally, the colleagues at other institutions who reviewed chapter drafts made significant contributions to this edition, and we would like to thank them for their generosity, both in time and in helpful ideas and specific suggestions:

Jamie Bronstein, *New Mexico State University*
Eliga H. Gould, *University of New Hampshire*
Donna Cooper Graves, *University of Tennessee—Martin*
Gaylen Lewis, *Bakersfield College*
Linda Przybyszewski, *University of Cincinnati*
Elizabeth Rose, *Trinity College*
Clarice Stasz, *Sonoma State University*
Michael Topp, *University of Texas—El Paso*
Lynn Y. Weiner, *Roosevelt University*
Robert S. Wolff, *Central Connecticut State University*

As with our four previous editions, we dedicate these volumes to all our colleagues who seek to offer a challenging and stimulating academic experience to their students, and to those students themselves, who make all our work worthwhile.

W. B. W.
S. D. B.

DISCOVERING THE AMERICAN PAST

1

Grant, Greeley, and the Popular Press: The Presidential Election of 1872

✱ THE PROBLEM ✱

By 1872, it appeared that Reconstruction was in serious trouble. Although Congress had increased the powers of military governors in the states of the former Confederacy, many southern whites remained fiercely unrepentant and resisted—sometimes violently— efforts to grant citizenship and voting rights to former slaves. For the most part African Americans remained landless and uneducated, making them highly vulnerable to white land- owners and unscrupulous election officials. More serious, among north- ern white voters the zeal for recon- structing the South was beginning to wane, as new issues and concerns, such as government corruption, civil service reform, continued westward expansion and conflict with Native Americans, currency inflation, and the rise of industry, vied with one another for people's attention.

In May 1872, a group of disillu- sioned men broke with the Grant ad- ministration and the Republican party and held their own convention in Cin- cinnati, Ohio. Calling themselves Liberal Republicans, they formally nominated the widely known and con- troversial *New York Tribune* editor Horace Greeley as the party's presi- dential candidate and Missouri Gover- nor B. Gratz Brown as his running mate. In a letter accepting the conven- tion's nomination, Greeley called for an end to the failed experiment of Re- construction, asserting that he had "the confident trust that the masses of our countrymen North and South are eager to clasp hands across the bloody chasm which has too long divided

CHAPTER 1

GRANT, GREELEY,
AND THE POPULAR
PRESS: THE
PRESIDENTIAL
ELECTION OF 1872

them. . . ."[1] Hoping to turn the Grant administration out of office, the Democrats also nominated Greeley and Brown.

What began as a contest over opposing philosophies and stands on issues such as Reconstruction, however, soon turned into one of the most vicious and personal presidential campaigns in American history. To be sure, some previous presidential contests had been ugly affairs as well (especially those of 1800 and 1828), but the campaign of 1872 seemed to descend to a new low in political vituperation and smear tactics. By November 1872, no office seeker was left unscathed.[2]

Although no one who participated in the 1872 presidential race escaped blame, two people in particular were among the most responsible: Thomas Nast and Matthew Somerville (Matt) Morgan. Nast (1840–1902) was the chief political cartoonist for the popular *Harper's Weekly,* while Morgan (1839–1890) was Nast's opposite on the rival *Frank Leslie's Illustrated Newspaper.* Two of the most talented illustrators of their time, Nast and Morgan were in large part responsible for their respective weekly publications reaching circulations of 100,000 by 1872, the year that both men were at the zeniths of their power and influence.

Your tasks in this chapter are to analyze the political cartoons of both Thomas Nast and Matt Morgan, and then, using those cartoons, to answer the following questions:

1. How did each side attempt to portray the other? the respective presidential candidates (Grant and Greeley)?
2. What were the principal issues the cartoons attempted to address? Which issues did they *not* address or avoid addressing?
3. How did each side attempt to deal with Reconstruction in the presidential election of 1872?

For those who maintain that recent presidential contests have reached a new level of personal attacks and general nastiness, the 1872 election is a much-needed corrective.

1. For Greeley's acceptance letter see William Gillette, "Election of 1872," in Arthur M. Schlesinger Jr., ed., *History of American Presidential Elections* (New York: Chelsea House, 1971), Vol. II, p. 1359.
2. An excellent book on the earliest "nasty" election is Bernard A. Weisberger's *America Afire: Jefferson, Adams, and the Revolutionary Election of 1800* (New York: William Morrow, 2000).

❉ BACKGROUND ❉

Although Radical Republicans[3] outdid each other in oratorical eulogies to Abraham Lincoln, secretly they were not altogether displeased by the death of the president. Not only could the Radical Republicans then use Lincoln as a martyr for their own cause, but also they had reason to believe that Lincoln's successor, Andrew Johnson of Tennessee, would be more sympathetic to their plans than the late president had been. After all, Johnson had been a harsh military governor of Tennessee (1862–1864) who had said many times that treason "must be made odious, and the traitors must be punished and impoverished."[4]

Yet it did not take Radical Republicans long to realize that President Andrew Johnson was not one of them. Although he had spoken harshly, he pardoned around 13,000 former Confederates, who quickly captured control of southern state governments and congressional delegations. Many northerners were shocked to see former Confederate officers and officials, and even former Confederate Vice President Alexander Stephens, returned to Washington. At the same time, the new southern state legislatures passed a series of laws, known collectively as black codes, that so severely restricted the rights of former slaves that they were all but slaves again. Moreover, Johnson privately told southerners that he opposed the Fourteenth Amendment to the Constitution, intended to confer full civil rights on the newly freed slaves. When Radical Republicans in Congress attempted to enact harsher measures, Johnson vetoed them and, simultaneously, appeared to do little to combat the widespread defiance of white southerners, including insulting federal troops, desecrating the American flag, and participating in organized resistance groups such as the Ku Klux Klan.

The congressional elections of 1866 gave Radical Republicans enough seats in Congress to override Johnson's vetoes. Beginning in March 1867, Congress passed a series of Reconstruction acts that divided the South into five military districts, to be ruled by military commanders under martial law. Southern states had to ratify the Fourteenth Amendment and institute African American suffrage before being allowed to take their formal places in the Union. The Freedmen's Bureau, founded in 1865, was given additional federal support to set up schools and hospitals for African Americans, negotiate labor contracts, and, with military assistance, monitor elections. When President Johnson attempted to block these acts and purposely violated the Tenure of Office Act and the Command of the Army Act (both of which were Radical Republican measures passed over his vetoes),

3. The Radical Republicans were the left wing of the Republican party. They favored the abolition of slavery, a harsher policy against the defeated South, and full equality for African Americans.
4. See his remarks on the fall of Richmond, April 3, 1865, in LeRoy P. Graf, ed., *The Papers of Andrew Johnson* (Knoxville: University of Tennessee Press, 1986), Vol. VII, p. 545.

CHAPTER 1

GRANT, GREELEY,
AND THE POPULAR
PRESS: THE
PRESIDENTIAL
ELECTION OF 1872

he was impeached by Congress in 1868, but fell one vote short of the two-thirds required to remove him.

With the impotent Johnson left to serve out the final months of his term, Radical Republicans picked the popular war hero General Ulysses Grant as the Republican party's 1868 presidential nominee. Although it was not widely known at the time, Grant had harbored presidential ambitions as early as 1863. At war's end, he set out on a series of national tours on which he attended celebrations in his honor, received honorary degrees, delivered carefully written noncontroversial speeches, and attended funerals of his comrades. A far more wily politician than he was credited with being, Grant simultaneously stayed on good terms with Andrew Johnson while privately cultivating the president's enemies. Only in early 1868 did Johnson fully realize what Grant was doing. In a conversation with Johnson, Gideon Welles told Johnson that "Grant is going over." Ruefully, Johnson replied, "Yes." The open break came in January of 1868.[5] After Grant won the 1868 presidential race in a very close vote (versus the Democratic governor of New York, Horatio Seymour), Johnson bitterly refused to attend the new president's inauguration.

The political skills that helped Grant reach the presidency seemed to abandon him once he got there. A series of scandals rocked the administration, two of the most prominent occurring before 1872 and involving the president's brother-in-law in a scheme to corner the gold market and his vice president Schuyler Colfax who, along with some Republican congressmen, was linked to a fraudulent construction company (the Credit Mobilier) designed to skim off government funds appropriated for the Union Pacific Railroad (Colfax was dropped from the Republican ticket in 1872). In addition, the Grant administration increased tariff rates in 1870 (thus driving up the prices for certain goods), reinstituted paper money in 1871 (to inflate the currency), opposed civil service reform, and advocated what one historian called a "farcical plan" to annex the Dominican Republic. As one disillusioned Republican said of Grant, the "rascals . . . know they can twist him around their thumb by flattering him."[6] Reconstruction in the South seemed as if it would never end.

By early 1872, a diverse group of editors, professional men, businessmen, disappointed office seekers, upper-class intellectuals, and reform-minded Republicans was determined to overthrow the Grant administration. Calling themselves Liberal Republicans, they gathered in Cincinnati in May 1872 to establish a new political party to oust the "stalwart" Republicans.

Deciding who would be the standard bearer of such a disparate conglomeration was no easy matter. U.S. Supreme Court Chief Justice Salmon P. Chase was available and eager, but he had been a perennial candidate who, it was felt, could never beat Grant. Venerable Senator Charles Sumner of Massachusetts was in poor health and former Minister to Great Britain Charles

5. See William S. McFeely, *Grant: A Biography* (New York: Norton, 1981), p. 263. Gideon Welles (1802–1878) was U.S. Secretary of the Navy, 1861–1869.

6. Gillette, "Election of 1872," pp. 1303, 1307.

Francis Adams (son of former President John Quincy Adams) was considered a poor campaigner and too aristocratic (he had opposed universal suffrage). Senator Carl Schurz of Missouri was one of the original founders of the Liberal Republicans, but he was ineligible because of his foreign birth (Germany). Missouri Governor B. Gratz Brown was widely known to be a heavy drinker, and U.S. Supreme Court Associate Justice David Davis had written some court decisions that were unpopular. Finally, on the sixth ballot, the Cincinnati convention nominated *New York Tribune* editor Horace Greeley.

Horace Greeley had made no secret of the fact that he yearned to be the Liberal Republicans' presidential candidate. Born into a poor New Hampshire family in 1811, Greeley was considered a child prodigy in the tiny community of Amherst. But the family was evicted from its farm when Horace was nine years old, and he was unable to attend school past the age of thirteen. Apprenticed to a printer, he worked his way up from apprentice to journeyman to printer and finally to editor of a number of newspapers, most of which folded for lack of readers. In 1841, his fortune turned, as he became editor of the *New York Tribune* and built that paper into one of the largest and most influential in the nation. Greeley knew great talent when he saw it, employing at various times Charles Dana, Margaret Fuller, and George Ripley. Authors whose work was accepted for inclusion in the *Tribune* included Ralph Waldo Emerson, Nathaniel Hawthorne, Walt Whitman (first published in the *Tribune*), and Karl Marx (on the revolutions of

1848). A three-month term in the U.S. House of Representatives (filling out the term of a congressman removed from office) was the only office Greeley had held previously, although he had sought a seat in the U.S. Senate and the governorship of New York.

The Greeley candidacy had several liabilities. To begin with, over the years Greeley's editorials in the *Tribune* had made him many enemies. As early as 1853, he had confessed to William Seward that a man "says so many things in the course of thirty years that may be quoted against him. . . ."[7] In addition, in his years at the *Tribune,* Greeley had advocated a number of causes, including prohibition (his father almost certainly was an alcoholic), vegetarianism, changing the name of the United States to Columbia, opposing women's corsets, and other ideas that made him appear to some people as an eccentric. Finally, Greeley was on record as criticizing the Democratic party, whose support he certainly would need to overthrow Grant, and being at odds with key provisions of his own party's platform. Hearing of Greeley's nomination, one politician exclaimed, "Six weeks ago I did not suppose that any considerable number of men, outside of a Lunatic Asylum, would nominate Greeley for President."[8]

No sooner had the Liberal Republicans' Cincinnati convention concluded than the nation's newspapers and newsmagazines began to take aim at one presidential candidate or the

7. Glyndon G. Van Deusen, *Horace Greeley, Nineteenth-Century Crusader* (Philadelphia: University of Pennsylvania Press, 1953), p. 414.
8. Gillette, "Election of 1872," p. 1316.

CHAPTER 1

GRANT, GREELEY,
AND THE POPULAR
PRESS: THE
PRESIDENTIAL
ELECTION OF 1872

other. By 1872, the illustrated weekly newspaper or newsmagazine was the most influential medium in the United States, and the editorial cartoonists or illustrators were the crown princes of that medium.

The first successful illustrated weekly newspaper in the United States was *Frank Leslie's Illustrated Newspaper,* whose first issue was published on December 15, 1855. The newspaper's founder, whose real name was Henry Carter, was born near London, England, in 1821. According to legend, Carter signed his illustrations with the pseudonym "Frank Leslie" so that his disapproving father would not discover that he had taken up a career in illustration. Immigrating to the United States in 1848 in search of more economic opportunity, Frank Leslie (as he now called himself) made a fortune publishing *Frank Leslie's Illustrated Newspaper* and other papers and magazines. At one time employing over a hundred artists, engravers, and printers, Leslie set the standards for illustrated newspapers and magazines that others followed. He brought in illustrator-cartoonist Matt Morgan from Great Britain specifically for the paper's coverage of the 1872 election.

Harper's Weekly was the brainchild of Fletcher Harper, one of four brothers who founded and operated Harper Brothers printing and publishing company.[9] By 1830, Harper Brothers was the largest book publisher in the United States. In 1857, Fletcher Harper established *Harper's Weekly* and in 1859, he lured illustrator-cartoonist Thomas Nast from rival Frank Leslie.

Born in the German Palatinate (one of the German states) in 1840, Nast immigrated with his family to New York City in 1846, and by the age of fifteen he was among Leslie's "stable" of artists. Throughout his career, Nast produced more than three thousand cartoons, book illustrations, and printings (he did 150 drawings for *Harper's Weekly* in 1872 alone). He is credited with originating the modern depiction of Santa Claus, the Republican elephant, and the Democratic donkey. Paid the princely sum of $18,000 by *Harper's Weekly* in 1872, Nast had the complete support of owner-publisher Fletcher Harper, even when editor George William Curtis "begged the artist to hold his fire."[10] When it came to holding his fire, Thomas Nast never did.

As you examine and analyze the political cartoons by Matt Morgan from *Frank Leslie's Illustrated Newspaper* and Thomas Nast from *Harper's Weekly*, consider the following questions:

1. How did each side attempt to portray the other? the respective presidential candidates (Grant and Greeley)?
2. What were the principal issues the cartoons attempted to address? Which issues did they *not* address or avoid addressing?
3. How did each side attempt to deal with Reconstruction in the presidential election of 1872?

Be sure to take notes as you go along.

9. The Harper firm was founded in 1817. Fletcher Harper joined Harper Brothers in 1825.

10. J. Chal Vinson, *Thomas Nast, Political Cartoonist* (Athens, Ga.: University of Georgia Press, 1967), p. 24.

✵ THE METHOD ✵

Although the presidential election of 1872 perhaps represents the zenith of the political cartoon as an influential art form, cartoons and caricatures had a long tradition of influence in both Europe and America before 1872. English artists established the cartoon style that eventually made *Punch* (founded in 1841) one of the liveliest periodicals on both sides of the Atlantic. In America, Benjamin Franklin is traditionally credited with publishing the first newspaper cartoon in the colonies, in 1754—the multidivided snake, each part of the snake representing one colony, with the ominous warning "Join or Die." By the time Andrew Jackson sought the presidency in the 1820s, the political cartoon had become a regular and popular feature of American political life. Lacking modern sophistication, these cartoons nonetheless influenced people far more than the printed word.

Like the newspaper editorial, the political cartoon is intended to do much more than objectively report events. Instead, the political cartoon is meant to express an opinion, a point of view, an approval or disapproval. Political cartoonists want to catch people's attention, make them laugh or feel angry, move them to action. In short, political cartoons do not depict exactly what is happening, but rather try to make people see what is happening from a particular point of view.

How can we hope to analyze political cartoons that deal with issues, events, and people from over 125 years ago? To begin with, using your text, The Problem and Background sec-

tions of this chapter, and assistance from your instructor, make a list of the most important issues having to do with the Reconstruction of the South, the Grant administration, the Liberal Republican revolt, and Horace Greeley himself. As you examine each of the cartoons in this chapter (seven cartoons from *Frank Leslie's Illustrated Newspaper* and seven from *Harper's Weekly*), try to determine what the artist is trying to say, what issue or event (or pseudo-issue or pseudo-event)[11] is being portrayed, and how the individuals are depicted. Sometimes a cartoon's caption, dialogue, or other words or phrases can help you determine the cartoon's focus.

Next, look closely at each cartoon for clues that will help you understand what Morgan or Nast was trying to say. People who saw these cartoons in 1872 did not have to study them so carefully—just as you do not have to spend a great deal of time studying contemporary political cartoons in today's newspapers or newsmagazines. The individuals and events depicted in each cartoon were immediately familiar to people in 1872, and the messages were obvious. But you are a *historian,* and you will be using these cartoons as historical evidence to help you understand the presidential election of 1872.

11. A pseudo-event is a sham event, one that never actually took place or took place as a staged event for the press. Both sets of cartoons are replete with such pseudo-events. Similarly, a pseudo-issue is a false issue, one that may have been created by the cartoonist or by other political partisans.

CHAPTER 1

GRANT, GREELEY,
AND THE POPULAR
PRESS: THE
PRESIDENTIAL
ELECTION OF 1872

As you will see, both Matt Morgan and Thomas Nast were talented artists. Both cartoonists often used *symbolism* to make their respective points, sometimes in the form of *allegory*. In an allegory, familiar figures (such as Grant or Greeley) are portrayed in a setting or situation that everyone knows—see, for example, Sources 4 and 10 in the Evidence section of this chapter. Thus, by placing these familiar figures in a well-known setting (a Bible story, a piece of mythology, Aesop's fables, and so forth) a deeper meaning or depiction of the figures is communicated.

Other, less complicated symbolism was employed in the 1872 cartoons as well. Both the American flag and military uniforms were powerful images that could be used by each cartoonist. Similarly, Columbia (a tall woman wearing a long classical dress) was a common representation of the United States itself, as was the emerging figure of Uncle Sam when it was used in cartoons in juxtaposition with such figures as Grant, Greeley, and others.

Both President Ulysses Grant and Liberal Republican-Democratic challenger Horace Greeley were instantly recognizable in both Morgan's and Nast's cartoons. How the two candidates were depicted in the cartoons will be crucially important to you as you attempt to analyze each cartoonist's approach to the presidential election of 1872. Other caricatures, however, will be less familiar to you. When identification of a caricatured individual is necessary for you to "read" a cartoon, it is provided in a footnote.

As you can see, a political cartoon must be analyzed in detail to get the full meaning the cartoonist was trying to convey. If you proceed with patience and care, you will be able to analyze the fourteen 1872 political cartoons and thereby to answer the three questions this chapter asks.

❋ THE EVIDENCE ❋

Sources 1 through 7 from *Frank Leslie's Illustrated Newspaper,* April 6, May 4, May 25, June 29, August 10, August 24, and November 2, 1872. Source 1: The Granger Collection. Sources 2 through 7: Courtesy of The University of Tennessee, Knoxville.

Political Cartoons by Matt Morgan

1. A Drunken Despot, April 6, 1872.

12. Roscoe Conkling (Republican, N.Y.), U.S. Senator.
13. President Ulysses Grant.

CHAPTER 1

GRANT, GREELEY,
AND THE POPULAR
PRESS: THE
PRESIDENTIAL
ELECTION OF 1872

2. Uncle Sam in Danger, May 4, 1872.

14. Carl Schurz (Liberal Republican, Mo.), U.S. Senator.
15. Horace Greeley.

3. Swords into Plowshares, May 25, 1872.

16. Schurz.
17. Greeley.

CHAPTER 1

GRANT, GREELEY,
AND THE POPULAR
PRESS: THE
PRESIDENTIAL
ELECTION OF 1872

4. Our King Canute, June 29, 1872.

5. The Bribe Refused, August 10, 1872.

THE BRIBE REFUSED.

"Notwithstanding the large sums of money which have been sent by the Administration to North Carolina (under the pretense that it was to pay Court expenses), the more intelligent portion of the Blacks are very enthusiastic for Mr. Greeley, and have succeeded in making many converts. They exercise a very controlling influence among their associates, which is one of the most encouraging signs of the campaign."—EX-SENATOR DOOLITTLE.

CHAPTER 1

GRANT, GREELEY,
AND THE POPULAR
PRESS: THE
PRESIDENTIAL
ELECTION OF 1872

6. Sumner as a Modern Moses, August 24, 1872.

18. Charles Sumner (Republican, Mass.), Radical Republican; broke with Grant. To the right of Sumner are Schurz and Greeley.

7. A Useless Appeal, November 2, 1872.

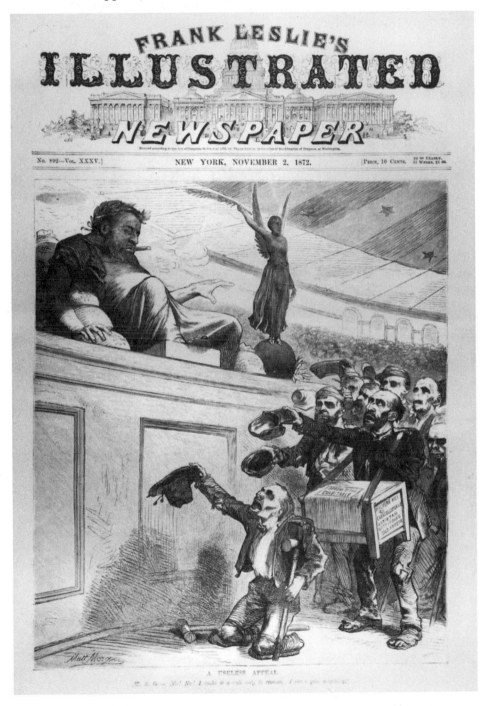

CHAPTER 1

GRANT, GREELEY,
AND THE POPULAR
PRESS: THE
PRESIDENTIAL
ELECTION OF 1872

Sources 8 through 14 from *Harper's Weekly*, April 13, April 20, August 10, September 14, September 21, and October 12, 1872. Courtesy of The University of Tennessee, Knoxville.

Political Cartoons by Thomas Nast

8. The Republic Is Not Ungrateful, April 13, 1872.

THE REPUBLIC IS NOT UNGRATEFUL.

"It is not what is *charged* but what is *proved* that damages the party defendant. Any one may be accused of the most heinous offenses; the Saviour of mankind was not only arraigned but convicted; but what of it? Facts alone are decisive."—*New York Tribune, March 13, 1872.*

9. Sumner as Robinson Crusoe, April 20, 1872.

CHAPTER 1

GRANT, GREELEY,
AND THE POPULAR
PRESS: THE
PRESIDENTIAL
ELECTION OF 1872

10. Any Thing to Get In, August 10, 1872.

11. Greeley and Booth, September 14, 1872.

19. John Wilkes Booth (1838–1865), assassin of President Lincoln.

CHAPTER 1

GRANT, GREELEY,
AND THE POPULAR
PRESS: THE
PRESIDENTIAL
ELECTION OF 1872

12. General Orders, September 21, 1872.

GENERAL ORDERS.

General Dix. "If any Man attempts to haul down the American Flag, Shoot him on the Spot!"

13. "Let Us Clasp Hands over the Bloody Chasm," September 21, 1872.

CHAPTER 1

GRANT, GREELEY,
AND THE POPULAR
PRESS: THE
PRESIDENTIAL
ELECTION OF 1872

14. More Secession Conspiracy, October 12, 1872.

MORE SECESSION CONSPIRACY.

THE VOICE OF THE PEOPLE. "Do you want another Uprising of the North—a still Bloodier Chasm—more Widows, Orphans, and Cripples, and
another National Debt, you Wh'ted Sepulchre?"

✱ QUESTIONS TO CONSIDER ✱

Begin by reviewing your list of important issues having to do with Reconstruction, the Grant administration, the Liberal Republican revolt, and Horace Greeley himself. Then, starting with the seven Morgan cartoons from *Frank Leslie's Illustrated Newspaper* (Sources 1 through 7) and moving on to the seven Nast cartoons from *Harper's Weekly* (Sources 8 through 14), answer the following questions for each cartoon:

1. What issue (or event) is represented by this cartoon?
2. Who are the principal figures, and how are they portrayed?
3. What *imagery* is used?
4. Is the cartoon an *allegory*? If so, what is the basis of that allegory?
5. What *symbols* (flag, Columbia, and Uncle Sam, for example) are used, and how are they used?
6. How were Morgan and Nast trying to influence public opinion through their respective cartoons?

You may find that making a chart is the easiest way to sort your answers.

Morgan's cartoons in Sources 3, 5, and 6 deal with Greeley's, Liberal Republicans', and the Democratic party's views of Reconstruction. With regard to Reconstruction, what do these three cartoons advocate? How is Greeley portrayed in each cartoon (notice, in Source 5, he is standing behind the glass voting receptacle to the far left)? How are President Grant and the stalwart Republicans portrayed? Sources 4, 6, and 7 are all allegories. Who was the legendary King Canute (Source 4)? Why is Grant portrayed as Canute? What is the allegory represented in Source 6 (from left to right, the caricatures depict Sumner, Schurz, and Greeley)? What is the message of this cartoon? Source 7 portrays Grant as a Roman emperor, apparently dispensing charity. Who are the beggars? What is the cartoon's message?

Grant is depicted in all but one of the Morgan cartoons (Source 6). How is he portrayed? Conversely, how is Greeley portrayed (see, especially, Sources 2, 3, 5, and 6)? What reasons does Morgan infer that voters should choose Greeley?

Now move on to the seven Nast cartoons from *Harper's Weekly* (Sources 8 through 14), again using the preceding six questions.

Nast's cartoons in Sources 9, 12, and 14 deal directly with Reconstruction (Sources 11 and 13 do so as well, albeit indirectly). Begin by examining Source 9, an allegory based on Daniel Defoe's 1719 novel *Robinson Crusoe.* You should notice almost immediately that Nast's cartoons are more filled with details than those of Morgan. In Source 9, Greeley is leading a party that is trying to lure respected abolitionist Charles Sumner of Massachusetts (Crusoe) away from the freed man (Friday) and into a rowboat that will take them to the ship "Democrat." Note that the original name of the ship, "Slavery," is crossed out. What do the four flags on the ship represent? Notice, too, that the papers in the African American man's hat are titled "Emancipated by A. Lincoln" and "Protected by U.S. Grant," and

CHAPTER 1

GRANT, GREELEY,
AND THE POPULAR
PRESS: THE
PRESIDENTIAL
ELECTION OF 1872

that the schoolhouse in the background is named "Lincoln School." What is Nast saying in Source 9 about Greeley's stand on Reconstruction? See Sources 12 and 14 as well.

In addition to the Robinson Crusoe allegory in Source 9, Nast makes use of allegory in Source 10. What does the Trojan horse represent in Virgil's account of the war between Greece and Troy? What does the Trojan horse represent here? Who is getting into the Trojan horse? Notice that B. Gratz Brown, Greeley's running mate, is portrayed as a slip of paper attached to Greeley's tail (see also Sources 11 through 14). It was said at the time that Nast had no photograph of Brown from which to draw a caricature, so he portrayed him as an insignificant slip of paper.

Nast's portrayals of Greeley are vicious and withering. In Sources 11 and 13, he distorts a phrase from Greeley's acceptance letter beyond recognition: Greeley is shown "clasp[ing] hands over the bloody chasm," a comment Greeley intended as an offer of reconciliation between the North and South. How does Nast use Greeley's phrase? In an 1869 essay titled "What I Know of Farming," Greeley celebrated life in rural America. How does

Nast twist that as well (see Sources 9, 11, 12, and 14)?

Like Morgan, Nast uses symbolism in his cartoons. How does Nast employ the symbols of the flag (in Sources 9 and, especially, 12) and Columbia (in Sources 8 and 14)? How does he use other symbols?

Grant is depicted in only one of the Nast cartoons (Source 8). How is he portrayed? What is the bust of Abraham Lincoln meant to represent? The feathers on the arrows aimed at Grant are labeled "slander," "malice," "misrepresentations," "insinuations," and "lies." How is Columbia protecting Grant? How, then, is Grant depicted by Nast?

Now put all your notes together to answer the three central questions of this chapter:

1. How did each side attempt to portray the other? the respective presidential candidates (Grant and Greeley)?
2. What were the principal issues the cartoons attempted to address? Which issues did they *not* address or avoid addressing?
3. How did each side attempt to deal with Reconstruction in the presidential election of 1872?

✳ EPILOGUE ✳

For Horace Greeley and Liberal Republicanism, the 1872 election campaign was a fiasco. As he himself had predicted, Greeley's comments in earlier speeches and writings (especially his willingness in 1860 to let the South

secede rather than fight a war, his 1867 offer to post a bond for Jefferson Davis, and his advocacy of a quick and gentle reconstruction of the South) virtually doomed his candidacy in the northern states. For its part, the Republican party hired three hundred researchers to dig up material against Greeley and then feed that material to people such as Thomas Nast.

Realizing his candidacy was in deep trouble, Greeley embarked on a physically punishing speaking tour through New Jersey, Pennsylvania, Ohio, Indiana, and Kentucky, delivering around two hundred speeches in ten days. Increasingly intemperate, in a speech in Jeffersonville, Indiana, on September 23, he lashed out at African Americans for supporting Grant, even asserting that his opposition to slavery "might have been a mistake!"[20]

The behavior of Greeley's running mate, B. Gratz Brown, did little to help the campaign. At a picnic, Brown became so intoxicated that he attempted to butter a watermelon. During a commencement address at Yale, his alma mater, Brown insulted the college, claimed he didn't know why he had gone there, and urged the graduates to vote for Greeley because "I believe he has the largest head in America."[21] Later in the campaign, the inebriated Brown passed out while delivering a speech in New York City.

The election was a rout of Greeley. Backed by the interests of new businessmen, the Grand Army of the Republic (a group of northern Civil War veterans), African Americans, and voters outraged by Greeley, Grant won the election with almost 56 percent of the popular vote and the electoral votes in all but six states (Georgia, Kentucky, Maryland, Missouri, Tennessee, and Texas).

Although the voters appeared to reject the Reconstruction plans of Greeley and embrace Grant and the Radical Republicans, after the 1872 presidential race, Radical Reconstruction deteriorated rapidly. The Amnesty Act of 1872, passed by Congress and signed by Grant to deprive Greeley of a campaign issue, restored the rights to vote and hold office to all but a handful of former Confederates. With northern support of Reconstruction declining and the Grant administration (in spite of its 1872 promises) losing interest in forcing the white South to respect the Fourteenth Amendment, southern Democrats quickly regained control of southern states. By late 1876, only Florida, Louisiana, and South Carolina had not been "redeemed," as southern Democrats referred to their political recapture of the South. By the presidential election of 1876, it was clear that Reconstruction was almost over, as both major party candidates pledged to end it in 1877.

Greeley returned to New York from his speaking tour a physically and mentally exhausted man. Then, on October 30, one week before the election, his wife died after a lingering illness. It was the final blow, and Greeley himself died on November 29, two weeks after the election. In its eulogy to Greeley, *Frank Leslie's Illustrated Weekly* mourned that "his life was worn out in his struggle to restore love between the sections." In a final touch of irony, the paper predicted that over Greeley's grave "the sections 'will clasp hands.'"[22]

20. Gillette, "Election of 1872," p. 1326.
21. *Ibid.*, p. 1327.

22. *Frank Leslie's Illustrated Newspaper,* December 14, 1872.

CHAPTER 1

GRANT, GREELEY,
AND THE POPULAR
PRESS: THE
PRESIDENTIAL
ELECTION OF 1872

As a gesture of good will and reconciliation, President Grant attended Greeley's funeral. But reconciliation would be long in coming. When Grant yearned for a third term in 1876, the abandonment of the Republican party by Greeley's supporters, combined with a fresh batch of second-term scandals, denied Grant the prize he so desperately sought. In retirement, he rushed to finish his memoirs (to provide for his wife Julia) before the throat cancer he had been diagnosed as having ultimately killed him. Grant died on July 23, 1885, and was interred in Central Park in New York City. In 1897, a magnificent tomb was dedicated to Grant and his remains were relocated there. When Julia died in 1902, President Theodore Roosevelt attended her funeral, and she was laid to rest in what grammatically should be called Grants' Tomb.[23]

Fletcher Harper died in 1877, but his brothers and heirs continued *Harper's Weekly* and, later, *Harper's* magazine. For his part, Frank Leslie created a scandal of his own when in 1873 he divorced his wife to marry a woman who simultaneously had divorced her husband. And when Leslie died in 1880 (like Grant, of throat cancer), his wife Miriam had her name legally changed to Frank Leslie. Soon after that, she married William Charles Wilde, the brother of Oscar Wilde, but they were divorced in 1893. When "Frank Leslie" (Miriam) died in 1914, she left her considerable estate to the cause of women's suffrage.

We know almost nothing about cartoonist-illustrator Matt Morgan after 1872, except that he died in 1890. But Thomas Nast is a different story. After the 1872 presidential election, Mark Twain told Nast that "you more than any other man have won a prodigious victory for Grant. . . . Those pictures were simply marvelous."[24] Taking advantage of his celebrity, Nast renegotiated his contract with *Harper's Weekly* and then went on a speaking tour that brought in $40,000 in seven months.[25]

But Nast was a spendthrift. Financially struggling, he appealed to friends, who ultimately influenced President Theodore Roosevelt to appoint him to a minor consular post in Ecuador. Nast died there of yellow fever in 1902.

23. In 1913 the Grants' son, Ulysses S. Grant, Jr., married a woman named America Mills. They were constantly introduced as "U.S. and America Grant." McFeely, *Grant,* p. 520.

24. Morton Keller, *The Art and Politics of Thomas Nast* (New York: Oxford Univ. Press, 1968), pp. 77–78.
25. $40,000 in 1873 would be approximately $452,000 in 1991 dollars.

2

The Road to True Freedom: African American Alternatives in the New South

✳ THE PROBLEM ✳

By 1895, when the venerable Frederick Douglass died, African Americans in the South had been free for thirty years. Yet in many ways, their situation had barely improved from that of servitude, and in some ways, it had actually deteriorated. Economically, very few had been able to acquire land of their own, and the vast majority continued to work for white landowners under various forms of labor arrangements and sometimes under outright peonage.[1] Political and civil rights supposedly had been guaranteed under the Fourteenth and Fifteenth amendments to the Constitution (ratified in 1868 and 1870, respectively), but those rights often were violated, federal courts offered little protection, and, beginning in the early 1890s, southern states began a successful campaign to disfranchise black voters and to institute legal segregation through legislation that collectively became known as Jim Crow laws.[2] In some ways more threatening, violence against African Americans

1. Whatever names were given to these labor arrangements (tenancy, sharecropping, and so on), in most of the arrangements a white landowner or merchant furnished farm workers with foodstuffs and fertilizer on credit, taking a percentage of the crops grown in return. For a fascinating description of how the system worked, see Theodore Rosengarten, *All God's Dangers: The Life of Nate Shaw* (New York: Alfred A. Knopf, 1974).

2. The term *Jim Crow,* generally used to refer to issues relating to African Americans, originated in the late 1820s with white minstrel singer Thomas "Daddy" Rice, who performed the song "Jump Jim Crow" in blackface makeup. By the 1840s, the term was used to refer to racially segregated facilities in the North.

CHAPTER 2

THE ROAD TO
TRUE FREEDOM:
AFRICAN
AMERICAN
ALTERNATIVES
IN THE NEW
SOUTH

was increasing and in most cases going unpunished. Between 1889 and 1900, 1,357 lynchings of African Americans were recorded in the United States, the vast majority in the states of the former Confederacy. In 1898, in New Bern, North Carolina, one white orator proposed "choking the Cape Fear River with the bodies of Negroes." In truth, by the 1890s it had become evident for all who cared to see that Lincoln's emancipation of southern slaves had been considerably less than complete.

A number of spokespersons offered significantly different strategies for improving the situation of African Americans in the South. For this chapter's Evidence section, we have chosen five such spokespersons, all of them well known to blacks in the New South. Ida B. Wells (1862–1931) was a journalist, lecturer, and crusader who was well known in both the United States and Europe. Booker T. Washington (1856–1915) was a celebrated educator, author, and political figure who many believed should have inherited the mantle of Frederick Douglass as the principal spokesperson for African Americans. Henry McNeal Turner (1834–1915) was a bishop of the African Methodist Episcopal Church and a controversial speaker and writer. W. E. B. Du Bois (pronounced *Du Boys'*, 1868–1963) was an academician and editor and one of the founders of the National Association for the Advancement of Colored People (NAACP). Finally, Frances Ellen Watkins Harper (1825–1911) was a popular poet and writer who gave numerous speeches in support of both African American and women's rights. Each of these spokespersons offered a contrasting alternative for African Americans in the New South.

In this chapter, you will be analyzing the situation that African Americans in the New South faced in the years after Reconstruction and identifying the principal alternatives open to them. What different strategies did Wells, Washington, Turner, Du Bois, and Harper offer African Americans? Were there other options they did not address? Based on your examination of the different alternatives advocated by these five African American spokespersons, what do you think were the strengths and weaknesses of each approach? Finally, keep in mind that the five spokepersons advocated taking different paths to the *same* ultimate goal: full equality for African Americans.

❋ BACKGROUND ❋

The gradual end of Reconstruction by the federal government left the South in the hands of political and economic leaders who chose to call themselves "Redeemers." Many of these men came from the same landowner and planter-lawyer groups that had led the South prior to the Civil War, thus giving the post-Reconstruction South a high degree of continuity with earlier eras. Also important, however, was a comparatively new group of southerners, men who called for a "New South" that would be highlighted by increased industrialization, urbanization, and diversified agriculture.

In many ways, the New South movement was an undisguised attempt to imitate the industrialization that was sweeping through the North just prior to, during, and after the Civil War. Indeed, the North's industrial prowess had been one reason for its ultimate military victory. As Reconstruction gradually came to an end in the southern states, many southern bankers, business leaders, and editors became convinced that the South should not return to its previous, narrow economic base of plantations and one-crop agriculture but instead should follow the North's lead toward modernization through industry. Prior to the Civil War, many of these people had been calling for economic diversification, but they had been overwhelmed by the plantation aristocracy that controlled southern state politics and had used that control to further its own interests. By the end of Reconstruction, however, the planter elite had lost a good deal of its power, thus creating a power vacuum into which advocates of a New South could move.

Nearly every city, town, and hamlet of the former Confederacy had its New South boosters. Getting together in industrial societies or chambers of commerce, the boosters called for the erection of mills and factories. Why, they asked, should southerners export their valuable raw materials elsewhere, only to see them return from northern and European factories as costly finished products? Why couldn't

southerners set up their own manufacturing establishments and become prosperous within a self-contained economy? And if the southerners were short of capital, why not encourage rich northern investors to put up money in return for promises of great profits? In fact, the South had all the ingredients required of an industrial system: raw materials, a rebuilt transportation system, labor, potential consumers, and the possibility of obtaining capital. As they fed each other's dreams, the New South advocates pictured a resurgent South, a prosperous South, a triumphant South, a South of steam and power rather than plantations and magnolias.

Undoubtedly, the leading spokesman of the New South movement was Henry Grady, editor of the *Atlanta Constitution* and one of the most influential figures in the southern states. Born in Athens, Georgia, in 1850, Grady was orphaned in his early teens when his father was killed in the Civil War. Graduating from his hometown college, the University of Georgia, Grady began a long and not particularly profitable career as a journalist. In 1879, aided by northern industrialist Cyrus Field, he purchased a quarter interest in the *Atlanta Constitution* and became that newspaper's editor. From that position, he became the chief advocate of the New South movement.

Whether speaking to southern or northern audiences, Grady had no peer. Addressing a group of potential investors in New South industries in New York in 1886, he delighted his audience by saying that he was glad the Confederacy had lost the Civil

CHAPTER 2

THE ROAD TO
TRUE FREEDOM:
AFRICAN
AMERICAN
ALTERNATIVES
IN THE NEW
SOUTH

War, for that defeat had broken the power of the plantation aristocracy and provided the opportunity for the South to move into the modern industrial age. Northerners, Grady continued, were welcome: "We have sown towns and cities in the place of theories, and put business above politics . . . and have . . . wiped out the place where Mason and Dixon's line used to be."[3]

To those southerners who envisioned a New South, the central goal was a harmonious, interdependent society in which each person and thing had a clearly defined place. Most New South boosters stressed industry and the growth of cities because the South had few factories and mills and almost no cities of substantial size. But agriculture also would have its place, although it would not be the same as the cash-crop agriculture of the pre–Civil War years. Instead, New South spokespersons advocated a diversified agriculture that would still produce cash crops for export but would also make the South more self-sufficient by producing food crops and raw materials for the anticipated factories. Small towns would be used for collection and distribution, a rebuilt railroad network would transport goods, and northern capital would finance the entire process. Hence each part of the economy and, indeed, each person would have a clearly defined place and role in the New South, a place and role that would ensure everyone a piece of the New South's prosperity.

But even as Grady and his counterparts were fashioning their dreams of a New South and selling those dreams to both northerners and southerners, a less beneficial, less prosperous side of the New South was taking shape. In spite of the New South advocates' successes in establishing factories and mills (for example, Knoxville, Tennessee, witnessed the founding of more than ninety such enterprises in the 1880s alone), the post-Reconstruction South remained primarily agricultural. Furthermore, many of the farms were worked by sharecroppers or tenant farmers who eked out a bare subsistence while the profits went to the landowners or to the banks. This situation was especially prevalent in the lower South, where by 1910 a great proportion of farms were worked by tenants: South Carolina (63.0 percent), Georgia (65.6 percent), Alabama (60.2 percent), Mississippi (66.1 percent), and Louisiana (55.3 percent).[4] Even as factory smokestacks were rising on portions of the southern horizon, a high percentage of southerners remained in agriculture and in poverty.

Undeniably, African Americans suffered the most. More than four million African American men, women, and children had been freed by the Civil War. During Reconstruction, some advances were made, especially in the areas of public education and voter registration. Yet even these gains were either impermanent or incomplete. By 1880 in Georgia, only 33.7 percent of the black school-age population was

3. Grady's speech is in Richard N. Current and John A. Garraty, eds., *Words That Made American History* (Boston: Little, Brown, 1962), Vol. II, pp. 23–31.

4. Bureau of the Census, *Farm Tenancy in the United States* (Washington: Government Printing Office, 1924), pp. 207–208.

enrolled in school, and by 1890 (twenty-five years after emancipation), almost half of all blacks aged ten to fourteen in the Deep South were still illiterate.[5] As for voting rights, the vast majority of African Americans chose not to exercise them, fearing intimidation and violence.

Many blacks and whites at the time recognized that African Americans would never be able to improve their situation economically, socially, or politically without owning land. Yet even many Radical Republicans were reluctant to give land to the former slaves. Such a move would mean seizing land from the white planters, a proposal that clashed with the notion of the sanctity of private property. As a result, most African Americans were forced to take menial, low-paying jobs in southern cities or to work as farmers on land they did not own. By 1880, only 1.6 percent of the landowners in Georgia were black, and most of them owned the most marginal and least productive land.

As poor urban laborers or tenant farmers, African Americans were dependent on their employers, landowners, or bankers and prey to rigid vagrancy laws, the convict lease system, peonage, and outright racial discrimination. Moreover, the end of Reconstruction in the southern states was followed by a reimposition of rigid racial segregation, at first through a return to traditional practices and later (in the 1890s) by state laws governing nearly every aspect of southern life. For example, voting by African Americans was discouraged, initially by intimidation and then by more formal means such as poll taxes and literacy tests. African Americans who protested or strayed from their "place" were dealt with harshly. Between 1880 and 1918, more than twenty-four hundred African Americans were lynched by southern white mobs, each action being a grim reminder to African Americans of what could happen to those who challenged the status quo. For their part, the few southern whites who spoke against such outrages were themselves subjects of intimidation and even violence. Indeed, although most African American men and women undoubtedly would have disagreed, African Americans' relative position in some ways had deteriorated since the end of the Civil War.

Many New South advocates openly worried about how potential northern investors and politicians would react to this state of affairs. Although the dream of the New South rested on the concept of a harmonious, interdependent society in which each component (industry or agriculture, for example) and each person (white or black) had a clearly defined place, it appeared that African Americans were being kept in their "place" largely by intimidation and force. Who would want to invest in a region in which the status quo of mutual deference and "place" often was maintained by force? To calm northern fears, Grady and his cohorts assured northerners that African Americans' position was improving and that southern society was

5. Roger L. Ransom and Richard Sutch, *One Kind of Freedom: The Economic Consequences of Emancipation* (Cambridge: Cambridge University Press, 1977), pp. 28, 30.

CHAPTER 2

THE ROAD TO
TRUE FREEDOM:
AFRICAN
AMERICAN
ALTERNATIVES
IN THE NEW
SOUTH

one of mutual respect between the races. "We have found," Grady stated, "that in the summing up the free Negro counts more than he did as a slave."[6] Most northerners believed Grady because they wanted to, because they had no taste for another bitter Reconstruction, and in many cases because they shared white southerners' prejudice against African Americans. Grady was able to reassure them because they wanted to be reassured.

Thus for southern African Americans, the New South movement had done little to better their collective lot. Indeed, in some ways their position had deteriorated. Tied economically either to land they did not own or to the lowest-paying jobs in towns and cities, subjects of an increasingly rigid code of racial segregation and loss of political rights, and victims of an upswing in racially directed violence, African Americans in the New South had every reason to question the oratory of Henry Grady and other New South boosters. Jobs in the New South's mills and factories generally were reserved for whites, so the opportunities that European immigrants in the North had to work their way gradually up the economic ladder were closed to southern blacks.

How did African Americans respond to this deteriorating situation? In the 1890s, numerous African American farmers joined the Colored Alliance, part of the Farmers' Alliance Movement that swept the South and Midwest in the 1880s and 1890s. This movement attempted to reverse the farmers' eroding position through the establishment of farmers' cooperatives (to sell their crops together for higher prices and to purchase manufactured goods wholesale) and by entering politics to elect candidates sympathetic to farmers (who would draft legislation favorable to farmers). Many feared, however, that this increased militancy of farmers—white and black—would produce a political backlash that would leave them even worse off. Such a backlash occurred in the South in the 1890s with the defeat of the Populist revolt.

Wells, Washington, Turner, Du Bois, and Harper offered southern African Americans five other ways to confront the economic, social, and political difficulties they faced. And, as African American men and women soon discovered, there were other options as well.

Your task in this chapter is to analyze the evidence in order to answer the following central questions:

1. What were the different alternatives offered by Wells, Washington, Turner, Du Bois and Harper?
2. Were there other options those five spokespersons did not mention?
3. What were the strengths and weaknesses of each alternative? Note: Remember that you are evaluating the five alternatives *not* from a present-day perspective but in the context and time in which they were advocated (1892–1906).
4. How would you support your assessment of the strengths and weaknesses of each alternative?

6. *The New South: Writings and Speeches of Henry Grady* (Savannah: The Beehive Press, 1971), p. 8.

THE METHOD

In this chapter, the evidence is from speeches delivered by five well-known African Americans or from their writings that were also given as speeches. Although all five spokespersons were known to southern African Americans, they were not equally well known. It is almost impossible to tell which of the five was the best known (or least known) in her or his time, although fragmentary evidence suggests that Washington and Harper were the most well-known figures among African Americans in various socioeconomic groups.

The piece by Ida B. Wells (Source 1) is excerpted from a pamphlet published simultaneously in the United States and England in 1892, but it is almost certain that parts of it were delivered as a speech by Wells in that same year. The selections by Booker T. Washington (Source 2), Henry NcNeal Turner (Source 3), W. E. B. Du Bois (Sources 4 and 5), and Frances E. W. Harper (Source 6) are transcriptions, or printed versions, of speeches delivered in September 1895, December 1895, 1903, 1906, and November 1892, respectively.

Ida Bell Wells was born a slave in Holly Springs, Mississippi, in 1862. After emancipation, her father and mother, as a carpenter and a cook, respectively, earned enough money to send her to a freedmen's school. In 1876, her parents died in a yellow fever epidemic. Only fourteen years old, Wells lied about her age and got a job teaching in a rural school for blacks, eventually moving to Memphis, Tennessee, to teach in the city's schools for African Americans. In 1884, she was forcibly removed from a railroad passenger car for refusing to move to the car reserved for "colored" passengers; she sued the railroad company.[7] About this time, Wells began writing articles for many black-owned newspapers, mostly on the subject of unequal educational opportunities for whites and blacks in Memphis. As a result, the Memphis school board discharged her, and she became a full-time journalist and lecturer. By 1892, she had become co-owner of the *Memphis Free Speech* newspaper. In 1895, she married black lawyer-editor Ferdinand Lee Barnett and from that time went by the name Ida Wells-Barnett, a somewhat radical practice in 1895.

Like Wells, Booker T. Washington was born a slave, in Franklin County, Virginia. Largely self-taught before entering Hampton Institute, a school for African Americans, at age seventeen, he worked his way through school, mostly as a janitor. At age twenty-five, he was chosen to organize a normal school for blacks at Tuskegee, Alabama. Washington spent thirty-four years as the guiding force at Tuskegee Institute, shaping the school into his vision of what African Americans must do to better their lot. In great demand as a speaker to white and black audiences alike, Washington received an honorary degree from

7. The Tennessee Supreme Court ruled in favor of the Chesapeake and Ohio Railroad and against Wells in 1887.

CHAPTER 2

THE ROAD TO
TRUE FREEDOM:
AFRICAN
AMERICAN
ALTERNATIVES
IN THE NEW
SOUTH

Harvard College in 1891. Four years later, he was chosen as the principal speaker at the opening of the Negro section of the Cotton States and International Exposition in Atlanta.

Henry McNeal Turner was born a free black near Abbeville, South Carolina. Mostly self-taught, he joined the Methodist Episcopal Church, South, in 1848 and was licensed to preach in 1853. In 1858, he abandoned that denomination to become a minister in the African Methodist Episcopal (AME) Church, and by 1862 he was the pastor of the large Israel church in Washington, D.C. In 1863, he became a chaplain in the Union army, assigned to the 1st U.S. Colored Regiment. After the war, he became an official of the Freedmen's Bureau in Georgia and afterward held a succession of political appointments. One of the founders of the Republican party in Georgia, Turner was made bishop of the AME Church in Georgia in 1880. In that position, he met and became a friend of Ida B. Wells, who also was a member of the AME Church.

William Edward Burghardt Du Bois was born in Great Barrington, Massachusetts, one of approximately fifty blacks in a town of five thousand people. He was educated with the white children in the town's public school and in 1885 was enrolled at Fisk University, a college for African Americans in Nashville, Tennessee. It was there, according to his autobiography, that he first encountered overt racial prejudice. Graduated from Fisk in 1888, he entered Harvard as a junior. He received his bachelor's degree in 1890 and his Ph.D. in 1895. His book

The Philadelphia Negro was published in 1899. In this book, Du Bois asserted that the problems African Americans faced were the results of their history (slavery and racism) and environment, not of some imagined genetic inferiority.

Frances Ellen Watkins Harper was born in Maryland in 1825, the only child of free parents. Orphaned at an early age, she was raised by an aunt, who enrolled her in a school for free blacks run by an uncle, who headed the Academy for Negro Youth and was a celebrated African American abolitionist (he was friends with both William Lloyd Garrison and Benjamin Lundy). Ending her formal education at the age of thirteen, Harper worked as a seamstress and needlework teacher. But she yearned to write and, in 1845, published her first book of poetry. It was later followed by ten more volumes of poetry (all commercially successful), a short story—the first to be published by a black woman—in 1859, and an immensely popular novel in 1892. She was a founder and vice president of the National Association of Colored Women. In 1860, she married Fenton Harper, who died in 1864. The couple had one child, a daughter, who was in continuous poor health and died in 1909.

This is not the first time that you have had to analyze speeches. Our society is almost literally bombarded by speeches delivered by politicians, business figures, educators, and others, most of whom are trying to convince us to adopt a set of ideas or actions. As we listen to such speeches, we invariably weigh the options presented to us, often using other available evidence (in this case, the Background section of this chapter) to help us make our decisions. One purpose of this exercise is to help you think more critically and use evidence more thoroughly when assessing different options.

It is logical to begin by analyzing each of the speeches in turn. As you read each selection, make a rough chart like the one below to help you remember the main points.

Once you have carefully defined the alternatives presented by Wells, Washington, Turner, Du Bois, and Harper, return to the Background section of this chapter. As you reread that section, determine the strengths and weaknesses of each alternative offered for African Americans living in the New South in the late nineteenth and early twentieth centuries. What evidence would you use to determine each alternative's strengths and weaknesses?

African American Alternatives			
Speaker	Suggested Alternatives	How Does Speaker Develop Her/His Arguments?	Strengths and Weaknesses (Fill in later)
Wells			
Washington			
Turner			
Du Bois			
Harper			

✳ THE EVIDENCE ✳

Source 1 from Ida B. Wells, *United States Atrocities* (London: Lux Newspaper and Publishing Co., 1892), pp. 13–18. In the United States, the pamphlet was titled *Southern Horrors*. See Jacqueline Jones Royster, ed., *Southern Horrors and Other Writings: The Anti-Lynching Campaign of Ida B. Wells, 1892–1900* (Boston: Bedford Books, 1997), pp. 49–72.

1. Ida B. Wells's *United States Atrocities,* 1892 (excerpt).

Mr. Henry W. Grady, in his well-remembered speeches in New England and New York, pictured the Afro-American as incapable of self-government. Through him and other leading men the cry of the South to the country has been "Hands off! Leave us to solve our problem." To the Afro-American

CHAPTER 2

THE ROAD TO
TRUE FREEDOM:
AFRICAN
AMERICAN
ALTERNATIVES
IN THE NEW
SOUTH

the South says, "The white man must and will rule." There is little difference between the Ante-bellum South and the New South. Her white citizens are wedded to any method however revolting, any measure however
extreme, for the subjugation of the young manhood of the dark race. They
have cheated him out of his ballot, deprived him of civil rights or redress
in the Civil Courts thereof, robbed him of the fruits of his labour, and are
still murdering, burning and lynching him.

The result is a growing disregard of human life. Lynch Law has spread
its insidious influence till men in New York State, Pennsylvania and on the
free Western plains feel they can take the law in their own hands with
impunity, especially where an Afro-American is concerned. The South is
brutalised to a degree not realised by its own inhabitants, and the very
foundation of government, law, and order are imperilled.

Public sentiment has had a slight "reaction," though not sufficient to stop
the crusade of lawlessness and lynching. The spirit of Christianity of the
great M. E. Church was sufficiently aroused by the frequent and revolting
crimes against a powerless people, to pass strong condemnatory resolutions
at its General Conference in Omaha last May. The spirit of justice of the
grand old party[8] asserted itself sufficiently to secure a denunciation of the
wrongs, and a feeble declaration of the belief in human rights in the Republican platform at Minneapolis, June 7th. A few of the great "dailies"
and "weeklies" have swung into line declaring that Lynch Law must go.
The President of the United States issued a proclamation that it be not
tolerated in the territories over which he has jurisdiction. . . .

These efforts brought forth apologies and a short halt, but the lynching
mania has raged again through the past twelve months with unabated fury.
The strong arm of the law must be brought to bear upon lynchers in severe
punishment, but this cannot and will not be done unless a healthy public
sentiment demands and sustains such action. The men and women in the
South who disapprove of lynching and remain silent on the perpetration of
such outrages are *particeps criminis*—accomplices, accessories before and
after the fact, equally guilty with the actual law-breakers, who would not
persist if they did not know that neither the law nor militia would be
deployed against them.

In the creation of this healthier public sentiment, the Afro-American can
do for himself what no one else can do for him. The world looks on with
wonder that we have conceded so much, and remain law-abiding under such
great outrage and provocation.

To Northern capital and Afro-American labour the South owes its re-
habilitation. If labour is withdrawn capital will not remain. The Afro-

8. *Grand old party* refers to the Republican party.

American is thus the backbone of the South. A thorough knowledge and judicious exercise of this power in lynching localities could many times effect a bloodless revolution. The white man's dollar is his god, and to stop this will be to stop outrages in many localities.

The Afro-Americans of Memphis denounced the lynching of three of their best citizens, and urged and waited for the authorities to act in the matter, and bring the lynchers to justice. No attempt was made to do so, and the black men left the city by thousands, bringing about great stagnation in every branch of business. Those who remained so injured the business of the street car company by staying off the cars, that the superintendent, manager, and treasurer called personally on the editors of the *Free Speech,* and asked them to urge our people to give them their patronage again. Other business men became alarmed over the situation, and the *Free Speech* was suppressed that the coloured people might be more easily controlled. A meeting of white citizens in June, three months after the lynching, passed resolutions for the first time condemning it. *But they did not punish the lynchers.* Every one of them was known by name because they had been selected to do the dirty work by some of the very citizens who passed these resolutions! Memphis is fast losing her black population, who proclaim as they go that there is no protection for the life and property of any Afro-American citizen in Memphis who will not be a slave. . . .

[*Wells then urged African Americans in Kentucky to boycott railroads in the state, since the legislature had passed a law segregating passenger cars. She claimed that such a boycott would mean a loss to the railroads of $1 million per year.*]

The appeal to the white man's pocket has ever been more effectual than all the appeals ever made to his conscience. Nothing, absolutely nothing, is to be gained by a further sacrifice of manhood and self-respect. By the right exercise of his power as the industrial factor of the South, the Afro-American can demand and secure his rights, the punishment of lynchers, and a fair trial for members of his race accused of outrage.

Of the many inhuman outrages of this present year, the only case where the proposed lynching did *not* occur, was where the men armed themselves in Jacksonville, Florida, and Paducah, Kentucky, and prevented it. The only times an Afro-American who was assaulted got away has been when he had a gun, and used it in self-defence. The lesson this teaches, and which every Afro-American should ponder well, is that a Winchester rifle should have a place of honour in every black home, and it should be used for that protection which the law refuses to give. When the white man, who is always the aggressor, knows he runs a great risk of biting the dust every time his Afro-American victim does, he will have greater respect for Afro-American

CHAPTER 2

THE ROAD TO
TRUE FREEDOM:
AFRICAN
AMERICAN
ALTERNATIVES
IN THE NEW
SOUTH

life. The more the Afro-American yields and cringes and begs, the more he has to do so, the more he is insulted, outraged, and lynched. . . .

Source 2 from Louis R. Harlan, ed., *The Booker T. Washington Papers* (Urbana: University of Illinois Press, 1974), Vol. III, pp. 583–587.

2. Booker T. Washington's Atlanta Exposition Address (standard printed version), September 1895.

[Atlanta, Ga., Sept. 18, 1895]

Mr. President and Gentlemen of the Board of Directors and Citizens:

One-third of the population of the South is of the Negro race. No enterprise seeking the material, civil, or moral welfare of this section can disregard this element of our population and reach the highest success. I but convey to you, Mr. President and Directors, the sentiment of the masses of my race when I say that in no way have the value and manhood of the American Negro been more fittingly and generously recognized than by the managers of this magnificent Exposition at every stage of its progress. It is a recognition that will do more to cement the friendship of the two races than any occurrence since the dawn of our freedom.

Not only this, but the opportunity here afforded will awaken among us a new era of industrial progress. Ignorant and inexperienced, it is not strange that in the first years of our new life we began at the top instead of at the bottom; that a seat in Congress or the state legislature was more sought than real estate or industrial skill; that the political convention or stump speaking had more attractions than starting a dairy farm or truck garden.

A ship lost at sea for many days suddenly sighted a friendly vessel. From the mast of the unfortunate vessel was seen a signal, "Water, water; we die of thirst!" The answer from the friendly vessel at once came back, "Cast down your bucket where you are." A second time the signal, "Water, water; send us water!" ran up from the distressed vessel, and was answered, "Cast down your bucket where you are." And a third and fourth signal for water was answered, "Cast down your bucket where you are." The captain of the distressed vessel, at last heeding the injunction, cast down his bucket, and it came up full of fresh, sparkling water from the mouth of the Amazon River. To those of my race who depend on bettering their condition in a foreign land or who underestimate the importance of cultivating friendly relations with the Southern white man, who is their next-door neighbour, I would say: "Cast down your bucket where you are"—cast it down in making friends in every manly way of the people of all races by whom we are surrounded.

Cast it down in agriculture, mechanics, in commerce, in domestic service, and in the professions. And in this connection it is well to bear in mind that whatever other sins the South may be called to bear, when it comes to business, pure and simple, it is in the South that the Negro is given a man's chance in the commercial world, and in nothing is this Exposition more eloquent than in emphasizing this chance. Our greatest danger is that in the great leap from slavery to freedom we may overlook the fact that the masses of us are to live by the productions of our hands, and fail to keep in mind that we shall prosper in proportion as we learn to dignify and glorify common labour, and put brains and skill into the common occupations of life; shall prosper in proportion as we learn to draw the line between the superficial and the substantial, the ornamental gewgaws of life and the useful. No race can prosper till it learns that there is as much dignity in tilling a field as in writing a poem. It is at the bottom of life we must begin, and not at the top. Nor should we permit our grievances to overshadow our opportunities.

To those of the white race who look to the incoming of those of foreign birth and strange tongue and habits for the prosperity of the South, were I permitted I would repeat what I say to my own race, "Cast down your bucket where you are." Cast it down among the eight millions of Negroes whose habits you know, whose fidelity and love you have tested in days when to have proved treacherous meant the ruin of your firesides. Cast down your bucket among these people who have, without strikes and labour wars, tilled your fields, cleared your forests, builded your railroads and cities, and brought forth treasures from the bowels of the earth, and helped make possible this magnificent representation of the progress of the South. Casting down your bucket among my people, helping and encouraging them as you are doing on these grounds, and to education of head, hand, and heart, you will find that they will buy your surplus land, make blossom the waste places in your fields, and run your factories. While doing this, you can be sure in the future, as in the past, that you and your families will be surrounded by the most patient, faithful, law-abiding, and unresentful people that the world has seen. As we have proved our loyalty to you in the past, in nursing your children, watching by the sick-bed of your mothers and fathers, and often following them with tear-dimmed eyes to their graves, so in the future, in our humble way, we shall stand by you with a devotion that no foreigner can approach, ready to lay down our lives, if need be, in defense of yours, interlacing our industrial, commercial, civil, and religious life with yours in a way that shall make the interests of both races

CHAPTER 2

THE ROAD TO
TRUE FREEDOM:
AFRICAN
AMERICAN
ALTERNATIVES
IN THE NEW
SOUTH

one. In all things that are purely social we can be as separate as the fingers, yet one as the hand in all things essential to mutual progress.

There is no defense or security for any of us except in the highest intelligence and development of all. If anywhere there are efforts tending to curtail the fullest growth of the Negro, let these efforts be turned into stimulating, encouraging, and making him the most useful and intelligent citizen. Effort or means so invested will pay a thousand per cent interest. These efforts will be twice blessed—"blessing him that gives and him that takes."

There is no escape through law of man or God from the inevitable:—

"The laws of changeless justice bind
    Oppressor with oppressed;
And close as sin and suffering joined
    We march to fate abreast."

Nearly sixteen millions of hands will aid you in pulling the load upward, or they will pull against you the load downward. We shall constitute one-third and more of the ignorance and crime of the South, or one-third [of] its intelligence and progress; we shall contribute one-third to the business and industrial prosperity of the South, or we shall prove a veritable body of death, stagnating, depressing, retarding every effort to advance the body politic.

Gentlemen of the Exposition, as we present to you our humble effort at an exhibition of our progress, you must not expect overmuch. Starting thirty years ago with ownership here and there in a few quilts and pumpkins and chickens (gathered from miscellaneous sources), remember the path that has led from these to the inventions and production of agricultural implements, buggies, steam-engines, newspapers, books, statuary, carving, paintings, the management of drug stores and banks, has not been trodden without contact with thorns and thistles. While we take pride in what we exhibit as a result of our independent efforts, we do not for a moment forget that our part in this exhibition would fall far short of your expectations but for the constant help that has come to our educational life, not only from the Southern states, but especially from Northern philanthropists, who have made their gifts a constant stream of blessing and encouragement.

The wisest among my race understand that the agitation of questions of social equality is the extremest folly, and that progress in the enjoyment of all the privileges that will come to us must be the result of severe and constant struggle rather than of artificial forcing. No race that has anything to contribute to the markets of the world is long in any degree ostracized.

It is important and right that all privileges of the law be ours, but it is vastly more important that we be prepared for the exercise of these privileges. The opportunity to earn a dollar in a factory just now is worth infinitely more than the opportunity to spend a dollar in an opera-house.

In conclusion, may I repeat that nothing in thirty years has given us more hope and encouragement, and drawn us so near to you of the white race, as this opportunity offered by the Exposition; and here bending, as it were, over the altar that represents the results of the struggles of your race and mine, both starting practically empty-handed three decades ago, I pledge that in your effort to work out the great and intricate problem which God has laid at the doors of the South, you shall have at all times the patient, sympathetic help of my race; only let this be constantly in mind, that, while from representations in these buildings of the product of field, of forest, of mine, of factory, letters, and art, much good will come, yet far above and beyond material benefits will be that higher good, that, let us pray God, will come, in a blotting out of sectional differences and racial animosities and suspicions in a determination to administer absolute justice, in a willing obedience among all classes to the mandates of law. This, coupled with our material prosperity, will bring into our beloved South a new heaven and a new earth.

Source 3 from Edwin S. Redkey, ed., *Respect Black: The Writings and Speeches of Henry McNeal Turner* (New York: Arno Press, 1971), pp. 167–171.

3. Henry McNeal Turner's "The American Negro and His Fatherland," December 1895 (excerpt).

It would be a waste of time to expend much labor, the few moments I have to devote to this subject, upon the present status of the Negroid race in the United States. It is too well-known already. However, I believe that the Negro was brought to this country in the providence of God to a heaven-permitted if not a divine-sanctioned manual laboring school, that he might have direct contact with the mightiest race that ever trod the face of the globe.

The heathen Africans, to my certain knowledge, I care not what others may say, eagerly yearn for that civilization which they believe will elevate them and make them potential for good. The African was not sent and brought to this country by chance, or by the avarice of the white man, single and alone. The white slave-purchaser went to the shores of that continent and bought our ancestors from their African masters. The bulk who were

[41]

CHAPTER 2

THE ROAD TO
TRUE FREEDOM:
AFRICAN
AMERICAN
ALTERNATIVES
IN THE NEW
SOUTH

brought to this country were the children of parents who had been in slavery a thousand years. Yet hereditary slavery is not universal among the African slaveholders. So that the argument often advanced, that the white man went to Africa and stole us, is not true. They bought us out of a slavery that still exists over a large portion of that continent. For there are millions and millions of slaves in Africa today. Thus the superior African sent us, and the white man brought us, and we remained in slavery as long as it was necessary to learn that a God, who is a spirit, made the world and controls it, and that that Supreme Being could be sought and found by the exercise of faith in His only begotten Son. Slavery then went down, and the colored man was thrown upon his own responsibility, and here he is today, in the providence of God, cultivating self-reliance and imbibing a knowledge of civil law in contradistinction to the dictum of one man, which was the law of the black man until slavery was overthrown. I believe that the Negroid race has been free long enough now to begin to think for himself and plan for better conditions [than] he can lay claim to in this country or ever will. *There is no manhood future in the United States for the Negro.* He may eke out an existence for generations to come, but he can never be a *man*—full, symmetrical and undwarfed. . . .

[Here Turner asserted that a "great chasm" continued to exist between the races, that whites would have no social contact with blacks, and (without using Booker T. Washington's name) that any black who claimed that African Americans did not want social equality immediately "is either an ignoramus, or is an advocate of the perpetual servility and degradation of his race. . . ."]

. . . And as such, I believe that two or three millions of us should return to the land of our ancestors, and establish our own nation, civilization, laws, customs, style of manufacture, and not only give the world, like other race varieties, the benefit of our individuality, but build up social conditions peculiarly our own, and cease to be grumblers, chronic complainers and a menace to the white man's country, or the country he claims and is bound to dominate.

The civil status of the Negro is simply what the white man grants of his own free will and accord. The black man can demand nothing. He is deposed from the jury and tried, convicted and sentenced by men who do not claim to be his peers. On the railroads, where the colored race is found in the largest numbers, he is the victim of proscription, and he must ride in the Jim Crow car or walk. The Supreme Court of the United States decided, October 15th, 1883, that the colored man had no civil rights under the general government,[9] and the several States, from then until now, have

9. On October 15, 1883, the Supreme Court handed down one decision that applied to five separate cases that had been argued before the Court, all of them having to do with racial

been enacting laws which limit, curtail and deprive him of his civil rights, immunities and privileges, until he is now being disfranchised, and where it will end no one can divine. . . .

The discriminating laws, all will concede, are degrading to those against which they operate, and the degrader will be degraded also. "For all acts are reactionary, and will return in curses upon those who curse," said Stephen A. Douglass [*sic*], the great competitor of President Lincoln. Neither does it require a philosopher to inform you that degradation begets degradation. Any people oppressed, proscribed, belied, slandered, burned, flayed and lynched will not only become cowardly and servile, but will transmit that same servility to their posterity, and continue to do so *ad infinitum,* and as such will never make a bold and courageous people. The condition of the Negro in the United States is so repugnant to the instincts of respected manhood that thousands, yea hundreds of thousands, of miscegenated will pass for white, and snub the people with whom they are identified at every opportunity, thus destroying themselves, or at least *unracing* themselves. They do not want to be black because of its ignoble condition, and they cannot be white, thus they become monstrosities. Thousands of young men who are even educated by white teachers never have any respect for people of their own color and spend their days as devotees of white gods. Hundreds, if not thousands, of the terms employed by the white race in the English language are also degrading to the black man. Everything that is satanic, corrupt, base and infamous is denominated *black,* and all that constitutes virtue, purity, innocence, religion, and that which is divine and heavenly, is represented as *white.* Our Sabbath-school children, by the time they reach proper consciousness, are taught to sing to the laudation of white and to the contempt of black. Can any one with an ounce of common sense expect that these children, when they reach maturity, will ever have any respect for their black or colored faces, or the faces of their associates? But, without multiplying words, the terms used in our religious experience, and the hymns we sing in many instances, are degrading, and will be as long as the black man is surrounded by the idea that *white* represents God and black represents the devil. The Negro should, therefore, build up a nation of his own, and create a language in keeping with his color, as the whites have done. Nor will he ever respect himself until he does it. . . .

What the black man needs is a country and surroundings in harmony with his color and with respect for his manhood. Upon this point I would

---

segregation by private businesses (inns, hotels, theaters, and a railroad). Writing for the majority, Justice Joseph P. Bradley ruled that the Thirteenth, Fourteenth, and Fifteenth amendments did not give the federal government the power to outlaw discriminatory practices by private organizations, but only by states. See 109 U.S. 3, 3 S. Ct., 18, 27, L. Ed. 835 (1883).

CHAPTER 2

THE ROAD TO
TRUE FREEDOM:
AFRICAN
AMERICAN
ALTERNATIVES
IN THE NEW
SOUTH

delight to dwell longer if I had time. Thousands of white people in this country are ever and anon advising the colored people to keep out of politics, but they do not advise themselves. If the Negro is a man in keeping with other men, why should he be less concerned about politics than any one else? Strange, too, that a number of would-be colored leaders are ignorant and debased enough to proclaim the same foolish jargon. For the Negro to stay out of politics is to level himself with a horse or a cow, which is no politician, and the Negro who does it proclaims his inability to take part in political affairs. If the Negro is to be a man, full and complete, he must take part in everything that belongs to manhood. If he omits a single duty, responsibility or privilege, to that extent he is limited and incomplete.

Time, however, forbids my continuing the discussion of this subject, roughly and hastily as these thoughts have been thrown together. Not being able to present a dozen or two more phases, which I would cheerfully and gladly do if opportunity permitted, I conclude by saying the argument that it would be impossible to transport the colored people of the United States back to Africa is an advertisement of folly. Two hundred millions of dollars would rid this country of the last member of the Negroid race, if such a thing was desirable, and two hundred and fifty millions would give every man, woman and child excellent fare, and the general government could furnish that amount and never miss it, and that would only be the pitiful sum of a million dollars a year for the time we labored for nothing, and for which somebody or some power is responsible. The emigrant agents at New York, Boston, Philadelphia, St. John, N.B., and Halifax, N.S., with whom I have talked, establish beyond contradiction, that over a million, and from that to twelve hundred thousand persons, come to this country every year, and yet there is no public stir about it. But in the case of African emigration, two or three millions only of self-reliant men and women would be necessary to establish the conditions we are advocating in Africa. . . .

Source 4 from Nathan Huggins, comp., *W. E. B. Du Bois Writings* (New York: Library of America, 1986), pp. 842, 846–848, 860–861.

4. W. E. B. Du Bois's "The Talented Tenth," 1903 (excerpt).

The Negro race, like all races, is going to be saved by its exceptional men. The problem of education, then, among Negroes must first of all deal with the Talented Tenth; it is the problem of developing the Best of this race that they may guide the Mass away from the contamination and death of the Worst, in their own and other races. Now the training of men is a difficult and intricate task. Its technique is a matter for educational experts, but its object is for the vision of seers. If we make money the object of man-training, we shall develop money-makers but not necessarily men; if we make technical skill the object of education, we may possess artisans but not, in nature, men. Men we shall have only as we make manhood the object of the work of the schools—intelligence, broad sympathy, knowledge of the world that was and is, and of the relation [of] men to it—this is the curriculum of that Higher Education which must underlie true life. On this foundation we may build bread-winning skill of hand and quickness of brain, with never a fear lest the child and man mistake the means of living for the object of life. . . .

[Here Du Bois argued against those who asserted that African American "leadership should have begun at the plow and not in the Senate" by stating that for 250 years blacks had been at the plow and were still "half-free serfs" without political rights. He then went on to say that many people focused their attention on "death, disease, and crime" among blacks, ignoring those who had achieved education, professions, homes, and the like.]

Can the masses of the Negro people be in any possible way more quickly raised than by the effort and example of this aristocracy of talent and character? Was there ever a nation on God's fair earth civilized from the bottom upward? Never; it is, ever was and ever will be from the top downward that culture filters. The Talented Tenth rises and pulls all that are worth the saving up to their vantage ground. This is the history of human progress; and the two historic mistakes which have hindered that progress were the thinking first that no more could ever rise save the few already risen; or second, that it would better the unrisen to pull the risen down.

How then shall the leaders of a struggling people be trained and the hands of the risen few strengthened? There can be but one answer: The best and most capable of their youth must be schooled in the colleges and universities of the land. We will not quarrel as to just what the university of the Negro should teach or how it should teach it—I willingly admit that each soul and each race-soul needs its own peculiar curriculum. But this is true: A university is a human invention for the transmission of knowledge and culture from generation to generation, through the training of quick minds and pure hearts, and for this work no other human invention will suffice, not even trade and industrial schools.

All men cannot go to college but some men must; every isolated group or nation must have its yeast, must have for the talented few centers of training where men are not so mystified and befuddled by the hard and necessary toil of earning a living, as to have no aims higher than their

CHAPTER 2

THE ROAD TO
TRUE FREEDOM:
AFRICAN
AMERICAN
ALTERNATIVES
IN THE NEW
SOUTH

bellies, and no God greater than Gold. This is true training, and thus in the beginning were the favored sons of the freedmen trained.

Thus, again, in the manning of trade schools and manual training schools we are thrown back upon the higher training as its source and chief support. There was a time when any aged and wornout carpenter could teach in a trade school. But not so to-day. Indeed the demand for college-bred men by a school like Tuskegee, ought to make Mr. Booker T. Washington the firmest friend of higher training. Here he has as helpers the son of a Negro senator, trained in Greek and the humanities, and graduated at Harvard; the son of a Negro congressman and lawyer, trained in Latin and mathematics, and graduated at Oberlin; he has as his wife, a woman who read Virgil and Homer in the same class room with me; he has as college chaplain, a classical graduate of Atlanta University; as teacher of science, a graduate of Fisk; as teacher of history, a graduate of Smith,—indeed some thirty of his chief teachers are college graduates, and instead of studying French grammars in the midst of weeds, or buying pianos for dirty cabins, they are at Mr. Washington's right hand helping him in a noble work. And yet one of the effects of Mr. Washington's propaganda has been to throw doubt upon the expediency of such training for Negroes, as these persons have had.

Men of America, the problem is plain before you. Here is a race transplanted through the criminal foolishness of your fathers. Whether you like it or not the millions are here, and here they will remain. If you do not lift them up, they will pull you down. Education and work are the levers to uplift a people. Work alone will not do it unless inspired by the right ideals and guided by intelligence. Education must not simply teach work—it must teach Life. The Talented Tenth of the Negro race must be made leaders of thought and missionaries of culture among their people. No others can do this work and Negro colleges must train men for it. The Negro race, like all other races, is going to be saved by its exceptional men. . . .

Source 5 from Herbert Atheker, ed., *Pamphlets and Leaflets by W. E. B. Du Bois* (White Plains, N.Y.: Kraus-Thomson Organization Ltd., 1986), pp. 63–65.

5. Du Bois's Niagara Address, 1906 (excerpt).[10]

. . . In detail our demands are clear and unequivocal. First, we would vote; with the right to vote goes everything: Freedom, manhood, the honor of your wives, the chastity of your daughters, the right to work, and the chance to rise, and let no man listen to those who deny this.

10. The Niagara Movement was organized by Du Bois in 1905. It called for agitation against all forms of segregation. This is a selection from Du Bois's address to the group in 1906.

We want full manhood suffrage, and we want it now, henceforth and forever.

Second. We want discrimination in public accommodation to cease. Separation in railway and street cars, based simply on race and color, is un-American, undemocratic, and silly. We protest against all such discrimination.

Third. We claim the right of freemen to walk, talk, and be with them that wish to be with us. No man has a right to choose another man's friends, and to attempt to do so is an impudent interference with the most fundamental human privilege.

Fourth. We want the laws enforced against rich as well as poor; against Capitalist as well as Laborer; against white as well as black. We are not more lawless than the white race, we are more often arrested, convicted and mobbed. We want justice even for criminals and outlaws. We want the Constitution of the country enforced. We want Congress to take charge of Congressional elections. We want the Fourteenth Amendment carried out to the letter and every State disfranchised in Congress which attempts to disfranchise its rightful voters. We want the Fifteenth Amendment enforced and no State allowed to base its franchise simply on color.

The failure of the Republican Party in Congress at the session just closed to redeem its pledge of 1904 with reference to suffrage conditions [in] the South seems a plain, deliberate, and premeditated breach of promise, and stamps that party as guilty of obtaining votes under false pretense.

Fifth. We want our children educated. The school system in the country districts of the South is a disgrace and in few towns and cities are the Negro schools what they ought to be. We want the national government to step in and wipe out illiteracy in the South. Either the United States will destroy ignorance or ignorance will destroy the United States.

And when we call for education we mean real education. We believe in work. We ourselves are workers, but work is not necessarily education. Education is the development of power and ideal. We want our children trained as intelligent human beings should be, and we will fight for all time against any proposal to educate black boys and girls simply as servants and underlings, or simply for the use of other people. They have a right to know, to think, to aspire.

These are some of the chief things which we want. How shall we get them? By voting where we may vote, by persistent, unceasing agitation, by hammering at the truth, by sacrifice and work.

We do not believe in violence, neither in the despised violence of the raid nor the lauded violence of the soldier, nor the barbarous violence of the mob, but we do believe in John Brown, in that incarnate spirit of justice, that hatred of a lie, that willingness to sacrifice money, reputation, and life itself on the altar of right. And here on the scene of John Brown's martyrdom we

CHAPTER 2

THE ROAD TO
TRUE FREEDOM:
AFRICAN
AMERICAN
ALTERNATIVES
IN THE NEW
SOUTH

reconsecrate ourselves, our honor, our property to the final emancipation of the race which John Brown died to make free.

Our enemies, triumphant for the present, are fighting the stars in their courses. Justice and humanity must prevail. We live to tell these dark brothers of ours—scattered in counsel, wavering and weak—that no bribe of money or notoriety, no promise of wealth or fame, is worth the surrender of a people's manhood or the loss of a man's self-respect. We refuse to surrender the leadership of this race to cowards and trucklers. We are men; we will be treated as men. On this rock we have planted our banners. We will never give up, though the trump of doom find us still fighting.

And we shall win. The past promised it, the present foretells it. Thank God for John Brown! Thank God for Garrison and Douglass! Sumner and Phillips, Nat Turner and Robert Gould Shaw,[11] and all the hallowed dead who died for freedom! Thank God for all those today, few though their voices be, who have not forgotten the divine brotherhood of all men, white and black, rich and poor, fortunate and unfortunate.

We appeal to the young men and women of this nation, to those whose nostrils are not yet befouled by greed and snobbery and racial narrowness: Stand up for the right, prove yourselves worthy of your heritage and whether born north or south dare to treat men as men. Cannot the nation that has absorbed ten million foreigners into its political life without catastrophe absorb ten million Negro Americans into that same political life at less cost than their unjust and illegal exclusion will involve?

Courage, brothers! The battle for humanity is not lost or losing. All across the skies sit signs of promise. The Slav is rising in his might, the yellow millions are tasting liberty, the black Africans are writhing toward the light, and everywhere the laborer, with ballot in his hand, is voting open the gates of Opportunity and Peace. The morning breaks over blood-stained hills. We must not falter, we may not shrink. Above are the everlasting stars.

Source 6 from Frances Smith Foster, ed., *A Brighter Coming Day: A Frances Ellen Watkins Harper Reader* (New York: Feminist Press, 1990), pp. 285–292.

6. Frances E. W. Harper's "Enlightened Motherhood," an Address to the Brooklyn Literary Society, November 15, 1892 (excerpt).

It is nearly thirty years since an emancipated people stood on the threshold of a new era, facing an uncertain future—a legally unmarried race, to be

11. Robert Gould Shaw was a Massachusetts white man who during the Civil War commanded African American troops. While leading those soldiers into battle, Shaw was killed on July 18, 1863. He was portrayed in the 1989 film *Glory*.

taught the sacredness of the marriage relation; an ignorant people, to be taught to read the book of the Christian law and to learn to comprehend more fully the claims of the gospel of the Christ of Calvary. A homeless race, to be gathered into homes of peaceful security and to be instructed how to plant around their firesides the strongest batteries against the sins that degrade and the race vices that demoralize. A race unversed in the science of government and unskilled in the just administration of law, to be translated from the old oligarchy of slavery into the new commonwealth of freedom, and to whose men came the right to exchange the fetters on their wrists for the ballots in their right hands—a ballot which, if not vitiated by fraud or restrained by intimidation, counts just as much as that of the most talented and influential man in the land.

While politicians may stumble on the barren mountain of fretful controversy, and men, lacking faith in God and the invisible forces which make for righteousness, may shrink from the unsolved problems of the hour, into the hands of Christian women comes the opportunity of serving the ever blessed Christ, by ministering to His little ones and striving to make their homes the brightest spots on earth and the fairest types of heaven. The school may instruct and the church may teach, but the home is an institution older than the church and antedates school, and that is the place where children should be trained for useful citizenship on earth and a hope of holy companionship in heaven. . . .

The home may be a humble spot, where there are no velvet carpets to hush your tread, no magnificence to surround your way, nor costly creations of painter's art or sculptor's skill to please your conceptions or gratify your tastes; but what are the costliest gifts of fortune when placed in the balance with the confiding love of dear children or the true devotion of a noble and manly husband whose heart can safely trust in his wife? You may place upon the brow of a true wife and mother the greenest laurels; you may crowd her hands with civic honors; but, after all, to her there will be no place like home, and the crown of her motherhood will be more precious than the diadem of a queen. . . .

Marriage between two youthful and loving hearts means the laying [of] the foundation stones of a new home, and the woman who helps erect that home should be careful not to build it above the reeling brain of a drunkard or the weakened fibre of a debauchee. If it be folly for a merchant to send an argosy, laden with the richest treasures, at midnight on a moonless sea, without a rudder, compass, or guide, is it not madness for a woman to trust her future happiness, and the welfare of the dear children who may yet nestle in her arms and make music and sunshine around her fireside, in the unsteady hands of a characterless man, too lacking in self-respect and self-control to hold the helm and rudder of his own

CHAPTER 2

THE ROAD TO
TRUE FREEDOM:
AFRICAN
AMERICAN
ALTERNATIVES
IN THE NEW
SOUTH

life; who drifts where he ought to steer, and only lasts when he ought to live?

The moment the crown of motherhood falls on the brow of a young wife, God gives her a new interest in the welfare of the home and the good of society. If hitherto she had been content to trip through life a lighthearted girl, or to tread amid the halls of wealth and fashion the gayest of the gay, life holds for her now a high and noble service. She must be more than the child of pleasure or the devotee of fashion. Her work is grandly constructive. A helpless and ignorant babe lies smiling in her arms. God has trusted her with a child, and it is her privilege to help that child develop the most precious thing a man or woman can possess on earth, and that is a good character. Moth may devour our finest garments, fire may consume and floods destroy our fairest homes, rust may gather on our silver and tarnish our gold, but there is an asbestos that no fire can destroy, a treasure which shall be richer for its service and better for its use, and that is a good character. . . .

Are there not women, respectable women, who feel that it would wring their hearts with untold anguish, and bring their gray hairs in sorrow to the grave, if their daughters should trail the robes of their womanhood in the dust, yet who would say of their sons, if they were trampling their manhood down and fettering their souls with cords of vice, "O, well, boys will be boys, and young men will sow their wild oats."

I hold that no woman loves social purity as it deserves to be loved and valued, if she cares for the purity of her daughters and not her sons; who would gather her dainty robes from contact with the fallen woman and yet greet with smiling lips and clasp with warm and welcoming hands the author of her wrong and ruin. How many mothers to-day shrink from a double standard for society which can ostracise the woman and condone the offense of the man? How many mothers say within their hearts, "I intend to teach my boy to be as pure in his life, as chaste in his conversation, as the young girl who sits at my side encircled in the warm clasp of loving arms?" How many mothers strive to have their boys shun the gilded saloon as they would the den of a deadly serpent? Not the mother who thoughtlessly sends her child to the saloon for a beverage to make merry with her friends. How many mothers teach their boys to shrink in horror from the fascinations of women, not as God made them, but as sin has degraded them? . . .

I would ask, in conclusion, is there a branch of the human race in the Western Hemisphere which has greater need of the inspiring and uplifting influences that can flow out of the lives and examples of the truly enlightened than ourselves? Mothers who can teach their sons not to love pleasure or fear death; mothers who can teach their children to embrace every opportunity, employ every power, and use every means to build up a future to contrast with the old sad past. Men may boast of the aristocracy of blood; they may glory in the aristocracy of talent, and be proud of the aristocracy of wealth, but there is an aristocracy which must ever outrank them all, and that is the aristocracy of character.

The work of the mothers of our race is grandly constructive. It is for us to build above the wreck and ruin of the past more stately temples of thought and action. Some races have been overthrown, dashed in pieces, and destroyed; but to-day the world is needing, fainting, for something better than the results of arrogance, aggressiveness, and indomitable power. We need mothers who are capable of being character builders, patient, loving, strong, and true, whose homes will be an uplifting power in the race. This is one of the greatest needs of the hour. No race can afford to neglect the enlightenment of its mothers. If you would have a clergy without virtue or morality, a manhood without honor, and a womanhood frivolous, mocking, and ignorant, neglect the education of your daughters. But if, on the other hand, you would have strong men, virtuous women, and good homes, then enlighten your women, so that they may be able to bless their homes by the purity of their lives, the tenderness of their hearts, and the strength of their intellects. From schools and colleges your children may come well versed in ancient lore and modern learning, but it is for us to learn and teach, within the shadow of our own homes, the highest and best of all sciences, the science of a true life. When the last lay of the minstrel shall die upon his ashy lips, and the sweetest numbers of the poet cease to charm his death-dulled ear; when the eye of the astronomer shall be too dim to mark the path of worlds that roll in light and power on high; and when all our earthly knowledge has performed for us its mission, and we are ready to lay aside our environments as garments we have outworn and outgrown: if we have learned the science of a true life, we may rest assured that this acquirement will go with us through the valley and shadow of death, only to grow lighter and brighter through the eternities.

✳ QUESTIONS TO CONSIDER ✳

The Background section of this chapter strongly suggests that the prospects for African Americans in the post-Reconstruction South were bleak. Although blacks certainly preferred sharecropping or tenancy to working in gangs as in the days of slavery, neither sharecropping nor

CHAPTER 2

THE ROAD TO
TRUE FREEDOM:
AFRICAN
AMERICAN
ALTERNATIVES
IN THE NEW
SOUTH

tenancy offered African Americans much chance to own their own land. Furthermore, the industrial opportunities available to European immigrants, which allowed many of them gradually to climb the economic ladder, for the most part were closed to southern blacks, in part because the South was never able to match the North in the creation of industrial jobs and in part because what jobs the New South industrialization did create often were closed to blacks. As we have seen, educational opportunities for African Americans in the South were severely limited—so much so that by 1890, more than 75 percent of the adult black population in the Deep South still was illiterate (as opposed to 17.1 percent of the adult white population). In addition, rigid segregation laws and racial violence had increased dramatically. Indeed, the prospects for southern blacks were far from promising.

Begin by analyzing Ida B. Wells's response (Source 1) to the deteriorating condition of African Americans in the South. In her view, how did blacks in Memphis and Kentucky provide a model for others? What was that model? In addition to that model, Wells tells us how blacks in Jacksonville, Florida, and Paducah, Kentucky, were able to prevent lynchings in those towns. What alternative did those blacks present? Was Wells advocating it? Finally, what role did Wells see the African American press playing in preventing lynchings?

The alternative offered by Booker T. Washington (Source 2) differs markedly from those offered by Wells. In his view, what *process* should African Americans follow to enjoy their full rights? How did he support his argument? What did Washington conceive the role of southern whites in African Americans' progress to be? Before you dismiss Washington's alternative, remember that his *goals* were roughly similar to those of Wells. Also use some inference to imagine how Washington's audiences would have reacted to his speech. How would southern whites have greeted his speech? Southern blacks? What about northern whites? Northern blacks? To whom was Washington speaking?

Now move on to Henry McNeal Turner's alternative (Source 3). At first Bishop Turner seems to be insulting blacks. What was he really trying to say? Why did he think that God ordained blacks to be brought to America in chains? In Turner's view, once blacks were freed, what was their best alternative? Why? Turner's view of whites is at serious odds with that of Washington. How do the two views differ on this point? How did Turner use his view of whites to support his alternative for blacks?

Taken together, the two speeches by W. E. B. Du Bois (Sources 4 and 5) present a consistent view, even though their subject matter and emphasis are different. What was the "talented tenth"? In Du Bois's view, what crucial role must that group play? How is that view at odds with Washington's view? In his Niagara Address of 1906, Du Bois states what the goals of the "talented tenth" should be. What are those objectives? How does his *process* differ from that of Washington? Furthermore, how does Du Bois's view differ from Washington's with respect to timing? Tactics? Tone? Remember, however, that the long-term goals of both men were similar.

Perhaps you have been struck by the fact that both Turner and Du Bois pinned their hopes for progress on African American *men*. Turner refers frequently to "manhood" and Du Bois to "exceptional men." Why do you think this was so? Why do you think the concept of African American manhood was important to these two thinkers?

For Frances E. W. Harper (Source 6), the hopes of African Americans lay not with black men but with black *women*. Why did she believe this was so? As opposed to education, work, or the political arena, in Harper's view what was the importance of the African American home? Would Harper have agreed or disagreed with Wells? Washington? Turner? Du Bois? How might African American men such as Washington, Turner, and Du Bois have reacted to her arguments?

After you have examined each of the alternatives, move on to your assessment of the strengths and weaknesses of each argument. As noted earlier, you will need to review the Background section of this chapter in order to establish the historical context in which the five arguments were made. Then, using that context, try to imagine the reactions that these alternatives might have elicited in the following situations:

1. What would have happened if southern African Americans had come to adopt Wells's alternatives? Where might the process outlined by Wells have led? Were there any risks for African Americans? If so, what were they?

2. What would have happened if southern African Americans had adopted Washington's alternative? How long would it have taken them to realize Washington's goals? Were there any risks involved? If so, what were they?

3. What would have happened if southern African Americans had adopted Turner's alternative? Were there any risks involved? How realistic was Turner's option?

4. What would have happened if southern African Americans had adopted Du Bois's alternative? How long would Du Bois's process have taken? Were there any risks involved?

5. Was white assistance necessary according to Wells? to Washington? to Turner? to Du Bois? How did each spokesperson perceive the roles of the federal government and the federal courts? How did the government and courts stand on this issue at the time? [*Clue:* What was the Supreme Court decision in *Plessy v. Ferguson* (1896)?]

6. How might blacks and whites have reacted to Harper's arguments? black women? black men? As with the ideas of Washington, how long would it have taken African Americans who embraced Harper's ideas to reach the goals of social, economic, and political equality?

To be sure, it is very nearly impossible for us to put ourselves completely in the shoes of these men and women. While racism still is a strong force in American life today, the intel-

CHAPTER 2

THE ROAD TO
TRUE FREEDOM:
AFRICAN
AMERICAN
ALTERNATIVES
IN THE NEW
SOUTH

lectual and cultural environment was dramatically different in the time these five spokespersons were offering their ideas to African Americans. Even so, by placing each spokesperson in a historical context, we should be able to evaluate the strengths and weaknesses of his or her argument.

❈ EPILOGUE ❈

For the advocates of a New South, the realization of their dream seemed to be just over the horizon, always just beyond their grasp. Many of the factories did make a good deal of money. But profits often flowed out of the South to northern investors. And factory owners often maintained profits by paying workers pitifully low wages, which led to the rise of a poor white urban class that lived in slums and faced enormous problems of malnutrition, poor health, family instability, and crime. To most of those who had left their meager farms to find opportunities in the burgeoning southern cities, life there appeared even worse than it had been in the rural areas. Many whites returned to their rural homesteads disappointed and dispirited by urban life.

For an increasing number of southern African Americans, the solution seemed to be to abandon the South entirely. Beginning around the time of World War I (1917–1918), a growing number of African Americans migrated to the industrial cities of the Northeast, Midwest, and West Coast (see Source 7). But there, too, they met racial hostility and racially inspired riots.

But in the North, African Americans could vote and thereby influence public policy. By the late 1940s, it had become clear that northern urban African American voters, by their very number, could force American politicians to deal with racial discrimination. By the 1950s, it was evident that the South would have to change its racial policies, if not willingly then by force. It took federal courts, federal marshals, and occasionally federal troops, but the crust of discrimination in the South began to be broken in the 1960s. Attitudes changed slowly, but the white southern politician draped in the Confederate flag and calling for resistance to change became a figure of the past. Although much work still needed to be done, changes in the South had been profound, laying the groundwork for more changes ahead. Indeed, by the 1960s the industrialization and prosperity (largely through in-migration) of the Sunbelt seemed to show that Grady's dream of a New South might become a reality.

And yet, for all the hopeful indications (black voting and officeholding in the South, for instance), in many ways the picture was a somber one. By the 1970s, several concerned observers, both black and white, feared that the poorest 30 percent of all black families, instead of climbing slowly up the economic ladder, were in the process of forming a permanent underclass, complete with a social pathology

Source 7 from U.S. Bureau of the Census, *Historical Statistics of the United States, Colonial Times to 1970* (Washington, D.C.: U.S. Government Printing Office, 1975), Vol. I, p. 95.

7. Estimated Net Intercensal Migration* of Negro Population by Region, 1870–1920 (in thousands).

Region	1870–1880	1880–1890	1890–1900	1900–1910	1910–1920
New England[1]	4.5	6.6	14.2	8.0	12.0
Middle Atlantic[2]	19.2	39.1	90.7	87.2	170.1
East North Central[3]	20.8	16.4	39.4	45.6	200.4
West North Central[4]	15.7	7.9	23.5	10.2	43.7
South Atlantic[5]	−47.9	−72.5	−181.6	−111.9	−158.0
East South Central[6]	−56.2	−60.1	−43.3	−109.6	−246.3
West South Central[7]	45.1	62.9	56.9	51.0	−46.2

*A net intercensal migration represents the amount of migration that took place between U.S. censuses, which are taken every ten years. The net figure is computed by comparing in-migration with out-migration to a particular state. A minus figure means that out-migration from a state was greater than in-migration.
1. Maine, New Hampshire, Vermont, Massachusetts, Rhode Island, and Connecticut.
2. New York, New Jersey, and Pennsylvania.
3. Ohio, Indiana, Illinois, Michigan, and Wisconsin.
4. Minnesota, Iowa, Missouri, North Dakota, South Dakota, Nebraska, and Kansas.
5. Delaware, Maryland, District of Columbia, Virginia, West Virginia, North Carolina, South Carolina, Georgia, and Florida.
6. Kentucky, Tennessee, Alabama, and Mississippi.
7. Arkansas, Louisiana, Oklahoma, and Texas.

that included broken families, crime, drugs, violence, and grinding poverty. Equally disturbing in the 1980s was a new wave of racial intolerance among whites, a phenomenon that even invaded many American colleges and universities. In short, although much progress had been made since the turn of the nineteenth century, in many ways, as in the New South, the dream of equality and tolerance remained just over the horizon.

By this time, of course, Wells, Washington, Turner, Du Bois, and Harper were dead. Wells continued to write militant articles for the African American press, became deeply involved in the women's suffrage movement, and carried on a successful crusade to prevent the racial segregation of the Chicago city schools. She died in Chicago in 1931. For his part, Washington publicly clung to his notion of self-help while secretly supporting more aggressive efforts to gain political rights for African Americans. He died in Tuskegee, Alabama, in 1915.

Turner's dream of thousands of blacks moving to Africa never materialized. In response, he grew more strident and was especially critical of African Americans who opposed his

CHAPTER 2

THE ROAD TO
TRUE FREEDOM:
AFRICAN
AMERICAN
ALTERNATIVES
IN THE NEW
SOUTH

ideas. In 1898, Turner raised a storm of protest when his essay "God Is a Negro" was published. The essay began, "We have as much right . . . to believe that God is a Negro, as you buckra, or white, people have to believe that God is a fine looking, symmetrical and ornamented white man."[12] He died while on a speaking trip to Canada in 1915. As for Du Bois, he eventually turned away from his championship of a "talented tenth" in favor of more mass protests. As a harbinger of many African Americans of the 1960s and 1970s, he embraced pan-Africanism, combining it with his long-held Marxist ideas. He died in Africa in 1963.

Harper was one of the most popular poets of her time. After her husband's death, she became increasingly vocal on feminist issues, was a friend and ally of Susan B. Anthony, and, in 1866, delivered a moving address before the National Women's Rights Convention. She died in Philadelphia, Pennsylvania, from heart disease in 1911. Her home has been preserved as a national historic landmark.

In their time, Wells, Washington, Turner, Du Bois, and Harper were important and respected figures. Although often publicly at odds with one another, they shared the same dream of African Americans living with pride and dignity in a world that recognized them as complete men and women. In an era in which few people championed the causes of African Americans in the New South, these five spokespersons stood out as courageous individuals.

12. Edwin S. Redkey, ed., *Respect Black: The Writings and Speeches of Henry McNeal Turner* (New York: Arno Press, 1971), pp. 176–177.

3

How They Lived:
Middle-Class Life, 1870–1917

❇ THE PROBLEM ❇

In the 1870s, Heinrich Schliemann, a middle-aged German archaeologist, astonished the world with his claim that he had discovered the site of ancient Troy. As all educated people of the time knew, Troy was the golden city of heroes that the blind poet Homer (seventh century B.C.E.) made famous in his *Iliad* and *Odyssey*. Although archaeologists continued to argue bitterly about whether it was really Troy or some other ancient city that Schliemann was excavating, the general public was fascinated with the vases, gold and silver cups, necklaces, and earrings that were unearthed.

Not only the relics and "treasure" interested Americans, however. As the magazine *Nation* pointed out in 1875, these discoveries offered an opportunity to know about Troy as it had actually existed and to understand something about the daily lives of the inhabitants. Nineteenth-century Americans were intensely curious about the art, religion, burial customs, dress, and even the foods of the ancient Greeks. "Real Trojans," noted a magazine editor in 1881, "were very fond of oysters." (He based his conclusion on the large amounts of oyster shells uncovered at the archaeological digs.)

Material culture study is the use of artifacts to understand people's lives. In this chapter, you will be looking at some artifacts of the late nineteenth and early twentieth centuries—advertisements and house plans—to try to reconstruct the lives of middle-class white Americans during a period when the country was changing rapidly. What were Americans' hopes and fears during this era? What were their values?

❋ BACKGROUND ❋

The age from approximately 1870 to 1900 was characterized by enormous and profound changes in American life. Unquestionably, the most important changes were the nation's rapid industrialization and urbanization. Aided and accelerated by the rapid growth of railroads, emerging industries could extend their tentacles throughout the nation, collecting raw materials and fuel for the factories and distributing finished products to the growing American population. By 1900, that industrial process had come to be dominated by a few energetic and shrewd men, captains of industry to their friends and robber barons to their enemies. Almost every conceivable industry, from steel and oil to sugar refining and meat packing, was controlled by one or two gigantic corporations that essentially had the power to set prices on the raw materials bought and the finished products sold. In turn, the successes of those corporations created a new class of fabulously rich industrialists, and names like Swift, Armour, Westinghouse, Pillsbury, Pullman, Rockefeller, Carnegie, and Duke literally became almost household words, as much for the notoriety of the industrialists as for the industries and products they created.

As America became more industrialized, it also became more urban. In the past, the sizes of cities had been limited by the availability of nearby food, fuel, and employment opportunities. But the network of railroads and the rise of large factories had removed those limitations, and American cities grew phenomenally. Between 1860 and 1910, urban population increased sevenfold, and by 1920 more than half of all Americans lived in cities.[1] These urban complexes not only dominated the regions in which they were located but eventually set much of the tone for the entire nation as well.

Both processes—industrialization and urbanization—profoundly altered nearly every facet of American life. Family size began to decrease; the woman who might have had five or six children in 1860 was replaced by the "new" woman of 1900 who had only three or four children. The fruits of industrialization, distributed by new marketing techniques, could be enjoyed by a large portion of the American population. Electric lights, telephones, and eventually home appliances virtually revolutionized the lives of the middle and upper classes, as did Ford's later mass production of the Model T automobile.

The nature of the work also was changed because factories required a higher degree of regimentation than did farm work or the "putting-out" system. Many industries found it more profitable to employ women and children than adult males, thus altering the home lives of many of the nation's working-class citizens. Moreover, the lure of employment brought millions of immigrants to the United States, most of whom huddled together in

1. The census defined *city* as a place with a population over twenty-five hundred people. Thus, many of the cities referred to in this chapter are what we would call towns, or even small towns.

cities, found low-paying jobs, and dreamed of the future. And as the cities grew grimy with factory soot and became increasingly populated by laborers, immigrants, and what one observer referred to as the "dangerous classes," upper- and middle-class Americans began to abandon the urban cores and retreat to fashionable suburbs on the peripheries, to return to the cities either in their automobiles or on streetcars only for work or recreation. In fact, the comforts of middle-class life were made possible, in part, by the exploitation of industrial workers.

Industrialization and urbanization not only changed how most Americans lived but how they *thought* as well. Faith in progress and technology was almost boundless, and there was widespread acceptance of the uneven distribution of wealth among Americans. Prior to the turn of the century, many upper- and middle-class Americans believed that life was a struggle in which the fittest survived. This concept, which applied Charles Darwin's discoveries about biological evolution to society, was called social Darwinism. The poor, especially the immigrant poor, were seen as biologically and morally inferior. It followed, then, that efforts to help the less fortunate through charity or government intervention were somehow tampering with both God's will and Darwinian evolution. In such a climate of opinion, the wealthy leaders of gigantic corporations became national heroes, superior in prestige to both preachers and presidents.

The response of the working classes varied; although many workers rejected the concepts of social Darwinism and Victorian morality, others aspired to middle-class status. In spite of long hours, low pay, and hazardous conditions, the men and women of the working classes engaged in a series of important labor protests and strikes during this period. A rich working-class culture developed in the saloons, vaudeville theaters, dance halls, and streets of medium-size and larger cities. Many workers sought alternatives in some form of socialism; many others, however, strove to achieve the standard of living of the rapidly expanding middle class. Across the country, young boys read the rags-to-riches tales of Horatio Alger, and girls learned to be "proper ladies" so that they would not embarrass their future husbands as they rose in society together.

Social critics and reformers of the time were appalled by the excesses of the "fabulously rich" and the misery of the "wretchedly poor." And yet a persistent belief in the opportunity to better one's position (or one's children's position) led many people to embrace an optimistic attitude and to focus on the acquisition of material possessions. New consumer goods were pouring from factories, and the housing industry was booming. Middle-class families emulated the housing and furnishing styles of the wealthy, and skilled blue-collar workers and their families aspired to own modest suburban homes on the streetcar line.

After 1900, widespread concern about the relationship of wages to the cost of maintaining a comfortable standard of living led to numerous studies of working-class families in various parts of the country. Could workers realistically hope to own homes and achieve decent standards of living as a result of their labor? In 1909, economist Robert Coit Chapin estimated that a family of five needed an annual income of about $900 to live in a decent home or apartment in New York City. A follow-up study of Philadelphia in 1917 estimated that same standard of living at approximately $1,600. Yet the average annual pay of adult male wage workers during these years ranged from only $600 to $1,700. Several other factors affected family income, however. Average wages are misleading, since skilled workers earned significantly more than unskilled or semiskilled workers. Even within the same industry and occupation, midwestern workers earned more than northeastern workers, and southern workers earned the lowest wages of all. Adult women workers, 80 percent of whom lived with families as wives or unmarried daughters, added their wages (approximately $300 to $600 a year) to the family income, as did working children. Many families, especially those of recent immigrants, also took in boarders and lodgers, who paid rent.

Finally, the cost of land and building materials was much more expensive in large cities than in smaller cities and towns. In his investigation of New York, Chapin found that 28 percent of working-class families in nine upstate cities owned their own homes, compared with only 1 percent in New York City. Another study in 1915 also sharply illustrated regional differences in homeownership. Twenty percent of Paterson, New Jersey, silk workers were homeowners, but only 10 percent of Birmingham, Alabama, steelworkers owned homes. Nineteen percent of Milwaukee's working-class families owned their own homes, compared to 4.4 percent of Boston's working-class families. Nor were all these homes in the central city. Working-class suburbs expanded along streetcar lines or were developed near industries on the fringes of a city, such as the suburb of Oakwood just outside Knoxville, Tennessee.[2] In this community near textile mills and a major railroad repair shop, house lots measuring 50 by 140 feet sold for less than one hundred dollars; most homes were built for under one thousand dollars. Nearly half of the one thousand families who moved to Oakwood between 1902 and 1917 came from the older industrial sections of Knoxville.

Completely reliable income and cost statistics for early twentieth-century America do not exist, but it seems reasonable to estimate that at least one-fourth of working-class families owned or were paying for homes and that many more aspired to homeownership. But fully half of all working-class families, usually concentrated in large cities, lived in or near poverty and could not hope to own their own homes. Those with middle-class white-collar occupations were more fortunate. Lawyers, doctors, businessmen, ministers, bank tellers, newspaper editors, and even schoolteachers could—through careful budgeting and saving—realistically expect to buy or build a house.

2. Knoxville's population in 1900 was 32,637; the city had experienced a 237 percent growth in population from 1880 to 1900.

Although technological advances and new distribution methods put many modern conveniences and new products within the reach of all but the poorest Americans, the economic growth of the period was neither constant nor steady. The repercussions from two major depressions—one in 1873 and one in 1893—made "getting ahead" difficult, if not impossible, for many lower-middle-class and blue-collar families. Furthermore, at times everything seemed to be changing so rapidly that many people felt insecure. Yet within middle-class families, this sense of insecurity and even fear often coexisted with optimism and a faith in progress.

One way to understand the lives of middle-class Americans during the post–Civil War era is to look at the *things* with which they surrounded themselves: their clothes, the goods and services they bought, and even their houses. Why did such fashions and designs appeal to Americans of the late nineteenth and early twentieth centuries? What kind of an impression were these people trying to make on other people? How did they really feel about themselves? Sometimes historians, like archaeologists, use artifacts such as clothes, furniture, houses, and so forth to reconstruct the lives of Americans in earlier times. Indeed, each year many thousands of tourists visit historic homes such as Jefferson's Monticello, retrace the fighting at Gettysburg, or stroll through entire restored communities such as Colonial Williamsburg. But historians of the post–Civil War period also may use advertisements (instead of the products or services themselves) and house plans (instead of the actual houses) to understand how middle-class Americans lived and what their values and concerns were.

Every day, Americans are surrounded, even bombarded, by advertising that tries to convince them to buy some product, use some service, or compare brand X with brand Y. Television, radio, billboards, magazines, and newspapers spread the message to potential consumers of a variety of necessary—and unnecessary—products. Underlying this barrage of advertisements is an appeal to a wide range of emotions: ambition, elitism, guilt, and anxiety. A whole new "science" has arisen, called market research, that analyzes consumers' reactions and predicts future buying patterns.

Yet advertising is a relatively new phenomenon, one that began to develop after the Civil War and did not assume its modern form until the 1920s. P. T. Barnum, the promoter and impresario of mid-nineteenth-century entertainment, pointed the way with publicity gimmicks for his museum and circuses and, later, for the relatively unknown Swedish singer Jenny Lind. (Barnum created such a demand for Lind's concert tickets that they sold for as much as two hundred dollars each.) But at the time of the Civil War, most merchants still announced special sales of their goods in simple newspaper notices, and brand names were virtually unknown.

Businesses, both large and small, expanded enormously after the Civil War. Taking advantage of the country's greatly improved transportation and communication systems, daring business leaders established innovative ways to distribute products, such as the mail-order firm and the department store. Sears Roebuck & Company was founded in 1893, and its "wish book," or catalogue, rapidly became popular reading for millions of people, especially those who lived in rural areas. Almost one thousand pages long, these catalogues offered a dazzling variety of consumer goods and were filled with testimonial letters from satisfied customers. Lewis Thomas from Jefferson County, Alabama, wrote in 1897,

> I received my saddle and I must say that I am so pleased and satisfied with my saddle, words cannot express my thanks for the benefit that I received from the pleasure and satisfaction given me. I know that I have a saddle that will by ordinary care last a lifetime, and all my neighbors are pleased as well, and I am satisfied so well that you shall have more of my orders in the near future.

And from Granite, Colorado, Mrs. Laura Garrison wrote, "Received my suit all right, was much pleased with it, will recommend your house to my friends."

For those who lived in cities, the department store was yet another way to distribute consumer goods. The massive, impressively decorated buildings erected by department store owners were often described as consumer "cathedrals" or "palaces." In fact, no less a personage than President William Howard Taft dedicated the new Wanamaker's department store in Philadelphia in 1911. "We are here," Taft told the crowd, "to celebrate the completion of one of the most impor-

tant instrumentalities in modern life for the promotion of comfort among the people."

Many of the products being manufactured in factories in the late nineteenth and early twentieth centuries represented items previously made at home. Tinned meats and biscuits, "store-bought" bread, ready-made clothing, and soap all represented the impact of technology on the functions of the homemaker. Other products were new versions of things already being used. For example, the bathtub was designed solely for washing one's body, as opposed to the large bucket or tub in which one collected rainwater, washed clothes, and, every so often, bathed. Still other products and gadgets (such as the phonograph and the automobile) were completely new, the result of a fertile period of inventiveness (1860–1890) that saw more than ten times more patents issued than were issued during the entire period up to 1860 (only 36,000 patents were issued prior to the Civil War, but 440,000 were granted during the next thirty years).

There was no question that American industry could produce new products and distribute them nationwide. But there *was* a problem: How could American industry overcome the traditional American ethic of thrift and create a demand for products that might not have even existed a few years earlier? It was this problem that the new field of advertising set out to solve.

America in 1865 was a country of widespread, if uneven, literacy and a vast variety of newspapers and magazines, all competing for readership. Businesses quickly learned that mass production demanded a national, even an international, market, and money spent on national advertising in newspapers and magazines rose from $27 million in 1860 to more than $95 million in 1900. By 1929, the amount spent on advertising had climbed to more than $1 billion. Brand names and catchy slogans vied with one another to capture the consumer's interest. Consumers could choose from among many biscuit manufacturers, as the president of National Biscuit Company reported to his stockholders in 1901: "We do not pretend to sell our standard goods cheaper than other manufacturers of biscuits sell their goods. They always undersell us. Why do they not take away our business?" His answer was fourfold: efficiency, quality goods, innovative packaging, and advertising. "The trademarks we adopted," he concluded, "their value we created."

Advertising not only helped differentiate one brand of a product from another, but it also helped break down regional differences as well as differences between rural and urban lifestyles. Women living on farms in Kansas could order the latest "New York–style frocks" from a mail-order catalogue, and people in small towns in the Midwest or rural areas in the South could find the newest furniture styles, appliances, and automobiles enticingly displayed in mass-circulation magazines. In this era, more and more people abandoned the old ways of doing things and embraced the new ways of life that resulted from the application of modern technology, mass production, and efficient distribution of products. Thus, some historians have argued that advertising acceler-

ated the transition of American society from one that emphasized production to one that stressed consumption.

The collective mentality, ideas, mood, and values of the rapidly changing society were reflected in nearly everything the society created, including its architecture. During the period from approximately 1865 to 1900, American architects designed public buildings, factories, banks, apartment houses, offices, and residential structures, aided by technological advances that allowed them to do things that had been impossible in the past. For instance, as American cities grew in size and population density, the value of real estate soared. Therefore, it made sense to design higher and higher buildings, taking advantage of every square foot of available land. The perfection of central heating systems; the inventions of the radiator, the elevator, and the flush toilet; and the use of steel framing allowed architects such as William Le Baron Jenney, Louis Sullivan, and others of the Chicago school of architecture to erect the modern skyscraper, a combined triumph of architecture, engineering, ingenuity, and construction.

At the same time, the new industrial elite were hiring these same architects to build their new homes—homes that often resembled huge Italian villas, French chateaux, and even Renaissance palaces. Only the wealthy, however, could afford homes individually designed by professional architects. Most people relied on contractors, builders, and carpenters who adapted drawings from books or magazines to suit their clients' needs and tastes. Such "pattern books," published by such men as Henry Holly, the Palliser brothers, Robert Shoppell, and the Radford Architectural Company, were extremely popular. It is estimated that in the mid-1870s, at least one hundred homes a year were being built from plans published in one women's magazine, *Godey's Lady's Book,* and thousands of others were built from pamphlets provided by lumber and plumbing fixture companies and architectural pattern books. Eventually, a person could order a complete home through the mail; all parts of the prefabricated house were shipped by railroad for assembly by local workers on the owner's site. George Barber of Knoxville, Tennessee, the Aladdin Company of Bay City, Michigan, and even Sears Roebuck & Company were all prospering in mail-order homes around the turn of the century.

From the historian's viewpoint, both advertising and architecture created a wealth of evidence that can be used to reconstruct our collective past.

By looking at and reading advertisements, we can trace Americans' changing habits, interests, and tastes. And by analyzing the kinds of emotional appeals used in the advertisements, we can begin to understand the aspirations and goals as well as the fears and anxieties of the people who lived in the rapidly changing society of the late nineteenth and early twentieth centuries.

Unfortunately, most people, including professional historians, are not used to looking for values and ideas in architecture. Yet every day we pass by houses and other buildings that could tell us a good deal about how people lived in a particular time period, as well as something about the values of the time. In this chapter, you will be examining closely both advertisements and house plans to reconstruct partially how middle-class Americans of the late nineteenth and early twentieth centuries lived.

❋ THE METHOD ❋

No historian would suggest that the advertisements of preceding decades (or today's advertisements, for that matter) speak for themselves—that they tell you how people actually lived. Like almost all other historical evidence, advertisements must be carefully analyzed for their messages. Advertisements are intended to make people want to buy various products and services. They can be positive or negative. Positive advertisements show the benefits—direct or indirect, explicit or implicit—that would come from owning a product. Such adver-

tisements depict an ideal. Negative or "scare" advertisements demonstrate the disastrous consequences of not owning the product. Some of the most effective advertisements combine both negative and positive approaches ("I was a lonely 360-pound woman before I discovered Dr. Quack's Appetite Suppressors—now I weigh 120 pounds and am engaged to be married!"). Advertisements also attempt to evoke an emotional response from potential consumers that will encourage the purchase of a particular product or service.

Very early advertisements tended to be primarily descriptive, simply picturing the product. Later advertisements often told a story with pictures and words. In looking at the advertisements in the Evidence section of this chapter, first determine whether the approach used in each one is positive, negative, or a combination of both factors. What were the expected consequences of using (or not using) the product? How did the advertisement try to sell the product or service? What emotional responses were expected?

The preceding evaluation is not too difficult, but in this exercise you must go even further with your analysis. You are trying to determine what each advertisement can tell you about earlier generations of Americans and the times in which they lived. Look at (and read) each advertisement carefully. Does it reveal anything about the values of the time period in which the advertisement appeared? About the roles of men and women? About attitudes concerning necessities and luxuries? About people's aspirations or fears?

House plans also must be analyzed if they are to tell us something about how people used to live. At one time or another, you have probably looked at a certain building and thought, "That is truly an ugly, awful-looking building! Whatever possessed the lunatic who built it?" Yet when that building was designed and built, most likely it was seen as a truly beautiful structure and may have been widely praised by its occupants as well as by those who merely passed by. Why is this so? Why did an earlier generation believe the building was beautiful?

All of us are aware that the standards for what is considered good art, good music, good literature, and good architecture change over time. What may be pleasing to the people of one era might be considered repugnant or even obscene by those of another time. But is this solely the result of changing fads, such as the sudden rises and declines in the popularity of movie and television stars, rock 'n' roll groups, or fashionable places to vacation?

The answer is partly yes, but only partly. Tastes do change, and fads such as the Hula-Hoop and the yo-yo come and inevitably go. However, we must still ask why a particular person or thing becomes popular or in vogue at a certain time. Do these changing tastes in art, music, literature, and architecture *mean* something? Can they tell us something about the people who embraced these various styles? More to the point, can they tell us something about the *values* of those who embraced them? Obviously, they can.

In examining these middle-class homes, you should first look for common exterior and interior features. Then look at the interior rooms and their functions, comparing them with rooms in American homes today. You also must try to imagine what impression these houses conveyed to people in the late nineteenth and early twentieth centuries. Finally, you will be thinking about all the evidence—the advertisements and the house plans—as a whole. What is the relationship between the material culture (in this case, the advertisements and the house plans) and the values and concerns of Americans in the late nineteenth and early twentieth centuries?

Sources 1 through 3 from Sears Roebuck & Company catalogues, 1897 and 1902.

1. Children's Reefer Jackets (1897) and Children's Toys (1902).

SEARS ROEBUCK & CO. INC.

85¢

$1.50

24171

24172

REEFER JACKETS FOR CHILDREN FROM 1 TO 5 YEARS OLD.

Reefer Jackets for little toddlers, from one to four years, nobby, stylish little coats at little bits of prices. As usual S. R. & Co. will save you money on these goods.

Do not forget to mention age and color desired when ordering.

DRESSED SAILOR DOLLS.

Sailor Girl Dolls.

No. 29R735 Sailor Girl Doll, bisque head, flowing hair, solid eyes, dressed to represent a girl in sailor costume. A very pretty doll. Length, 13 inches.
Price, each.................50c

Sailor Boy Dolls.

No. 29R739 Sailor Boy Doll, dressed to represent a boy in sailor costume, companion doll to sailor girl. Length, 13 inches.
Price, each.....................50c

The Penny Saver.

No. 29R147 A perfect register-ing bank; no key, no combination. Each time a cent is dropped into the bank the bell rings and the register indicates. Opens automatically at each 50 cents. The total always in sight. They are attractive and in-teresting to children. The mechanism is made of steel, and will not break or get out of order. It is highly interesting to children, and for this reason will encourage them to save. Shipping weight, 5 pounds. Price, each........85c

2. Boys' Wash Suits and Girls' Wash Dresses,[3] 1902.

Suits can only be fully appreciated by those who order from this department. A trial order will surely convince you that we are able to furnish new, fresh, up to date, stylish and well made wash suits at much lower prices than similar value can be had from any other house.

NOTE.—Boys' wash suits can be had only in the sizes as mentioned after each description. Always state age of boy and if large or small of age.

Boy's Wash Crash Suit, 35 Cents.

Navy Blue and White Percale Wash Suit, 40 Cents.

38R2128
98c

38R2130
$1.39

38R2131
$1.48

GIRLS' WASH DRESSES.

AGES FROM 4 TO 14 YEARS.

WHEN ORDERING please state Age, Height, Weight and Number of Inches around Bust.

SCALE OF SIZES, SHOWING PROPORTION OF BUST AND LENGTH TO THE AGE OF CHILD

Age	4	6	8	10	12	14
Bust	24	27	28	29	30	31
Skirt length	18	20	22	24	26	28

No. 38R2126 GIRLS' DRESS. Some made of Madras and some made of ginghams in fancy stripes and plaids, round yokes, "V" shape yokes, some trimmed with braid, ruffles and embroidery. We show no illustration of this number on account of the differ-

3. Washable, casual clothing.

3. Hip Pad and Bustle, 1902.

Parisienne Hip Pad and Bustle.

No. 18R4880 The **Parisienne Hip Pad and Bustle,** made of best tempered, black enameled, woven wire with hip pads of padded cloth. Perfect in shape, and light in weight. Very durable.
Price, each...**40c**
If by mail, postage extra, each, 10 cents.

Sources 4–7 and 10–26 may also be found in Edgar R. Jones, *Those Were the Good Old Days: A Happy Look at American Advertising 1880–1930* (New York: Simon & Schuster, 1959).

Source 4 from an 1893 advertisement.

4. Corsets.

Source 5 from an 1884 advertisement.

5. Beauty Advice Book.

A SCRAP-BOOK
FOR
"HOMELY WOMEN" ONLY.

We dedicate this collection of toilet secrets, not to the pretty women (they have advantages enough, without being told how to double their beauty), but to the plainer sisterhood, to those who look in the glass and are not satisfied with what they see. To such we bring abundant help.

CONTENTS. Part 1—Part 2.

Practical devices for ugly ears, mouths, fingertips, crooked teeth. To reduce flesh, etc. How to bleach and refine a poor skin. Freckles, Pimples, Moles, etc. Mask of Diana of Poictiers. Out of 100 Cosmetics, which to choose. How to make and apply them for daylight, evening, and the stage (one saves two thirds, and has a better article by making instead of buying Cosmetics). What goes to constitute a belle. Madame Vestris's methods for private Theatricals. How to sit for a photograph successfully, and other toilet hints.

Send $1.00, 2 two-cent stamps, and an envelope addressed to yourself.

BROWN, SHERBROOK, & CO.,
27 Hollis Street, Boston, Mass.

Source 6 from a 1912 advertisement.

6. Massage Cream for the Skin.

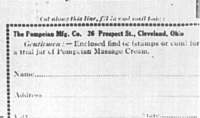

"Mother, here she is"

OF all moments the most try-ing—when the son brings *her* to his mother, of all critics the most exacting. Mother-love causes her to look with penetrating glance, almost *trying* to find flaws. No quality of beauty so serves to win an older woman as a skin smooth, fresh and healthy *in a natural way*, as easily provided by

POMPEIAN MASSAGE CREAM

Where artificial beautifiers—cosmetics and rouges—would only antagonize; and an uncared-for, pallid, wrinkled skin prove a negative influence—the Pompeian complexion immediately wins the mother, as it does in every other instance in social or business life.

You can have a beautiful complexion—

that greatest aid to woman's power and influence. A short use of Pompeian will surprise you and your friends. It will improve even the best complexion, and retain beauty and youthful appearance against Time's ravages.

"Don't *envy* a good complexion; use Pompeian and *have* one."

Pompeian is not a "cold" or "grease" cream, nor a rouge or cosmetic, and positively can not grow hair on the face. Pompeian simply affords a natural means toward a complete cleanliness of the facial pores. And in pores that are "Pompeian clean" lies skin health.

TRIAL JAR

sent for 6c (stamps or coin). Find out for yourself, now, why Pompeian is used and prized in a million homes where the value of a clear, fresh, youthful skin is appreciated. Clip coupon now.

All dealers 50c, 75c, $1

Cut along this line, fill in and mail today.

The Pompeian Mfg. Co. 36 Prospect St., Cleveland, Ohio

Gentlemen: — Enclosed find 6c (stamps or coin) for a trial jar of Pompeian Massage Cream.

Name.....................................

Address...................................

City......................... State..........

7. **Croup Remedy (1895), Garment Pins (1888), and *American Boy* Magazine (1912).**

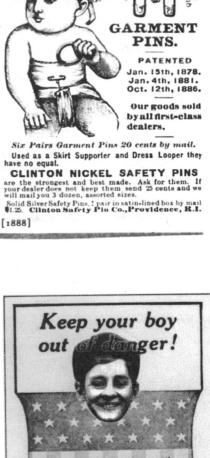

Sources 8 and 9 from Sears Roebuck & Company catalogues, 1897 and 1902.

8. Women's and Men's Hats, 1897.

LATEST DESIGNS IN STYLISH TRIMMED HATS.
AT 99 CENTS, $2.35, $3.25 AND UPWARDS.

WE SUBMIT ON THESE FOUR PAGES, the very newest effects in fashionable trimmed hats made especially for us from original designs, the same styles as will be shown by fashionable city milliners in large cities; styles that it will be impossible for you to secure in the stores in smaller towns, such goods as can be had only from the big millinery emporiums in metropolitan cities and there at two to three times our prices. These illustrations are made by artists direct from the hats, but it is impossible in a plain black and white drawing to give you a fair idea of the full beauty of these new hat creations. We ask you to read the descriptions carefully, note the illustrations and send us your order with the understanding that if the hat, when received, is not all and more than we claim for it, perfectly satisfactory, you are at liberty to return it to us at our expense and we will immediately return your money.

Wonderful Value.

99c

No. 39R101 Is a black dress shape fancy straw, slightly raised on the left. Very tastefully trimmed in the front with six large muslin roses and shaded foliage. Trimmed high to the right is a large rosette consisting of silk finished pink mull in half wheel effect, same extending all around the crown and falling over the back and caught on bandeau with loops of the same material. A very stylish young or middle aged ladies' hat. Shape can be ordered only in black or white, trimmings in any color desired, but looks very handsome as described. Price, each........99c

$1.95

No. 39R107 This is a hand made fancy straw braid dress hat, drooping slightly to front and back. The wire frame is covered with an imported hand made straw braid, trimmed fully to the left with artistically designed rosettes draped in plume effect. The entire crown is covered with an imported tinted foliage and buds. The facing is neat drawn work of narrow folds of pink silk finished mull, and the bandeau is covered with nicely made loops of the same material. An exceedingly becoming and effectively designed hat. Can be ordered in all colors, Price, each................ ....$1.95

...HAT DEPARTMENT...

DO NOT BE SATISFIED WITH ANY STYLE HAT when you can have at no additional expense a hat that will be becoming and at the same time stylish and in good form. Different sections of the country have their styles, due mainly to their difference in occupation and environment. If you live on a ranch and want the proper hat for such a life, we have it. If you wish the fashionable derby or stiff hat, we can supply this.
OUR LINE OF SOFT AND FEDORA SHAPES CANNOT BE EXCELLED.
VALUE. We can sell you a hat at almost any price, but by our manufacturer to the wearer plan we are able to sell to you at almost the same price your home merchant pays for the same quality. We want your order, because we can save you 25 to 40 per cent, and at the same time fill your order with NEW, CLEAN, UP TO DATE GOODS.

MEN'S DERBY OR STIFF HATS, $1.50.
No. 33R2010 Young Men's Stiff Hat, in fashionable shape. Is a very neat block, not extreme, but stylish. Crown, 4¾ inches; brim, 1¾ inches. Fine silk band and binding. Colors, black or brown. Sizes, 6¾ to 7½.
Price, each.... $1.50
If by mail, postage extra, 34 cents.
A Fashionable Block in Men's Stiff Hats for $2.00.

Men's Large or Full Shape Stiff Hats.
No. 33R2040 A style particularly suited to large men. A shapely, staple hat, as shown in illustration. Crown, 5½ inches; brim, 2¼ inches. Fine silk band and binding. Sizes, 6¾ to 7¾. Color, black only.
Each.... $1.50
If by mail, postage extra, 34 cents.

Our Men's $2.25 Quality Full Shape Hat.
No. 33R2046 Men's Full Shape Hat, same style and dimensions as the above, in the high grade non-breakable stock, with very fine silk band and binding; imported leather sweatband. Color, black only. Sizes, 6¾ to 7¾. Price, each............$2.25
If by mail, postage extra, 34 cents.

9. Men's Underwear, 1902.

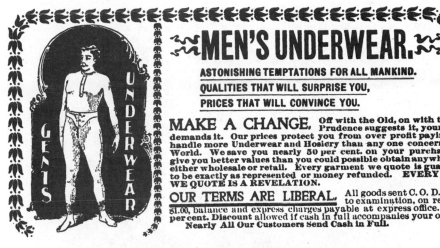

MEN'S UNDERWEAR.

ASTONISHING TEMPTATIONS FOR ALL MANKIND.

QUALITIES THAT WILL SURPRISE YOU,

PRICES THAT WILL CONVINCE YOU.

MAKE A CHANGE, Off with the Old, on with the New. Prudence suggests it, your health demands it. Our prices protect you from over profit paying. We handle more Underwear and Hosiery than any one concern in the World. We save you nearly 50 per cent. on your purchases and give you better values than you could possible obtain anywhere else either wholesale or retail. Every garment we quote is guaranteed to be exactly as represented or money refunded. **EVERY PRICE WE QUOTE IS A REVELATION.**

OUR TERMS ARE LIBERAL. All goods sent C. O. D., subject to examination, on receipt of $1.00, balance and express charges payable at express office. **Three** per cent. Discount allowed if cash in full accompanies your order. Nearly All Our Customers Send Cash in Full.

Ventilated Health Underwear.

Summer Weight Balbriggan.

No. 2830 Men's Ventilated Natural Gray Mixed Summer Undershirts. The most comfortable as well as the most healthful balbriggan underwear ever made; fine gauge and soft finish; fancy collarette neck, pearl buttons and ribbed cuffs; ventilated all over with small drop stitch openings. Highly recommended by the best physicians as conducive to good health. Sizes 34 to 42 only. Price each..**$0.58**

MEN'S FANCY UNDERWEAR.

Men's Striped Balbriggan Underwear, 41 Cents.

No. 16R5078 Men's Fine Fancy Balbriggan Undershirts, knit from fine Egyptian cotton, made in a very narrow ½-inch alternating white and blue stripe. A very pretty garment that never fails to give satisfaction. Fast color. Trimmed with collarette neck and pearl buttons. Perfect fitting ribbed cuffs. Never retails for less than 50 to 65 cents. Stitched throughout with never-rip seams' Sizes, 34 to 44 breast measure.

Price, each........................**41c**

Source 10 from an 1893 advertisement.

10. Shaving Soaps.

WILLIAMS' SHAVING SOAPS have enjoyed an unblemished reputation for excellence—for over HALF A HUNDRED YEARS—and are to-day the *only* shaving soaps—of absolute purity, with well-established claims for healing and antiseptic properties.

"CHEAP" and impure Shaving Soaps—are composed largely of refuse animal fats—abound in scrofulous and other disease germs—and if used —are almost sure to impregnate the pores of the skin—resulting in torturing cutaneous eruptions and other forms of blood-poisoning.

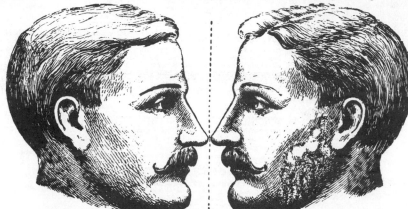

This view shows face—as shaved daily for years—with the famous WILLIAMS' Shaving Soap—always soft—fresh —bright and healthy. Not a sore or pimple in over 20 years of Shaving Experience.

This view shows the effect of being shaved ONCE with an impure—so-called "Cheap" Shaving Soap. Blood-poison—caused by applying impure animal fats to the tender cuticle of the face.

MR. CHAS. A. FOSTER,

34 SAVIN STREET,

BOSTON, MASS., writes:

"Never again will I allow a Barber to shave me unless I am *sure* he is using the only safe and reliable shaving soap made—namely WILLIAMS'. The other day—being in a hurry—I went into a shop near the Boston and Maine depot—to get a shave.

"I noticed a rank odor when the lather was put on my face, and asked the Barber if he used WILLIAMS' Shaving Soap. He said, 'No—I do not—because it costs a little more than other kinds.'

"A few days after this experience—my face was all broken out—terribly sore and smarting like fire.

"I consulted my Physician who told me it was a bad case of 'BARBER'S ITCH'—caused by the use of the Cheap Shaving Soap—containing diseased animal fats.

"I have suffered the worst kind of torture for two weeks—but I have learned a lesson."

Ask your Barber if *he* uses WILLIAMS'. Take no chances. Blood-poisoning—in some form or other is the almost sure result of using a cheaply made and impure Shaving Soap. While shaving—the pores of the Skin are open—and quickly drink in—any of the disease germs which may be contained in the diseased animal fats—so largely used in all "cheap"—inferior Toilet and Shaving Soaps. Ask for WILLIAMS'—and *insist* that you have it—and enjoy a feeling of SECURITY—as well as of comfort—while shaving or being shaved.

In providing for the safety and comfort of visitors—it has been officially ordered that

WILLIAMS' SHAVING SOAPS

shall be used EXCLUSIVELY—in all of the Barber Shops located on the Grounds of the World's Columbian Exposition. Thus AT THE VERY START—it receives the highest possible Honor.

WILLIAMS' "JERSEY CREAM" TOILET SOAP.

Something new with us. The result of 50 years of costly and laborious experiment. Send for circular. A most exquisite—healing and beautifying toilet soap. Containing the rich yellow cream of *our own herd* of imported Jersey Cattle. A full size cake mailed to any address for 25c. in stamps. Do not fail to try it. Ask your Druggist—or send to us.—Address,

The J. B. Williams Co., Glastonbury, Conn., U. S. A.

"WILLIAMS' SOAPS have for a foundation—over half a hundred years of unblemished reputation."

Source 11 from a 1908 advertisement.

11. Safety Razor.

"Shave Yourself"

"The man who shaves himself before breakfast in the morning has a pleasure which is never known by those whose faces are not familiar with the razor or for whom it is wielded by another.

"The operation creates a sense of cleanliness, opens one's eyes to things as they are, dissipates the cobwebs in the brain which accumulate during the night, and assists in establishing amicable relations with the world for the beginning of the day."

Well lathered, you can shave yourself with the "GILLETTE" in three to five minutes any and every morning in the year at a fraction of a cent per day. The blade of my Razor, the "GIL-LETTE," is the only new idea in Razor Blades for over 400 years. This double-edged, thin-as-a-wafer blade is held by the Gillette frame in a perfectly rigid manner (which avoids all possibility of vibration), thus ensuring a comfortable, safe and uniform shave — which conditions are not obtainable with any other make of razor.

With the "GILLETTE" a slight turn of the handle adjusts the blade (which is always in position) for a light or close shave with a soft or hard beard.

The "GILLETTE" holder triple silver plated will last you a lifetime, and when the blades become dull, throw away and buy —

10 Brand New Double-Edged "GILLETTE" Blades for 50c.

No blades re-sharpened or exchanged. The price of the "GILLETTE" set is $5.00 everywhere.

Sold by the leading Jewelry, Drug, Cutlery and Hardware Dealers.

Ask for the "GILLETTE" and booklet. Refuse all substitutes and write me to-day for special 30-day free trial order.

King C Gillette

Care of Gillette Sales Co.

279 Times Building, New York City.

Gillette Safety Razor
NO STROPPING. NO HONING.

Source 12 from a 1912 advertisement.

12. Watch Chains.

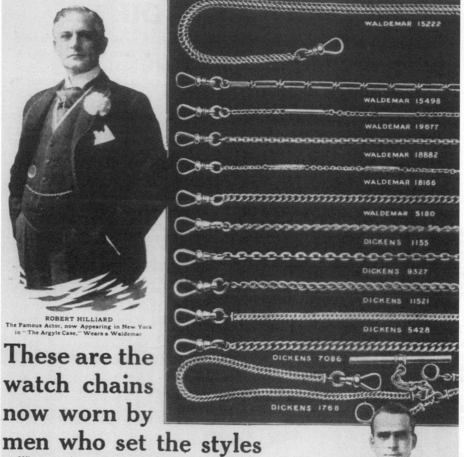

ROBERT HILLIARD
The Famous Actor, now Appearing in New York
in "The Argyle Case," Wears a Waldemar

These are the watch chains now worn by men who set the styles

When a man buys a watch chain he chooses a *pattern* to suit his individual taste—but he wants a *style* which will always be in good taste.

A watch chain is the only piece of jewelry worn universally by men. It is the most prominent piece a man can wear. Every man with any regard for his personal appearance wants his watch chain right.

SIMMONS CHAINS
TRADE MARK

are always "correct" in style. That is one reason why first-class jewelers have handled them for forty years. A man in the smaller cities and towns can be just as sure as a New Yorker that he is getting the "proper thing" if he buys a *Simmons Chain*.

Waldemar and Dickens are the most popular styles this year. Lapels, vests and fobs are also in good taste. For women there are chatelaines, neck, eyeglass and guard chains and bracelets.

The beauty of design and finish and the satisfactory service of the *Simmons Chains*, have made them a standard among well-dressed men and women.

The surface of a *Simmons Chain* is not a wash or plate. It is a rolled tube of 12 or 14 karat *solid* gold, of sufficient thickness to withstand the wear of years.

If your jeweler hasn't *Simmons Chains* write us for Style Book—make your selection and we'll see that you are supplied.

R. F. Simmons Co. (Established 1873) 177 N. Main St., Attleboro, Mass.
Look for SIMMONS stamped on each piece—your protection and guarantee for wear.

DOUGLAS FAIRBANKS
The Popular Actor who Made a Great
New York Success in "Officer 666,"
Wearing a Dickens

Source 13 from a 1916 advertisement.

13. Colt Revolver.

Source 14 from an 1891 advertisement.

14. One-Volume Book Collection.

NONE ARE TOO BUSY TO READ

IN ONE VOLUME.

"The Best Fifty Books of the Greatest Authors."

CONDENSED FOR BUSY PEOPLE.

BENJAMIN R. DAVENPORT, EDITOR.

NO EXCUSE FOR IGNORANCE.

Born 1564.   William Shakespeare.   Died 1616.

THIS WORK of 771 pages covers the whole range of Literature from Homer's Iliad, B. C. 1200 to Gen. Lew. Wallace's Ben Hur, A. D. 1880, including a Brief Biographical Sketch and FINE FULL-PAGE PORTRAIT OF EACH AUTHOR. Every one of the Fifty Books being so thoroughly reviewed and epitomized, as to enable the READERS OF THIS VOLUME TO DISCUSS THEM FULLY, making use of Familiar Quotations properly, and knowing the connection in which they were originally used by their Great Authors.

THIS BOOK is made from material furnished by Homer, Shakespeare, Milton, Bunyan, Dickens, Stowe, Gen. Lew. Wallace, and the other great authors of thirty centuries.

BY IT A LITERARY EDUCATION MAY BE ACQUIRED WITHIN ONE WEEK, ALL FROM ONE VOLUME.

A BOOK FOR BUSY AMERICANS.

TIME SAVED. MONEY SAVED.

KNOWLEDGE IN A NUTSHELL.

NEW YORK WORLD, March 15th.—"The book is one destined to have a great sale, because it supplies, IN THE FULLEST SENSE, A LONG FELT LITERARY WANT."

Born 1783.   Washington Irving.   Died 1859.

Opinions expressed by practical, busy and successful self-made men, as to the great value and merit of Mr. Davenport's condensations:

Mr. PHILIP D. ARMOUR writes: "I am pleased to own 'Fifty Best Books.' It certainly should enable the busy American, at small expenditure of time, to gain a fairly comprehensive knowledge of the style and scope of the authors you have selected."

GEN. RUSSELL A. ALGER writes: "I have received the beautiful volume. It is surely a very desirable work."

GOV. JOSEPH E. BROWN, of Georgia, writes: "You have shown great power of condensation. This is eminently a practical age; men engaged in the struggle for bread have no time to enter much into details in literature. What the age wants is to get hold of the substance of a book. This work entitles you to be understood as a benefactor."

BOSTON DAILY GLOBE, April 2, 1891.—"Men of the present generation have not time to wade through from 2,000 to 3,000 pages of any of literature's standard volumes, and as a result they do not undertake it at all, and are often placed in an embarrassing position."

BUFFALO EXPRESS, March 1st.—"The Best Fifty Books of the Greatest Authors. Condensed for Busy People," edited by Benjamin R. Davenport, deserves high praise. It not only gives busy people an introduction to literature, but takes them to its very sanctum sanctorum and bids them be at home. The editor has selected his best fifty books with the advice of the most eminent literary men in England and America. These masterpieces, from Homer's 'Iliad' to Lew. Wallace's 'Ben Hur,' he has condensed into one volume of 771 pages, working in all of the famous passages and supplying a narrative in good, straightforward, unpretentious English. The story of each book is accompanied with a brief biographical sketch and a portrait of each author. No matter how familiar one is with any of these fifty books, be it for instance, 'Don Quixote,' 'Rasselas,' 'Les Miserables,' 'Paradise Lost,' or any other, he will be forced to admit, after reading the dozen pages devoted to each one in this condensation, that there is little, if anything, to add, either with regard to plot, characters, scenes, situations, quotations, or anything else that is ever discussed by people. The result of days or weeks of reading will be the possession of hardly one single bit of information or one tangible idea concerning the book in hand that is not to be acquired by reading the dozen pages in this condensation within a half hour."

Born 1812.   Charles Dickens.   Died 1870.

SOLD BY SUBSCRIPTION ONLY.   AGENTS WANTED EVERYWHERE.

CANVASSERS who desire to represent a book which sells rapidly and without argument should send for CIRCULARS. Books forwarded, postage paid, to any address upon receipt of price.

Fine English Muslin, Sprinkled Edges, $3 75.   Full Sheep, Library Style, Marbled Edges, $4.75.
Seal Russia, Gilt Edges, $6.75.

19th CENTURY BOOK CONCERN, 40 Exchange St., Buffalo, N. Y.

1891]

Source 15 from a 1906 advertisement.

15. Correspondence School.

What are You Worth
From The
NECK
UP?

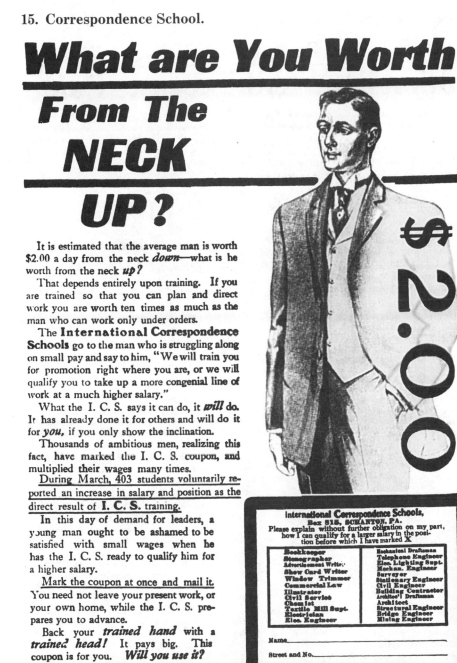

It is estimated that the average man is worth $2.00 a day from the neck *down*—what is he worth from the neck *up?*

That depends entirely upon training. If you are trained so that you can plan and direct work you are worth ten times as much as the man who can work only under orders.

The **International Correspondence Schools** go to the man who is struggling along on small pay and say to him, "We will train you for promotion right where you are, or we will qualify you to take up a more congenial line of work at a much higher salary."

What the I. C. S. says it can do, it *will do.* It has already done it for others and will do it for *you,* if you only show the inclination.

Thousands of ambitious men, realizing this fact, have marked the I. C. S. coupon, and multiplied their wages many times.

During March, 403 students voluntarily reported an increase in salary and position as the direct result of **I. C. S.** training.

In this day of demand for leaders, a young man ought to be ashamed to be satisfied with small wages when he has the I. C. S. ready to qualify him for a higher salary.

Mark the coupon at once and mail it. You need not leave your present work, or your own home, while the I. C. S. prepares you to advance.

Back your *trained hand* with a *trained head!* It pays big. This coupon is for you. *Will you use it?*

International Correspondence Schools,
Box 818, SCRANTON, PA.
Please explain without further obligation on my part, how I can qualify for a larger salary in the position before which I have marked X

Bookkeeper	Mechanical Draftsman
Stenographer	Telephone Engineer
Advertisement Writer	Elec. Lighting Supt.
Show Card Writer	Mechan. Engineer
Window Trimmer	Surveyor
Commercial Law	Stationary Engineer
Illustrator	Civil Engineer
Civil Service	Building Contractor
Chemist	Architec'l Draftsman
Textile Mill Supt.	Architect
Electrician	Structural Engineer
Elec. Engineer	Bridge Engineer
	Mining Engineer

Name_____

Street and No._____

City_____ State_____

Source 16 from a 1906 advertisement.

16. The Oliver Typewriter.

A Course in Practical Salesmanship Tuition FREE ~ All Expenses Paid

IN these times of keen business rivalry, the services of the Trained Salesman command a high premium.

The Oliver Sales Organization is the finest body of Trained Salesmen in the world. It is composed of picked men, and is under the guidance of Sales Experts.

In less than ten years it has placed the Oliver Typewriter where it belongs—in a position of absolute leadership.

Its aggregate earnings are enormous and the individual average is high.

The scope of its activities is as wide as civilization and the greatest prizes of the commercial world are open to its membership.

The organization is drilled like an army. It affords a liberal education in actual salesmanship, and increases individual earning power many per cent, by systematic development of natural talents.

Its ranks are recruited from every walk of life. Men who had missed their calling and made dismal failures in the over-crowded professions have been developed in the Oliver School of Practical Salesmanship into phenomenal successes.

The Oliver Typewriter puts the salesman in touch with the men worth knowing—the human dynamos who furnish the brain power of the commercial world.

Because every Business Executive is interested in the very things the Oliver stands for—economy of time and money—increase in efficiency of Correspondence and Accounting Departments.

The OLIVER Typewriter

The Standard Visible Writer

is simple in principle, compactly built, durable in construction, and its touch is beautifully elastic and most responsive.

In versatility, legibility, perfect alignment, visibility, etc., it is all that could be desired in a writing machine.

It's a constant source of inspiration to the salesman, as every day develops new evidence of its wide range of usefulness.

Just as the winning personality of a human being attracts and holds friends, so does the Oliver, by its responsiveness to all demands, gain and hold an ever-widening circle of enthusiastic admirers.

If you wish to learn actual salesmanship and become a member of the Oliver Organization, send in your application **immediately,** as the ranks are rapidly being filled.

You can take up this work in spare time, or give us your entire time, just as you prefer.

Whether you earn $300 a year, or **twelve times** $300 a year, depends entirely upon **yourself.**

We offer to properly qualified applicants the opportunity to earn handsome salaries and to gain a knowledge of salesmanship that will prove of inestimable value.

Can you afford to vegetate in a poorly-paid position, when the way is open to a successful business career?

Address at once.

THE OLIVER TYPEWRITER CO., 161 Wabash Ave., Chicago

WE WANT LOCAL AGENTS IN THE UNITED STATES AND CANADA.
PRINCIPAL FOREIGN OFFICE—75 QUEEN VICTORIA ST., LONDON.

Source 17 from a 1908 advertisement.

17. Life Insurance Club.

Don't Depend on Your Relatives When You Get Old

If you let things go kind o' slip-shod *now*, you may later have to get out of the 'bus and set your carpet-bag on the stoop of some house where your arrival will hardly be attended by an ovation.

If you secure a membership in the Century Club this sad possibility will be nipped in the bud. It is very, very comfortable to be able to sit under a vine and fig-tree of your own.

The Club has metropolitan headquarters and a national membership of self-respecting women and men who are building little fortunes on the monthly plan. Those who have joined thus far are a happy lot—it would do your heart good to read their letters.

We would just as soon send our particulars to you as to anybody else, and there is no reason in the world why you shouldn't know all about everything. You'll be glad if you do and sorry if you don't.

Be kind to those relatives—*and to yourself*.

Address, stating without fail your occupation and the exact date of your birth,

Century Life-Insurance Club
Section O

5, 7 and 9 East 42d Street, New York

RICHARD WIGHTMAN, Secretary

Source 18 from 1881 and 1885 advertisements.

18. Columbia Bicycles (1881) and Tricycles (1885).

COLUMBIA BICYCLES

The Art of wheelmanship is a gentlemanly and fascinating one, once acquired never forgotten, which no young man should neglect to acquire.

The Bicycle is practical everywhere that a buggy is, and enables you to dispense with the horse and the care and cost of keeping him. It is destined to be the prevailing light, quick, ready conveyance in country towns.

The Youth take to bicycles like ducks to water. They ride it quickly, easily, safely and gracefully. They can get more pleasure out of it than out of a horse, a boat, and a tennis or cricket outfit all together.

Parents should favor bicycle riding by their boys, because it gives them so much enjoyment, makes them lithe and strong, keeps them from evil associations, and increases their knowledge and their self-reliance. There is no out-door game or amusement so safe and wholesome.

The above paragraphs are but fragmentary suggestions; ask those who have ridden: read "The American Bicycler" (50 cts.), the "Bicycling World" (7 cts. a copy), our illustrated catalogue (3-ct. stamp).

The Columbia bicycles are of elegant design, best construction, fine finish, and are warranted. They may be had with best ball-bearings, finest nickel plate, and other specialties of construction and finish, according to choice.

The Mustang is a less expensive, plain and serviceable style of bicycle made by us for boys and youths.

Physicians, clergymen, lawyers, business men of every class, are riding our Columbias in nearly every State and Territory to-day, with profit in pocket, with benefit in health, and with delightful recreation. The L.A. W. Meet at Boston brought 800 men together on bicycles; but the boys, who outnumber them, and who have their own clubs and associations in so many places, were at school and at home. Why don't every boy have a bicycle?

Send 3-cent stamp for our 24-page illustrated catalogue and price-list, with full information.

THE POPE M'F'G CO.,
**598 Washington Street,
BOSTON MASS.**

COLUMBIA BICYCLES.

FOR HEALTH—BUSINESS—PLEASURE.

"Having examined somewhat carefully the 'wheels' of England and France, I do not believe that a better roadster is made in the world than the 'Expert Columbia.'"—ALONZO WILLIAMS, Professor of Mathematics, Brown University, Providence, R. I.

"A contractor and builder in Pennsylvania writes: 'I am using my 'wheel' night and day to make business calls, and conveying hardware and other things. . . . I would not exchange my bicycle for the best horse in the country.'"—The Wheelman.

"From the practical results which I determined by subjecting the different qualities of steel from which it is constructed to the recognized standard of Government tests, I am free to assert that you may justly claim that the 'Columbia' has not its equal in quality of material and finish; all of which is shown in the tabulated results in your possession."—F. J. DRAKE, U. S. Inspector of Material.

"A LADY'S TESTIMONY.—A recent recruit from the fair sex, in bearing evidence as to the utility of the tricycle, writes: 'My sister and myself have just returned from a tour, having ridden from Leeds to Woodbridge (Suffolk), and home again by Halstead and Walden (Essex), or a total of 470 miles whilst we have been away; and, as we have had such a successful time of it in every respect, we intend having another tour next year.'"—The C. T. C. Gazette.

EVERY BOY AND MAN SHOULD HAVE A

EVERY LADY SHOULD RIDE A

COLUMBIA BICYCLE.

COLUMBIA TRICYCLE.

"I want to lift my voice in favor of the 'wheel' as a thing of beauty, as an instrument of pleasure, and as one of the most practical of modern inventions, looking towards practical ends."—REV. GEO. F. PENTECOST.

"But the bicycle and tricycle are not only enjoyable modes of locomotion, they are also without a peer in their hygienic capacity."—DR. S. M. WOODBURN.

"I am of the opinion that no exercise for women has ever been discovered that is to them so really useful. Young and middle-aged ladies can learn to ride the tricycle with the greatest facility, and they become excellently skilful. The tricycle is, in fact, now with me a not uncommon prescription, and is far more useful than many a dry, formal, medicinal one which I had to write on paper."—B. W. RICHARDSON, M. D., F. R. S.

Illustrated Catalogue Sent Free.

THE POPE M'F'G CO., Principal Office, 597 Washington St., Boston, Mass.

[1885] BRANCH HOUSES: 12 Warren St., New York; 179 Michigan Ave., Chicago.

Source 19 from 1896 and 1914 advertisements.

19. Gramophone (1896) and Victrola (1914).

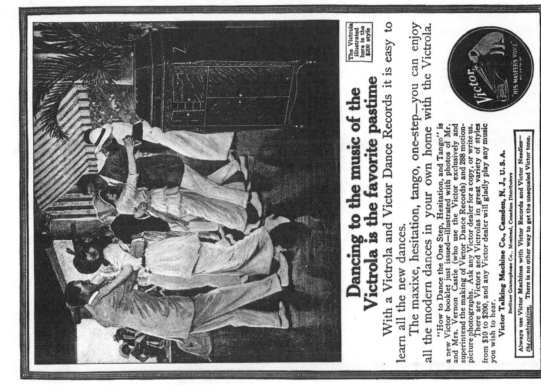

Dancing to the music of the Victrola is the favorite pastime

With a Victrola and Victor Dance Records it is easy to learn all the new dances.

The maxixe, hesitation, tango, one-step—you can enjoy all the modern dances in your own home with the Victrola.

"How to Dance the One Step, Hesitation, and Tango" is a new Victor booklet just issued—illustrated with photos of Mr. and Mrs. Vernon Castle (who use the Victor exclusively and superintend the making of Victor Dance Records) and 288 motion-picture photographs. Ask any Victor dealer for a copy, or write us.

There are Victors and Victrolas in great variety of styles from $10 to $200, and any Victor dealer will gladly play any music you wish to hear.

Victor Talking Machine Co., Camden, N. J., U.S.A.
Berliner Gramophone Co., Montreal, Canadian Distributors

Always use Victor Machines with Victor Records and Victor Needles—the combination. There is no other way to get the unequaled Victor tone.

The Victrola illustrated here is the $200 style

The Berliner Gramophone.

HOME is the place for your boys and girls to have a good time; amuse them and give them what they call fun and they will not want to go out; evenings. A talking machine is one of the wonders of the world; Mr. Berliner, of telephone fame, has by his recent invention brought this marvellous machine to a point where it may be purchased by every household. It is simple in construction, anybody can use it and it does not get out of order. It sings solos, duets and quartette music; it reproduces exactly the cornet, clarione; the banjo and in fact every instrument, including an orchestra or brass band. The talking and singing records are upon indestructible disks which are easily handled and do not wear out. We have an endless variety of these disks, including practically every song you are acquainted with.

The accompanying illustration shows exactly how the machine looks and how it is operated and the pleasure it is giving the people who are hearing it. $10.00 purchases this marvel of the ages, including two records. Extra records 60 cents each, $6.00 per dozen.

DESCRIPTION OF OUTFIT. The outfit includes the talking machine, Style No. 7½, which has a 5-inch revolving table covered with felt, nickel-plated edge, a large fly-wheel nickel-plated, balanced so as to turn evenly. Attached to the standard which holds the fly-wheel is the arm for the sound-box with reproducing diaphragm; attached to this diaphragm are the rubber tubes, which are provided with a double connection so that two people may hear at the same time. (Extra tubes, 75 cents each person.)

With each machine we enclose 3 records and 100 needles. Nicely packed in box and is sent express prepaid to any express office in the United States upon receipt of price.

Send Money by Postal Note, Express Money Order or New York Draft.

Special Offer. With each Machine ordered before Nov. 20th, we will include an Amplifying Horn.

For Sale by all Music Dealers.

Send for Catalogue. Free of Course.

NATIONAL GRAMOPHONE COMPANY, 874 to 880 Broadway, New York City.

[1896]

Source 20 from 1907 and 1912 advertisements.

20. Ford Automobile (1907) and Inter-State Electric Car for Women (1912).

FORD RUNABOUT
"Built for Two"

Two's company and a crowd frequently spoils a motoring trip.

When you have a large car you feel like filling up the seats—seems stingy for two to usurp so much luxury; so your tonneau is always full. Everybody's happy but—

Did you ever feel as if you'd just like to go alone—you and she—and have a day all your own? Go where you please, return when you please, drive as fancy dictates, without having to consult the wishes or the whims of others?

Ford Runabouts are ideal for such trips. Just hold two comfortably; ride like a light buggy, control easily and you can jog along mile after mile and enjoy the scenery.

Of course you can scorch if you want to—40 miles an hour easily—but you won't want to. You'll get used to the soft purr of the motor and the gentle motion of the car over the rolling country roads and—well, it's the most luxurious sensation one can imagine.

"We've enjoyed motoring more since we've had the Ford Runabout than we ever did before," says one lady whose purse can afford anything she desires. "Got the big car yet, but 'two's company,' and most times that's the way we go."

$600, F.O.B. Detroit

Model N. 4 Cyl. 15 H.P.

FORD MOTOR COMPANY,
25 Piquette Ave., - Detroit, Mich.

BRANCH RETAIL STORES—New York, Philadelphia, Boston, Chicago, Buffalo, Cleveland, Detroit and Kansas City. Standard Motor Co., San Francisco, Oakland and Los Angeles, distributors for California. Canadian trade supplied by Ford Motor Company of Canada, Walkerville, Ont.

The Automobile for Women

Inter-State

Electrically Started and Lighted

Controls Itself Pumps Its Own Tires

THE advent of the Inter-State, with its marvellously simple mechanism, its electrical self-starter and its self-controller has brought a revolution in motoring. Now the powerful and magnificent Inter-State starts and obeys the will of the woman driver as readily, as easily and as simply as an electric coupe. Without moving from the driver's seat or shifting gears she starts the engine by a turn of the switch — regulates the mixture by a simple movement of the lever on the steering column, and the magnificent Inter-State is under way and under perfect and absolute control, with no more trouble than turning on an electric light. The Inter-State electric self-starter is **part of the system** and **built into it**, and the motor dynamo turns the engine itself until it picks up under its own power.

No labor to start the Inter-State

Electric Lights as in Your Own Home

Any or all lights on by turning switch

ONE of the greatest features of the Inter-State is its electric light system—not a single light or two—but an entire and reliable system, front—side—rear, all correlated and so arranged that by a turn of the switch, without leaving the driver's seat, any or all of the lights may be turned on in all their brilliancy. No more gas tanks, no more oil filling, no more lamp trimming or adjusting. The system is simply perfect. The front headlights are provided with a dimming feature so that driving in city streets may be done with a medium diffused light.

Write Today for Art Catalog

This describes fully the six 40 and 50 H. P. completely equipped Models which cost from $2,400 to $3,400. Gives complete details of all the equipment and features, and also shows the Inter-State Models 30-A and 32-B, 40 H. P., costing $1,750 and $1,700 respectively.

THAT greatest nuisance of motoring—tire pumping—is *totally eliminated* with the Inter-State equipment. Any woman can attach the valve to the tire, turn on the pump and in a few minutes have tires just as solid and as perfectly filled as if done by the greatest tire expert in the world.

The Inter-State *does* the work. You *direct* it. There is nothing to it at all and you are forearmed for any emergency with the complete and thorough equipment of the Inter-State.

Inter-State Tire Pumping—No Work

Motoring Now All Pleasure

THIS great car performs all the labor itself—electrically self-started—electric lights and ignition, tire pumping and the automatic regulation of fuel consumption.

For the first time in the history of the automobile, electricity plays its *real part* in the entire mechanism. The Inter-State Electric System is really the *nerve system* commanding the energy and motion of the powerful steel muscles that make the Inter-State such a masterpiece of construction. Every conceivable accessory and feature is built into or included in the Inter-State. The Inter-State is truly the *only complete car* in this country or abroad—and this statement is made advisedly.

The *Only Complete Car*—Equipment and Features Unequalled

INTER-STATE AUTOMOBILE COMPANY, Dept. X, Muncie, Indiana
Boston Branch: 153 Massachusetts Avenue   *Omaha Branch:* 310 South 18th Street

21. Musical Automobile Exhaust Horn.

Source 22 from 1884 and 1908 advertisements.

22. Cooking Stove (1884) and Electric Washer and Wringer (1908).

ASK YOUR DEALER FOR THE
"GLENWOOD"

WITH PATENT MAGIC GRATE.

There is nothing more essential to the healthy happy home than well cooked food—which you may always be sure of by using the Glenwood Range. 100 styles! Illustrated Circular and Price List sent free.
WEIR STOVE CO., Taunton, Mass.

The Electric Washer and Wringer

YOU can now have your washings done by electricity. The 1900 Electric Washer Outfit (Washer, Wringer and Motor complete) does all the heavy work of washing and wrings out the clothes.
Any electric light current furnishes the power needed. You connect up the washer the same way you put an electric light globe into its socket. Then all there is to do to start the washer is—turn on the electricity. The motion of the tub (driven by the electricity) and the water and soap in the tub wash the clothes clean.   Washing is done quicker and easier, and more thoroughly and economically this way than ever before.

Washing

30 Days' FREE Trial—Freight Prepaid

Wringing

Servants will stay contented—laundry bills will be saved—clothes will last twice as long—where there is a 1900 Electric Washer to do the washing.
These washers save so much work and worry and trouble, that they *sell themselves.* This is the way of it—
We ship you an Electric Washer and *prepay the freight.*
Use the washer a month. Wash your linens and laces — wash your blankets and quilts—wash your rugs.
Then—when the month is up, if you are not convinced the washer is all we say— don't keep it. Tell us you don't want the washer and that will settle the matter. We won't charge anything for the use you have had of it.
This is the *only* washer outfit that does *all* the drudgery of the washing—*washes* and *wrings* clothes—saves them from wear and tear—and keeps your servants contented.
Our Washer Book tells how our washers are made and how they work. Send for this book today.
Don't mortgage your pleasure in life to dread of wash-day and wash-day troubles with servants. Let the 1900 Electric Washer and Wringer shoulder your wash-day burden—save your clothes and money, and keep your servants contented.
Write for our Washer Book at once. Address—
The 1900 Washer Co. 3133 Henry Street. Binghamton, N. Y. (If you live in Canada, write to the Canadian 1900 Washer Co., 355 Yonge Street, Toronto, Ont.)

Source 23 from 1909 and 1913 advertisements.

23. Vacuum Cleaner (1909) and Bathroom Closet (1913).

SIWELCLO Noiseless Siphon Jet CLOSET

The Noiselessness of the Siwelclo Is an Advantage Found in No Other Similar Fixture.

This appeals particularly to those whose sense of refinement is shocked by the noisy flushing of the old style closet. The Siwelclo was designed to prevent such embarrassment and has been welcomed whenever its noiseless feature has become known. When properly installed it cannot be heard outside of its immediate environment.

Every sanitary feature has been perfected in the Siwelclo—deep water seal preventing the passage of sewer gas, thorough flushing, etc.

The Siwelclo is made of Trenton Potteries Co. Vitreous China, with a surface that actually repels dirt like a china plate. It is glazed at a temperature 1000 degrees higher than is possible with any other material.

The most sanitary and satisfactory materials for all bathroom, kitchen and laundry fixtures are Trenton Potteries Co. Vitreous China and Solid Porcelain. Your architect and plumber will recommend them. If you are planning a new house or remodeling, you ought to see the great variety and beauty of design such as are shown in our new free booklet "Bathrooms of Character." Send for a copy now.

The Trenton Potteries Co.
Trenton, N. J., U. S. A.

The largest manufacturers of sanitary pottery in the U.S.A.

Why stir up the Dust Demon to Frenzy like this?

The Man	The Woman
always wonders why some way of cleaning can't be found without tormenting him with choking clouds of dust.	thinks she is performing praiseworthy and necessary work in an unavoidable manner.

You can Escape all this for $25

EVERY MAN AND WOMAN

should now realize that such laborious and tormenting "cleaning" methods, not only are absolutely unnecessary, but are **a relic of barbarism and a farce.** "Cleaning" with broom and carpet-sweeper merely scatters more of the dirt over a wider area. Old dirt has to be *pounded again and again.* The house is never thoroughly clean. Disease germs are left to multiply, then are sent flying to infect all those whose powers of resistance may be lowered.

THE IDEAL VACUUM CLEANER
(Fully Protected by Patents)

Operated by Hand puts no tax on the strength. Price $25	"IT EATS UP THE DIRT"	Or by Electric Motor, at a cost of 2 cents per hour. Price $55 or $60

"IT EATS UP THE DIRT" literally sucks out all the dust, grit, germs, moths and eggs of vermin that are *on* the object as well as *in* it—gobbles them down into its capacious maw, never to trouble you again.

This machine places in your hands a method of cleaning carpets, rugs, curtains, upholstery, wall decorations, etc., that hitherto has been limited to the very rich. It does exactly the same work as the Vacuum Cleaning systems that cost from $500 up—*and does it better and with more convenience.*

The Ideal Vacuum Cleaner is the perfection of the Vacuum Cleaning principle.

OPERATED BY HAND

Weighs only 20 pounds. Anybody can use it. Everybody can afford it. Compared with sweeping **it is ease itself.**

It is absolutely dustless.

Every machine guaranteed.

Our free Illustrated Booklet tells an interesting story of a remarkable saving in money, time, labor, health, and strength. Send for it to-day.

The American Vacuum Cleaner Company
225 Fifth Avenue, New York City

PRICES $25 to $60

Source 24 from an 1882 advertisement.

24. Musical Organ.

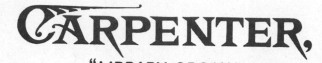

CARPENTER,

"LIBRARY ORGAN."

Containing the Celebrated Carpenter Organ Action.

Something Entirely New!   The Æsthetic Taste Gratified!

THIS IS ONLY ONE OF ONE HUNDRED DIFFERENT STYLES.

This effective and beautiful design in the modern Queen Anne Style is intended to meet the demands of those desiring an instrument of special elegance, and in harmony with the fittings and furnishings of the Study or Library Room, combining as it does, in a substantial and tasteful manner, the Organ, the Library cases, and the cabinet for bric-a-brac and articles of virtu.

It is well adapted to find favor in homes of culture and refinement, and will be championed by the music lover and connoisseur.

The composition is one of well balanced proportions, chaste subordination of ornamentation, and of artistic arrangement in constructive details, imparting to the design a rich simplicity and substantial worth

This beautiful organ contains the Celebrated Carpenter Organ Action. The action is to an Organ what the works are to a watch. The merits of the Carpenter Organ were fully proved on page 158 of the YOUTH'S COMPANION of April 20th, to which special attention is directed.

A beautiful 80-page Catalogue, the finest of its kind ever published, is now ready and will be sent free to all applying for it.

Nearly all reliable dealers sell the Carpenter Organs, but if any do not have them to show you, write to us for a Catalogue and information where you can see them. DO NOT BUY ANY ORGAN UNTIL YOU HAVE EXAMINED "THE CARPENTER." In writing for a Catalogue always state that you saw this advertisement, in the *Youth's Companion.*

Address or call on E. P. CARPENTER, Worcester, Mass., U. S. A.

25. Reed and Rattan Furniture.

ESTABLISHED 1826

Heywood-Wakefield

TRADE MARK

FACSIMILE OF OUR TAG

THE name *Heywood-Wakefield* appearing on Reed and Rattan Furniture signifies quality, style, and workmanship, that individualizes our brands of goods and has made them world-renowned. The best in Rattan Furniture is *not* the best unless it bears the tag *Heywood-Wakefield*.

Our furniture enhances the beauty of any home. Its presence lends an influence of dignity, comfort, and artisticness that harmonizes with any color treatment or architectural effect. So numerous are the styles made by us in Reed and Rattan Furniture, covering every known desire for the household, club, or hotel, and to which our design creators are constantly adding new effects in shapes and patterns, that you are practically sure of possessing, when selecting our goods, ideas that are exclusive and original.

We are also producers of the well-known line of

Heywood *Wakefield*

go-carts and baby carriages. Made in every conceivable style, including our celebrated collapsible, room-saving go-carts.

We have prepared attractive illustrated catalogs showing and describing our Reed and Rattan Furniture. Before purchasing, *write for catalog G.*

We also furnish, free, interesting catalog of our go-carts and baby carriages. If interested, *write for catalog 7.*

Write to our nearest store.

HEYWOOD BROTHERS AND WAKEFIELD COMPANY

BOSTON, BUFFALO, NEW YORK, PHILADELPHIA, BALTIMORE, CHICAGO, SAN FRANCISCO, LOS ANGELES, PORTLAND, ORE.

J. C. PLIMPTON & CO., Agts. LONDON AND LIVERPOOL, ENG.

Style 6830 B

Source 26 from 1887 and 1892 advertisements.

26. Houses in New York (1887) and Tennessee (1892): Exterior Views and Floor Plans.

* * * This marvelous house has been built more than 300 times from our plans; *it is so well planned* that it affords ample room even for a large family. 1st floor shown above; on 2d floor are 4 bedrooms and in attic 2 more. Plenty of Closets. The whole warmed by one chimney.

Large illustrations and full description of the above as well as of 39 other houses, ranging in cost from $400 up to $6,500, may be found in "SHOPPELL'S MODERN LOW-COST HOUSES," a large quarto pamphlet, showing also how to select sites, get loans, &c. Sent postpaid on receipt of 50c. Stamps taken, or send $1 bill and we will return the change. Address, BUILDING PLAN ASSOCIATION. (Mention this paper.) 24 Beekman St. (Box 2702,) N. Y.

27. Advice for Couples Buying a Home.

This is the house the young couple saved and paid for in five years.

A Young Couple
Were Married 5 Years Ago

He had a moderate salary. They started simply and saved. But they didn't skimp. They gave little dinners and heard the best lectures. In five years they had saved enough to pay for the house at the head of this page.

Another Young Couple Were Married, Too

They put by $7 a week, and the house at the bottom of this page is now theirs, —entirely paid for. A third young couple's income was $16 per week. They saved $8 of it, and bought and paid for the house at the bottom of this page.

How these and 97 others did it, step by step, dollar by dollar, is all told in the great series, "*How We Saved For a Home*,"— 100 articles by 100 people who saved for and now own their own homes on an

Average Salary of $15 a Week: None Higher Than $30

This great series will run for an entire year in

The Ladies' Home Journal

For ONE DOLLAR, for a year's subscription, you get the whole series.

THE CURTIS PUBLISHING COMPANY, PHILADELPHIA, PA.

This is the house saved for on $7 a week and now all paid for.

This is the house paid for out of a salary of $16 per week, saving $8.

Sources 28 through 31 from *Palliser's Model Homes*, 1878.

28. Cottage for a Mill Hand at Chelsea, Massachusetts (cost $1,200).

This is a very attractive design, and intended to give ample accommodation at a low cost for an ordinary family.

The cellar is placed under the Kitchen and Hall, which was thought in this instance to be sufficient to meet all requirements, though it is generally considered, in the Eastern States at least, to be poor economy not to have a cellar under the whole house, as it only requires about one foot in depth of additional stone work to secure a cellar, it being necessary to put down the stone work in any case, so that it will be beyond the reach of frost. The Kitchen is without a fire-place, the cooking to be done by a stove, which, if properly contrived, is a very effective ventilator, and preferred by many housekeepers for all Kitchen purposes.

The Parlor and Dining-room or general Living-room are provided with the healthy luxury of an open fire-place, and we know of no more elegant, cleanly and effective contrivance for this purpose than the one adopted in this instance; they are built of buff brick, with molded jambs and segment arch, and in which a basket grate or fire dogs can be placed for the desired fire, and in this way large rooms are kept perfectly comfortable in cold weather without heat from any other source. These fire-places are also provided with neat mantels constructed of ash, and which are elegant compared with the marbelized slate mantel, which is a sham, and repulsive to an educated taste.

On entering nearly every house in the land we find the same turned walnut post at the bottom of the stairs with tapering walnut sticks all the way up, surmounted with a flattened walnut rail having a shepherd's crook at the top; however, in this instance it is not so, but the staircase is surmounted with an ash rail, balusters and newel of simple, though unique design; and now that people are giving more attention to this important piece of furniture, we may look for a change in this respect.

This house is supplied with a cistern constructed with great care, the Kitchen sink being supplied with water by a pump, and there is no more easy method of procuring good water for all purposes of the household.

For a compact, convenient Cottage with every facility for doing the work with the least number of steps, for a low-priced elegant Cottage, we do not know of anything that surpasses this. Cost, $1,200.

Mr. E. A. Jones of Newport, Ohio, is also erecting this Cottage with the necessary changes to suit points of compass. Such a house as this if tastefully furnished, and embellished with suitable surroundings, as neat and well-kept grounds, flowers, etc., will always attract more attention than the uninviting, ill-designed buildings, no matter how much money may have been expended on them.

It is not necessary that artistic feeling should have always a large field for its display; and in the lesser works and smaller commissions as much art may find expression as in the costly façades and more pretentious structures.

29. Floor Plan and Exterior View of Cottage for a Mill Hand, 1878.

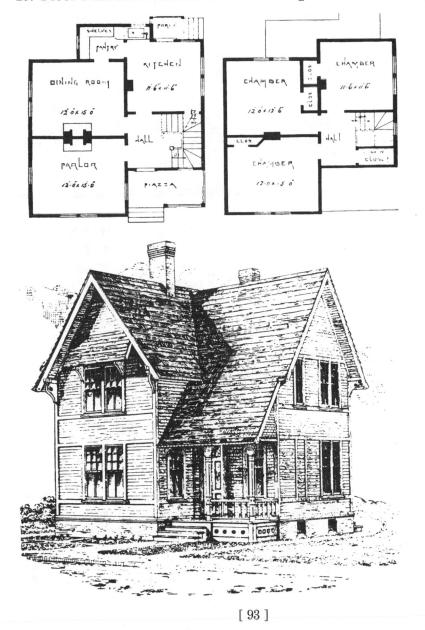

30. Residence of Rev. Dr. Marble, Newtown, Connecticut (cost $2,925), 1878.

This house commands a particularly fine view from both sides and the front, and is situated in one of the pleasantest country towns in New England, the hotels of this town being crowded during the summer months with people from the cities.

The exterior design is plain, yet picturesque, and at once gives one an idea of ease and comfort. The roofing over the Hall and Sitting-room is a particularly fine feature, and the elevation of the rear is very striking, the roof over the porch being a part of the main roof.

The interior arrangements are very nice, the Hall being very spacious, and in it we have a very easy and handsome stair-case of plain design, constructed of Georgia pine; the newel extends up to ceiling of first floor, while the other two posts extend up to ceiling of second floor. In all country houses one of the first things to be aimed at is to secure ample stair-cases, and until a man can afford space for an easy ascent to a second floor he should stay below; and to-day we find in houses, where there is no necessity for it, stairs that are little better than step-ladders, making a pretence of breadth at the bottom with swelled steps, and winding the steps on approaching the floor above, thus making a trap for the old and for the children.

The corner fire-place between Parlor and Dining-room is a feature we indulge in to a great extent in these days of economy, sliding doors and fire-places, although we sometimes have clients who object to this, thinking it would not look as well as when placed in center of side wall; but when they are asked how this and that can be provided for with the best and most economical results, they readily give in.

There is no water-closet [toilet] in the house, but an Earth-Closet is provided in the rear Hall, which is thoroughly ventilated.

The Dining-room is a very cheerful room and the Kitchen is reached through a passage also connecting with side veranda. The pantry is lighted with a window placed above press; each fire-place is furnished with a neat hard-wood mantel, and the Hall is finished in Georgia pine, the floor being laid with this material, and finished in natural color.

The exterior is painted as follows: Ground, light slate; trimmings, buff, and chamfers, black. Cost, $2,925.

The sight of this house in the locality in which it is built is very refreshing, and is greatly in advance of the old styles of rural box architecture to be found there. When people see beautiful things, they very naturally covet them, and they grow discontented in the possession of ugliness. Handsome houses, other things equal, are always the most valuable. They sell quickest and for the most money. Builders who feign a blindness to beauty must come to grief.

31. Floor Plan and Exterior View of a Clergyman's Residence, 1878.

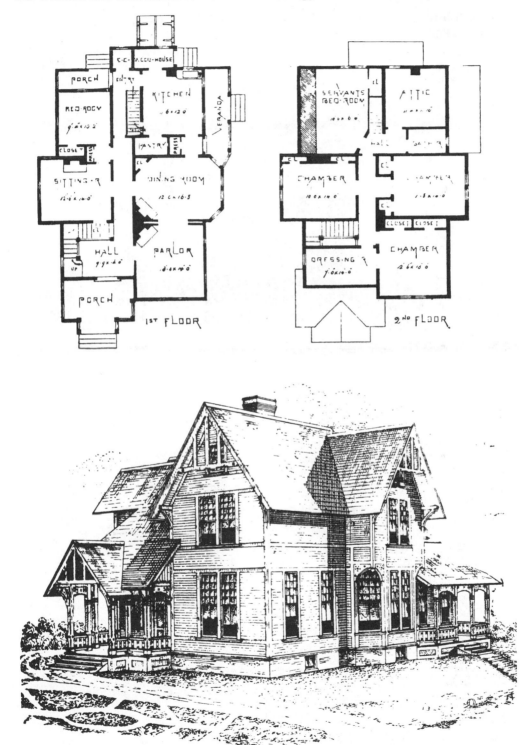

32. Exterior View and Floor Plan for a Suburban Middle-Class Home (cost $3,600), 1900.

PERSPECTIVE.

DESCRIPTION.

For explanation of all symbols (* † etc.) see supplement page 120.

GENERAL DIMENSIONS: Width, including veranda, 43 ft.; depth, including veranda, 49 ft. 6 ins.

HEIGHTS OF STORIES: Cellar, 7 ft.; first story, 10 ft.; second story, 9 ft.; attic, 8 ft.

EXTERIOR MATERIALS: Foundation, brick; first story, clapboards; second story, gables, roofs and lower portion of veranda railing, shingles.

INTERIOR FINISH: Two coat plaster for papering; plaster, cornices and centers in hall, parlor and dining-room. Soft wood flooring and trim throughout. Main stairs, ash. Kitchen and bath-room, wainscoted. Chair-rail in dining-room. Picture molding in hall, parlor and dining-room. All interior woodwork grain filled and finished with hard oil.

COLORS: All clapboards, first story, Colonial yellow. Trim, including water-table, corner boards, casings, cornices, bands, veranda posts and rails, outside doors, conductors, etc., ivory white. Veranda floor and ceiling, oiled. Shingles on side walls and gables stained dark yellow. Roof shingles, dark red.

ACCOMMODATIONS: The principal rooms, and their sizes, closets, etc., are shown by the floor plans. Cellar under whole house with inside and outside entrances and concrete floor. One room finished in attic, remainder of attic floored for storage. Double folding doors between parlor and hall and parlor and dining-room. Direct communication from hall with dining-room, parlor and kitchen. Bathroom, with complete plumbing, in second story. Open fire-places in dining-room, parlor and hall. Wide veranda. Bay-window in hall and bed-room over. Two stationary wash-tubs in cellar under kitchen.

COST: $3,600, including mantels, range and heater. The estimate is based on † New York prices for labor and materials.

Price of working plans, specifications, detail drawings, etc., $35.
Price of †† bill of materials, ... 10.

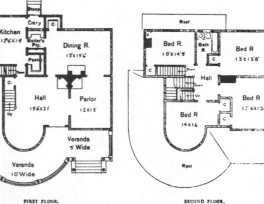

FIRST FLOOR.   SECOND FLOOR.

FEASIBLE MODIFICATIONS: General dimensions, materials and colors may be changed. Cellar may be decreased in size or wholly omitted. Sliding doors may be used in place of folding doors. Portable range may be used instead of brick-set range. Servants' water-closet could be introduced in cellar. Fireplaces may be reduced in number.

The price of working plans, specifications, etc., for a modified design, varies according to the alterations required and will be made known upon application to the Architects.

Address, CO-OPERATIVE BUILDING PLAN ASSOCIATION, Architects, 203 Broadway and 164–6–8 Fulton Street, New York, N. Y.

33. Excerpts on the New Business of Advertising, 1898–1927.

"Photographs in Advertising," *Printers' Ink,* August 17, 1898, p. 18.

It may have been noticed that the trend of modern magazine advertising is toward the use of photographs. . . . An advertisement that contains the photograph of a beautiful woman is certain to be attractive, and consequently its success is largely guaranteed. . . . But there are a host of articles on the market that can be advertised to great advantage by the introduction of a lady into the picture, and many advertisers have already seen this. . . .

But though the photographs of pretty women are only supposed to be attractive to the male sex, the picture of a baby or "cute" child will immediately captivate ninety-nine per cent of humanity. . . . Whatever he or she is supposed to advertise, we feel kindly toward, even if it is only for introducing us to the baby. . . .

Earnest Elmo Calkins, *The Business of Advertising* (1915; reprint, New York: D. Appleton and Co., 1920), pp. 1, 9.

It is hard to find a satisfactory definition of advertising. A picturesque way of putting it is to call it business imagination, an imagination that sees in a product possibilities which can be realized only by appealing to the public in new ways to create a desire where none existed before. . . .

Advertising modifies the course of the people's daily thoughts, gives them new words, new phrases, new ideas, new fashions, new prejudices and new customs. In the same way it obliterates old sets of words and phrases, fashions and customs. It may be doubted if any other one force, the school, the church and the press excepted, has so great an influence as advertising. To it we largely owe the prevalence of good roads, rubber tires, open plumbing, sanitary underwear, water filters, hygienic waters, vacuum cleaners, automobiles, kitchen cabinets, pure foods. These are only a few of the things which the public has been taught by advertising to use, to believe in, and to demand.

S. Roland Hall, *The Advertising Handbook: A Reference Work Covering the Principles and Practice of Advertising* (New York: McGraw-Hill, 1921), pp. 79–80, 101–103.

In other words, certain thoughts have become fixed in our minds in connection with certain other thoughts, and when we bring up one end of the connection the other is likely to follow. . . .

There is a motive, and a good one, in calling an automobile the "Lincoln," for that suggests sturdy, honest qualities.

No writer would undertake to make a real hero out of a character known as "Percy," for this name suggests "sissiness.". . .

Man is the stronger, as a rule. He is the bread-winner, to a large extent. His job is more in the outside world. He grows up to severer tasks, as a rule. He is more accustomed to rebuffs.

Though woman has progressed a long way in taking her place on an equal plane with that of man in business, politics and the professions, yet she is still to a large extent more sheltered than man. Her affairs are more within the home. Her sex makes her interest in clothes, home-furnishings, and the like keener than man's as a general thing. . . .

Because of her years of comparative non-acquaintance with mechanical matters, woman is generally less apt in understanding mechanical description and directions, and such advertisers must use greater care when appealing to women. . . .

On the other hand it is generally admitted that men are more democratic, more gregarious, than women—that women move more within their own circle or "clique."

A man is not likely to care if several other men in his circle have a hat exactly like his own. A woman would hardly care to buy a hat exactly like one worn by several other women in her town or community. A woman ordinarily will think nothing of shopping at several places to look at hats. A man is likely to visit only one shop. . . .

Claude C. Hopkins, *My Life in Advertising* (1927), reprinted as Claude C. Hopkins, *My Life in Advertising and Scientific Advertising* (Chicago: Advertising Publications, 1966), pp. 8–9, 119.

I am sure that I could not impress the rich, for I do not know them. I have never tried to sell what they buy. . . . But I do know the common people. I love to talk to laboring-men, to study housewives who must count their pennies, to gain the confidence and learn the ambitions of poor boys and girls. Give me something which they want and I will strike the responsive chord. My words will be simple, my sentences short. Scholars may ridicule my style. The rich and vain may laugh at the factors which I feature. But in millions of humble homes the common people will read and buy. They will feel that the writer knows them. And they, in advertising, form 95 per cent of our customers. . . .

People are like sheep. They cannot judge values, nor can you and I. We judge things largely by others' impressions, by popular favor. We go with the crowd. So the most effective thing I have ever found in advertising is the trend of the crowd.

✳ QUESTIONS TO CONSIDER ✳

For convenience, the evidence is divided into three sections. Sources 1 through 25 are advertisements from popular magazines and the 1897 and 1902 Sears Roebuck & Company catalogues. The prices probably seem ridiculously low to you, but these items were reasonably priced and affordable—although not really cheap—for most middle-class Americans in cities and towns and on farms. Sources 26 through 32 all deal with houses and buying a house, including house plans readily available by mail and through pattern books. Again, the prices seem very low, but working-class homes could be built for less than one thousand dollars (excluding the cost of the land) and middle-class homes for as little as two thousand dollars during this period. Source 33 focuses on the business of advertising.

As you read each advertisement, you will find it helpful to jot down notes. First, try to determine the message of the ad. What is the advertiser trying to sell? What emotion(s) does the ad appeal to? What fears? What hopes? Then ask what the ad tells you about society during that time. Does it tell you anything about men's roles? About women's roles? About the relationships between men and women? Does it tell you anything about children or young people? About adults' concerns about young people? About elderly people? Finally, do you see any changes occurring during the time period—for example, in the ads for the Gramophone and the Victrola (Source 19) or in the ads for automobiles (Source 20)? If so, what do these changes tell you about the roles of men, women, and young people between the 1880s and 1917?

Source 26 contains two advertisements for houses. Source 27 is an advertisement for a magazine series giving advice on how to buy a home. What do they tell you about people's needs and wants with regard to housing? What advice is offered to young married people? What values are emphasized by these advertisements for housing? Sources 28 through 32 consist of house plans and descriptions from architectural pattern books, arranged chronologically from 1878 to 1900. Look carefully at the exterior features of these houses. How would you describe them to a student who had not seen the pictures? Next, look at the interior rooms and their comparative sizes. What use or uses would each room probably have had? What rooms did these houses have that our own modern houses do not have? Do modern houses have rooms that these houses lacked? What similarities do you find in all the houses, from the mill hand's cottage ($1,200) in Sources 28 and 29 to the suburban middle-class home ($3,600) in Source 32? What differences are there? Finally, what kinds of things seemed to be important to the owners of these houses? What kind of impression did they wish to make on other people?

The excerpts in Source 33 are drawn from an advertising journal, two textbooks, and the autobiography of a famous advertising pioneer. *Printers' Ink* was a weekly journal of advertising founded in the second half of the nineteenth century. What kinds of photographs does the author recommend using? Why? What is the relationship between the photographs and the item being sold? Earnest Calkins first published a book on "modern" advertising in 1895, which he later rewrote as a textbook, *The Business of Advertising*. How does he define advertising? In what ways does he believe that advertising affects people?

S. Roland Hall had worked in advertising and later taught both salesmanship and advertising. Why does he believe that the names of products are important? What does he think are the major differences between men and women? How might these differences affect people who wrote advertisements? Finally, Claude Hopkins was a self-made man who became one of the highest-paid advertising copywriters of the late nineteenth and early twentieth centuries, at one time earning over $100,000 a year. In this excerpt from his autobiography, he explains the basic elements in his approach to advertising. To what factors does he attribute his success?

To conclude, consider what you have learned from the evidence as a whole. Can you describe how white middle-class Americans lived during this period? How the new business of advertising promoted material goods and houses? What these advertisements reveal about white middle-class values, hopes, and fears during this era of rapid changes?

❋ EPILOGUE ❋

Of course, not all Americans could live like the middle-class families you just studied. The poor and the immigrants who lived in the cities were crowded into windowless, airless tenement buildings that often covered an entire block. Poor rural black and white sharecroppers in the South lived in one- or two-room shacks, and many farmers in the western plains and prairies could afford to build only sod houses. During the Great Depression of the 1930s, many people, including middle-class families, lost their homes entirely through foreclosure, and the 1960s and 1970s saw the price of houses increase so rapidly that many families were priced out of the housing market. Even today, the problem of the homeless has not been solved.

The early twentieth century saw the captains of industry come under attack for what many came to believe were their excesses. Evidence of their disdain for and defiance of the public good, as well as of their treatment of workers, their political influence, and their ruthless business practices, came more and more to light due to the efforts of reformers and muckraking journalists. The society that once had venerated the industrial barons began to worry that they had too much power and came to believe that such power should be restricted.

Architecture also was undergoing a rapid transformation. Neoclassical, Georgian, colonial, and bungalow styles signaled a shift toward less ostentation and increased moderation in private dwellings. Perhaps the most striking work was done by Chicago architect Frank Lloyd Wright, who sought to give functional and social meaning to his designs and to make each structure blend into its unique landscape. According to Wright's concepts, there was no standard design for the "perfect house." Wright's ideas formed the basis for a series of movements that ultimately changed the perspective and direction of American architecture.

Progressive muckrakers also criticized advertising, particularly the claims of patent medicine advertisements. Such salesmanship, however, was described as "the brightest hope of America" by the 1920s. Bruce Barton, a talented salesman and founder of a huge advertising agency, even discovered "advertisements" in the Bi-
ble, which he described as the first "best seller." Although its image was slightly tarnished by the disillusionment accompanying the Great Depression, advertising helped "sell" World War II to the American public by encouraging conservation of scarce resources, and it emerged stronger and more persuasive than ever in the 1950s. Americans were starved for consumer goods after wartime rationing, and their rapid acceptance of a new entertainment medium—television—greatly expanded advertising opportunities.

But advertising still had (and has) its critics. Writing in 1954, historian David Potter, in *People of Plenty,* characterized advertising as the basic "institution of abundance." Advertising, he maintained, had become as powerful as religion or education had been in earlier eras. Advertising, he said, now actually *created* the standards and values of our society. Because advertising lacked social goals or social responsibility, however, he believed that its power was dangerous. We must not forget, Potter warned, "that it ultimately regards man as a consumer and defines its own mission as one of stimulating him to consume."

CHAPTER

4

Justifying American Imperialism: The Louisiana Purchase Exposition, 1904

✳ THE PROBLEM ✳

On April 30, 1904, in the White House in Washington, D.C., President Theodore Roosevelt pressed a telegraph key. Over 750 miles away, in St. Louis, Missouri, Roosevelt's signal officially opened the Louisiana Purchase International Exposition, in terms of acreage the largest world's fair that has ever been held. At the president's signal, a battery of artillery fired a salute in the direction of the nation's capital, ten thousand flags were unfurled, bands struck up their numbers, fountains sprayed into the air, and the opening-day crowd of 200,000 people heard Missouri Governor David R. Francis exclaim, "Enter here, ye sons of men." The 1904 St. Louis World's Fair was underway.[1]

From the formal end of Reconstruction in 1877 to the United States' entry into the First World War in 1917, Americans appeared to fall in love with world's fairs. Between 1876 and 1916, various U.S. cities hosted fourteen international expositions that were attended by nearly 100 million eager visitors.[2] Intended to stimulate

---

1. The actual centennial of the Louisiana Purchase was 1903, but construction of the

fair was so vast that the exposition opened one year late. The St. Louis Exposition commemorated the acquisition of the Louisiana Territory from France. The treaty between the United States and France was signed in Paris on April 30, 1803; the U.S. Senate ratified the treaty on October 20, 1803; and the United States took formal possession of the Louisiana Territory on December 20, 1803.
2. The first international exposition was held in London's Crystal Palace in 1851. Between 1876 and 1916, American expositions were held in Philadelphia, New Orleans, Chicago, Atlanta, Nashville, Buffalo, Charleston, St.

economic development in the host cities as well as provide opportunities for manufacturers to show their newest products to millions of potential consumers, these expositions or world's fairs also acquainted provincial Americans with machines and technology (the Corliss engine, electric lights, the air brake, refrigeration, the dynamo, x-rays, the telephone), new delights (the Ferris wheel, ice cream cones, the hoochie-koochie dance), and spectacular architecture, art, and historical artifacts (the Liberty Bell was brought from Philadelphia to both the New Orleans and Atlanta expositions). As President William McKinley commented at the 1901 Pan-American Exposition in Buffalo (where he was soon after assassinated), "Expositions are the time keepers of progress."

Visitors to the Louisiana Purchase Exposition in St. Louis in 1904 saw all this and more. More than nineteen million people[3] attended the largest world's fair ever held (1,272 acres, 75 buildings, 70,000 exhibits). Visitors could examine a display of one hundred automobiles or watch demonstrations of totally electric cooking. But the highlight of the St. Louis Exposition was its Anthropology Department, headed by the preeminent Smithsonian Institution ethnologist

W. J. McGee. The department brought to St. Louis representatives of "all the races of the world," who lived on the fairgrounds in villages designed to reproduce their "native habitats." For example, twelve hundred people were brought from the Philippine Islands, an area acquired from Spain in the Spanish-American War of 1898 and where American soldiers recently (1902) had subdued a Filipino rebellion. On a 47-acre site, six villages were constructed for these people, where American visitors could observe them and their customs.

In this chapter, you will be analyzing several photographs taken at the 1904 Louisiana Purchase Exposition in St. Louis. It is likely that a majority of the nineteen million people who attended the exposition visited the six Filipino villages set up on the fairgrounds. In addition, millions of Americans were able to view photographs of those villages taken by the Anthropology Department's official photographers. As noted earlier, in 1898 the United States had acquired a colonial empire from Spain, part of which was the Philippine Islands. How did the exhibits at the 1904 St. Louis Exposition—and the photographs taken of those exhibits—attempt to justify or create a climate for the United States' rise to imperial power status? How do you think Americans might have reacted to these exhibits and photographs?

This chapter shows how imaginative historians can analyze public events such as world's fairs, parades, patriotic celebrations, and so forth to understand the thoughts and attitudes of the events' organizers, participants,

Louis, Jamestown, Portland, Seattle, San Francisco, and San Diego. Numerous regional expositions and fairs also were held.
3. Nineteen million people (the official count; others were lower) represented 23.1 percent of the total U.S. population in 1904. Of course, not all visitors were Americans, and some people visited the exposition more than once and thus were counted more than once in the total figure.

CHAPTER 4

JUSTIFYING
AMERICAN
IMPERIALISM:
THE LOUISIANA
PURCHASE
EXPOSITION,
1904

and audiences. Such analyses are especially valuable in uncovering the collective mentality of people at a particular point in time. As you examine evidence from the Louisiana Purchase International Exposition of 1904, think of how the methods you are using might be applied to other large public events *and* how photographs of those events present both great opportunities as well as potential problems for historians.

❋ BACKGROUND ❋

Until the late nineteenth century, the United States' transoceanic foreign policy clearly had been of minor concern to the nation's citizens. Westward expansion and settlement, the slavery controversy and the Civil War, postwar reconstruction of the republic, and industrialization and urbanization had alternately captured the attention of Americans and pushed foreign affairs into the background. But beginning in the late nineteenth century, the United States became increasingly interested in expansion beyond its own shores, and by the end of that century had become a world power complete with a modest empire.

To be sure, the United States was not the only nation bitten by the imperialist bug. From the 1870s until around 1905, most Western nations engaged in a brief but extremely intense period of imperial expansion, a phenomenon that may have been one important factor leading to the outbreak of World War I in 1914. As the comparatively new nations of Italy (formed in 1870) and Germany (1871) joined the traditional colonial powers of England, France, Spain, Belgium, and the Netherlands in what appeared to be a headlong scramble for new possessions in Africa and Asia, many

Americans came to believe that the United States' newly gained status as a world power required that it join in the imperialist fury before all the territories ripe for colonization were snapped up by others. At the same time, advances in technology, medicine, and weaponry made it increasingly possible for Westerners to subdue non-Western peoples and live for extended periods in their newly won possessions. Great Britain, for example, acquired the Upper Nile River area in 1898, but only after slaughtering twenty thousand tribesmen at Omdurman, thanks to the recently invented machine gun (the "Maxim" gun, named for British engineer Sir Hiram Maxim). As Hilaire Belloc's "Modern Traveler" would sing,

> Whatever happens, we have got
> The Maxim gun, and they have not.[4]

In the 1890s, American public opinion began to shift from an anti-imperialist to a pro-expansion position. This shift was readily seen in the

4. Quoted in Roland Oliver and G. N. Sanderson, *The Cambridge History of Africa* (Cambridge: Cambridge University Press, 1985), Vol. VI, p. 98. See James A. Field Jr., "American Imperialism: The 'Worst Chapter' in Almost Any Book," in *American Historical Review* 83 (June 1978): 644–683.

business community, which initially had opposed the drift toward expansion and colonialism, believing that American industry would do well just meeting the needs of the rapidly growing population and fearing that a colonial empire would mean large armies and navies, increased government expenses, and the possibility of the nation's involvement in war. However, by the mid-1890s, American business leaders were beginning to have second thoughts. The apparent cycle of economic depressions (1819, 1837, 1857, 1873, 1893) made some businesspeople believe that American prosperity could be maintained only by selling surpluses of manufactured goods in foreign markets. Business leaders also were constantly looking for areas in which to invest their surplus capital. Investments beyond the borders of the United States, they believed, would be more secure if the American government would act to stabilize the areas in which they invested. In 1895, the newly organized National Association of Manufacturers sounded both those chords at its convention, where the keynote speaker was soon-to-be-president William McKinley, an Ohio governor with decided expansionist leanings.

In addition to economic arguments, a number of intellectual currents of the time dovetailed to create powerful arguments for and justifications of America's imperialist ventures. Those who advocated military growth, for example, argued persuasively that national self-preservation depended on the protection of international trade by a large and powerful navy with worldwide bases and refueling sta-

tions. Especially vocal was Captain Alfred Thayer Mahan, author of *The Influence of Sea Power upon History* (1890). Although Mahan's work was not widely known, his disciples included Theodore Roosevelt and Henry Cabot Lodge, men who eventually achieved positions whereby they could put Mahan's philosophy to work, Roosevelt as president and Lodge as a powerful U.S. senator from Massachusetts.

A religious current also influenced and justified American expansion. The technological and medical improvements that had helped Western armies subdue and occupy non-Western territories also made possible the dramatic increase in missionary activity. Working through both individual denominations and powerful congressional lobbies, missionaries argued that it was their duty to "Christianize" the world.[5] In the United States, Methodists, Baptists, Presbyterians, and Congregationalists were especially active, giving money and attention to their denominational missionary boards as well as to those who went out to convert the "heathen." In large part, these missionaries were selfless, committed men and women. Some, however, attempted to Westernize as well as Christianize their flocks, often denigrating or destroying indigenous cultures and traditions even as they brought modern health and educational institutions with them. All ar-

5. Because the majority of Filipinos were Roman Catholics (making the Philippines the only Christian "nation" in Asia), obviously American missionaries to the Philippines after 1899 meant *Protestantize* when they said "Christianize."

CHAPTER 4

JUSTIFYING
AMERICAN
IMPERIALISM:
THE LOUISIANA
PURCHASE
EXPOSITION,
1904

gued for the U.S. government to protect the missionaries more actively and open up other areas around the world to missionary work.

Accompanying this religious zeal were two other intellectual strains that in some ways were contradictory but that both justified American expansion. The first was that of social Darwinism. An application of Charles Darwin's theories of biological evolution to human affairs, social Darwinism taught that peoples, like species, were engaged in a life-or-death struggle to determine the "survival of the fittest." Those classes or nations that emerged triumphant in this struggle were considered the best suited to carry on the evolution of the human race. Therefore, the subjugation of weak peoples by strong ones was not only in accordance with the laws of nature but was bound to result in a more highly civilized world as well. Most celebrated among the social Darwinists was the Englishman Herbert Spencer, a diminutive and eccentric man who became a worldwide celebrity through his writings. (A letter was once addressed to him, "Herbert Spencer. England. And if the postman doesn't know the address, he ought to." It was delivered.)

Although Spencer himself disapproved of imperialism, it is easy to see how his writings could be used as a justification for empire building. One reflection of the intellectual strain of social Darwinism was reflected in the writings of the American author Josiah Strong. As he predicted in his book *Our Country: Its Possible Future and Its Present Crisis* (1885),

this race of unequaled energy . . . will spread itself over the earth. If I read

not amiss, this powerful race will move down upon Mexico, down upon Central and South America, out upon the islands of the sea, over upon Africa and beyond. And can anyone doubt that the result of this competition of races will be the "survival of the fittest"?

Spencer and Strong, however, were only two of a host of individuals in both Europe and the United States who employed "scientific" arguments that could be used to justify expansion and colonialism. Whatever their special areas of research (craniometry, craniology, polygeny, and so on), these "scientists" attempted to find biological determinants (such as intelligence) that would allow them to rank humans by race and/or ethnic group, or to rank humans from what Spencer might have called the "fittest" to the most "unfit." It does not take a great deal of imagination to see how such "scientific research" could be used to justify imperialism.[6]

Paralleling this notion of struggle for survival between the "fittest" and the "unfit" (a doctrine with strong racist overtones) was the concept of the "White Man's Burden." This concept held that it was the duty of the "fittest" not so much to destroy the "unfit" as to "civilize" them. White people, according to this view, had a responsibility to educate the rest of the world to the norms of Western society. As racist as social Darwinism, the belief in the White Man's Burden

6. For an informative survey of these "scientific" strains as well as for definitions and explanations of craniometry, craniology, and so on, see Stephen Jay Gould, *The Mismeasure of Man* (New York: W. W. Norton, 1981). Charles Darwin himself believed in racial differences in mental capacities; see *ibid.*, p. 35.

downplayed the idea of a struggle for survival between peoples and emphasized the "humanitarian" notion of bringing the benefits of "civilization" to the "uncivilized." Using this argument, many in the West justified imperialism as an obligation, a sacrifice that God had charged the "fittest" to make. Although the doctrine differs in tone from that of social Darwinism, one can see that its practical results might well be the same.

All these ideological impulses (economic, military, religious, "scientific," paternalistic) rested on one common assumption: that the world was a great competitive battlefield and that those nations that did not grow and expand would wither and die. Indeed, this "growth mania," or fascination with growth and the measurement of growth, was perhaps the most powerful intellectual strain in all of American society. For those who accepted such an assumption, the world was a dangerous, competitive jungle in which individuals, races, religions, nations, corporations, and cities struggled for domination. Those that grew would continue to exist; those that did not grow would die.

The convergence of these intellectual strains in the late nineteenth century prompted Americans to view the outside world as an area into which the United States' influence should expand. This expansionist strain was not an entirely new phenomenon; it had been an almost regular feature of American life nearly since the nation's beginning. Yet except for the purchase of Alaska, this was the first time that large numbers of Americans seemed to favor the extension of U.S. influence into areas that would not be settled

subsequently by Americans and would not eventually become states of the Union. In that sense, the American imperialism of the late nineteenth century was a new phenomenon, different from previous expansionist impulses. Instead, it more nearly resembled the "new" imperialism that engulfed European nations in the late nineteenth and early twentieth centuries, in which those nations rushed to carve out colonies or spheres of influence in Africa and Asia.

The Spanish-American War of 1898 was the event that helped the various impulses for U.S. expansion and colonization to converge. When Cubans began a revolt to secure their independence from Spain in 1895, most Americans were genuinely sympathetic toward the Cuban underdogs. Those genuine feelings were heightened by American newspaper reporters and editors, some of whom wrote lurid (and knowingly inaccurate) accounts of the Spanish "monsters" and the poor, downtrodden Cubans. President William McKinley tried to pressure Spain into making concessions and sent the American battleship *Maine* to Havana on a "courtesy call," an obvious move to underscore the United States' position toward Spain. But on February 15, 1898, the *Maine* blew up in Havana harbor. Although we now know (as a result of a 1976 study) that the explosion on the *Maine* was an internal one, almost surely the result of an accident, at the time many Americans, fired up by the press, were convinced that the Spanish had been responsible. Yet war with Spain did not come immediately and, in the opinion of some, was not inevitable, even after the *Maine* incident. How-

CHAPTER 4

JUSTIFYING
AMERICAN
IMPERIALISM:
THE LOUISIANA
PURCHASE
EXPOSITION,
1904

ever, on April 11, 1898, after two months of demands, negotiations, and arguments in which it sometimes appeared that war might be avoided, McKinley asked Congress for authorization to intervene in Cuba "in the name of humanity and civilization." On April 20, Congress granted authorization, and the Spanish-American War began.

If the Spanish-American War had not begun as an imperialistic venture, the convergence of the economic, military, religious, and racist impulses mentioned previously and the weak condition of Spain gave American leaders the opportunity to use the war and victory for expansionist purposes.

Once the United States had achieved a comparatively bloodless[7] victory against nearly impotent Spain, a general debate began over whether the United States should demand from Spain the surrender of its colonial empire, the jewels of which were Cuba and the Philippine Islands. Although President McKinley admitted that he had to consult a globe to find out where the Philippine Islands were, he was never in doubt that they should become a part of a new American empire. McKinley thus pressured the Spanish to include the surrender of their empire in the peace treaty (signed in Paris on December 10, 1898) and submitted that treaty to the U.S. Senate on January 4, 1899. After a brisk debate in which opponents of acquisition charged that acquiring

colonies went against America's history and morality, that acquiring the Philippines would embroil the United States in future wars, and that Filipinos would be able to migrate to the United States, where they would compete with American labor, on February 6, 1899, the Senate ratified the treaty by a vote of 57–27, just one vote more than the two-thirds necessary for ratifying a treaty.[8] Learning of the vote, an exultant McKinley boasted that the Philippines would become

a land of plenty and increasing possibilities; a people redeemed from savage and indolent habits, devoted to the arts of peace, in touch with commerce and trade of all nations, enjoying the blessings of freedom, of civil and religious liberty, of education, and of homes, and whose children's children shall for ages hence bless the American republic because it emancipated their fatherland, and set them in the pathway of the world's best civilization.[9]

The Senate vote, however, did not end the debate over whether the United States should become a colonial power. Two days before the Senate voted, fighting broke out between U.S. troops and Filipinos under Emilio Aguinaldo, who had helped American soldiers overthrow the Spanish and who expected the United States to grant the Philippines immediate inde-

7. The Spanish-American War lasted less than three months. The United States suffered only 362 battle or battle-related deaths (an additional 5,100 died of either disease or food poisoning), and the war cost only $250 million.

8. Outside the Senate, opponents of imperialism included Carl Schurz, William James, Mark Twain, Andrew Carnegie, Charles Francis Adams, Jane Addams, and William Jennings Bryan.
9. "Speech at Dinner of the Home Market Club," Feb. 16, 1899, in *Speeches and Addresses of William McKinley* (New York: Doubleday & McClure, 1900) p. 193.

pendence. Before the United States broke Aguinaldo's insurrection, approximately 125,000 American troops served in the Philippines, 4,200 were killed in action, and 2,800 were wounded, but an alleged 220,000 Filipinos died in battle, from disease and famine, and through torture. Government censors kept war-related atrocities from the American people. By 1902, the Philippine insurrection had been broken.

In 1900, Democratic presidential nominee William Jennings Bryan campaigned against McKinley on an anti-imperialist platform. The incumbent won easily (probably because of the fairly widespread prosperity that American voters enjoyed in 1900), but Bryan carried 45.5 percent of the vote, a better showing for a loser than in all but five presidential elections from 1900 to the present. By the time the St. Louis Exposition opened in 1904, anti-imperialist rhetoric had lost much of its appeal, but the issue was far from dead.

At the St. Louis Exposition, the Philippine Reservation exhibit was sponsored almost totally by the U.S. government. (It cost approximately $1 million.) Undoubtedly, this delighted the exposition's organizers, for they knew that similar attractions (called ethnological villages) had been extremely popular at the Paris Exposition of 1889, the Columbian Exposition of 1893, and the Pan-American Exposition of 1901. Former civil governor of the Philippines William Howard Taft (who in 1904 became secretary of war) supported the Philippine Reservation completely, as did Pedro A. Paterno, president of the Philippine Senate, who hoped that such an exhibit would attract investment capital to the islands. Federal agents scoured the Philippines, collecting materials to exhibit and "inviting" various Filipinos to journey to St. Louis. Those who agreed to come were allowed to make money by diving for coins, selling handicrafts, demonstrating their prowess with bows and arrows, and having their photographs taken with visitors to the exposition.

As expected, the Philippine Reservation exhibit was one of the highlights of the St. Louis Exposition. How did the Philippine Reservation seek to justify American imperialism? How do you think visitors might have reacted to what they saw? According to a 1904 *Harper's* magazine article, the St. Louis Exposition "fills a visitor full of pictures . . . that keep coming up in his mind for years afterwards." The same could be said about the photographs of the Philippine Reservation exhibit. What were those "pictures"?

THE METHOD

According to historian Robert W. Rydell, who wrote an excellent book about American international expositions in the late nineteenth and early twentieth centuries, expositions "propagated the ideas and values of the country's political, financial, corporate, and intellectual leaders and offered these ideas as the proper interpretation of social and political real-

CHAPTER 4

JUSTIFYING
AMERICAN
IMPERIALISM:
THE LOUISIANA
PURCHASE
EXPOSITION,
1904

ity."[10] In other words, the millions of Americans who visited exhibits that the Anthropology Department had created at the 1904 exposition saw what someone else wanted them to see. At the Philippine Reservation exhibit, visitors made their way through six Filipino villages erected by the U.S. government in which representatives of "all the races of the Philippine Islands" could be "studied" by scientists and where most Americans had their only opportunity to see Filipinos with their own eyes. Keep in mind the prevailing "scientific" theories and research that affected not only the scientists of the Anthropology Department but the general public as well. Thus the Philippine villages allowed the American government to use the reservation to justify its imperialistic ventures in the Philippines and elsewhere.

The evidence that you will be examining and analyzing in this chapter consists of fourteen photographs taken at the Louisiana Purchase International Exposition (Sources 1 through 14) and an excerpt from an essay by W. J. McGee, head of the exposition's Anthropology Department (Source 15). Through photographs taken by official exposition photographers, you will see some of what the fair's visitors saw. Similarly, McGee's essay is intended to help you understand some of the thinking behind the Anthropology Department's exhibits.

From its invention in 1839 by French painter Louis Jacques Da-

guerre (hence its original name) the daguerreotype or photograph was enthusiastically embraced by nearly everyone. By 1851 the word *photograph* was in common usage, and by 1853 there were eighty-six galleries in New York City alone where people could come to have their photographic portraits made.

Unlike the painting or the drawing, the photograph is generally thought of as an objective and completely neutral depiction of reality (a real-life person, family, or scene, for example). As Susan Sontag notes in her insightful book *On Photography,* "the photographer [is] thought to be an acute but non-interfering observer—a scribe, not a poet."[11] And yet, as we know, a photographer can arrange subjects in ways so as to communicate a particular point of view, a subjective opinion, an *interpretation* of reality rather than reality itself. Civil War photographer Mathew Brady, for example, would reposition corpses on the battlefield to create photographic images that were more visually shocking than were the actual battlefield scenes.

As you examine the photographs in Sources 1 through 14, keep in mind that you are seeing what someone else wants you to see. In analyzing each photograph, try to determine the photographer's point of view or bias. What message does the photographer hope to communicate to viewers? The Philippine Islands in 1904 contained an enormous diversity of peoples, from the most "primitive" to the most technologically and culturally sophisticated. About seventy-five linguistic

10. Robert W. Rydell, *All the World's a Fair: Visions of Empire at American International Expositions, 1876–1916* (Chicago: University of Chicago Press, 1984), p. 3.

11. Susan Sontag, *On Photography* (New York: Farrar, Straus and Giroux, 1977), p. 88.

groups were represented, as well as a plethora of Western and non-Western religious (under Spanish rule, most Filipinos had become Roman Catholics) and social customs. Yet of the many peoples who inhabited the Philippine Islands, the U.S. government selected only six groups to inhabit the reservation's villages. Five of the six groups are photographically depicted in Sources 5 through 13.[12] Why do you think each group was selected to go to St. Louis? What impressions do you think each group left in the minds of American visitors?

Although you may not be used to thinking of photographs as historical evidence, photographs and other visual documents (drawings, paintings, movies) often can yield as much information as more traditional sources. As Charles F. Bryan Jr. and Mark V. Wetherington note,

Through the eye of the camera, the researcher can examine people and places "frozen" in time. . . . Photographs can tell us much about the social preferences and pretensions of their subjects, and can catch people at work, at play, or at home. In fact, you can "read" a photograph in much the same manner as any other historical document.[13]

As you examine and analyze each photograph in the Evidence section,

ask the following questions. Take notes as you go along.

1. What message is the photographer attempting to convey? How does the photographer convey that message (there may well be more than one way)?
2. Is the photographer biased in any way? How? What is the purpose of the photograph?
3. Are there buildings in the photograph? What impressions of these buildings does the photographer intend that viewers should get? How does the photograph seek to elicit those impressions?
4. Are there people in the photograph? Are they posed or "natural"? How does the photographer portray these people? What are the people doing (if anything)? What impressions of these people does the photographer intend that viewers of the photograph should retain?
5. Examine the people in more detail. What about their clothing? Their facial expressions? *Note:* Because the exposition photographers expected their subjects to strike artificial poses in order to be photographed, many of the pictures appear rigid and posed. Indeed, they were. If you have an old family album, see how similar some of the poses are to those in these photographs.

After you have examined each photograph, look at all the photographs together. What message is the photographer (or photographers) intending to convey? Most professional photographers judge whether a photograph is good or poor by the responses it

12. Negro pygmies (or Negritos), Igorots, Tagalos, Bontocs, and Visayans. The sixth group was the Moros.
13. Charles F. Bryan Jr., and Mark V. Wetherington, *Finding Our Past: A Guidebook for Group Projects in Community History* (Knoxville: East Tennessee Historical Society, 1983), p. 26.

CHAPTER 4

JUSTIFYING
AMERICAN
IMPERIALISM:
THE LOUISIANA
PURCHASE
EXPOSITION,
1904

evokes in the viewer's mind. What is the relationship between the responses you imagine these photographs might have elicited in American viewers and the United States' justification for imperialism? The excerpt from McGee's essay also is extremely illuminating. What, if any, cultural bias or prejudice can you identify in his thinking?

❋ THE EVIDENCE ❋

Sources 1 through 3 from *The World's Fair, Comprising the Official Photographic Views of the Universal Exposition Held in St. Louis, 1904* (St. Louis: N. D. Thompson Publishing Co., 1903), pp. 6, 56, 67.

1. Opening-Day Ceremonies, April 30, 1904, in the Plaza of St. Louis (Palace of Varied Industries in the background).

2. **Palace of Liberal Arts (the United States Government Building in the background), 1904.**

3. Palace of Machinery and Palace of Electricity (260-foot-high Ferris wheel in the background), 1904.

Source 4 from J. W. Buel, ed., *Louisiana and the Fair: An Exposition of the World, Its People, and Their Achievements* (St. Louis: World's Progress Publishing Co., 1904), Vol. V, frontispiece. Photo: Missouri Historical Society.

4. Types and Development of Man, 1904.

CHAPTER 4

JUSTIFYING
AMERICAN
IMPERIALISM:
THE LOUISIANA
PURCHASE
EXPOSITION,
1904

Source 5 from Robert W. Rydell, *All the World's a Fair: Visions of Empire at American International Expositions, 1876–1916* (Chicago: University of Chicago Press, 1984), p. 175. Photo: Library of Congress.

5. Negrito Tribesman from the Philippines (exposition officials named this man "Missing Link"), 1904.

Source 6 from *The World's Fair, Comprising the Official Photographic Views,*
p. 149. Photo: Missouri Historical Society.

6. Igorots from the Philippines, 1904.

Sources 7 and 8 from Buel, ed., *Louisiana and the Fair*, Vol. V, p. 1721. Photos: Missouri Historical Society.

7. Tagalo Women Washing, 1904.

8. Igorots Performing a Festival Dance, 1904.

Source 9 from Rydell, *All the World's a Fair,* p. 174. Photo: Library of Congress.

9. Igorot Dancers and American Spectators, 1904.

Source 10 from Buel, ed., *Louisiana and the Fair,* Vol. V, p. 1737. Photo: Missouri Historical Society.

10. Igorots Preparing a Feast of Dog, 1904.

Source 11 from *The World's Fair, Comprising the Official Photographic Views,* p. 169. Photo: Missouri Historical Society.

11. Bontoc Head-Hunters from the Philippines, 1904.

Sources 12 and 13 from *The World's Fair, Comprising the Official Photographic Views,* pp. 161, 163. Photos: Missouri Historical Society.

12. Visayan Mothers with Their Children (two of whom were born at the exposition), 1904.

CHAPTER 4

JUSTIFYING
AMERICAN
IMPERIALISM:
THE LOUISIANA
PURCHASE
EXPOSITION,
1904

13. A Visayan Troupe of Singers, Dancers, and Orchestra Players, 1904.

Source 14 from Rydell, *All the World's a Fair,* p. 176. Photo: Missouri Historical Society.

14. Reproduction of an American School for Filipinos in the Philippines, 1904.

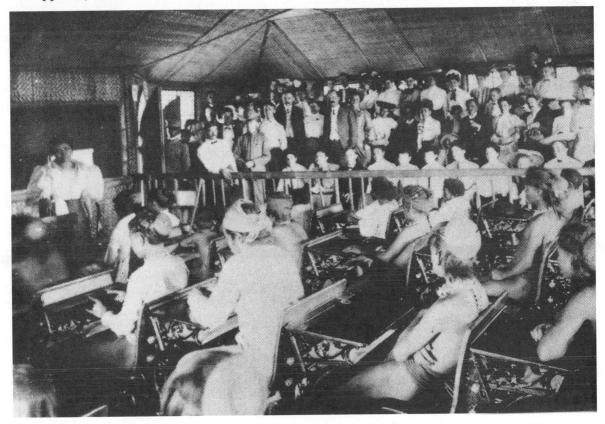

CHAPTER 4

JUSTIFYING
AMERICAN
IMPERIALISM:
THE LOUISIANA
PURCHASE
EXPOSITION,
1904

Source 15 from Buel, ed., *Louisiana and the Fair,* Vol. V, pp. 1567–1572.

15. Excerpt from W. J. McGee's, "Anthropology—A Congress of Nations at the Fair," 1904.

It is possible for the naturalist to build from the smallest bone of an extinct animal the very form, size, appearance, in short a reconstruction and reproduction of the animal as it appeared in life. So it is possible for the ethnologist to estimate, from any object fashioned by the art of man, the degree of civilization that produced it, and in many cases to establish a reasonable hypothesis respecting the customs, the religion, and even the achievements of the people of which the object referred to is a relict.

The story of the birth of man cannot be told in geologic records, but his growth from primitive savagery to the attainments that distinguish and aggrandize our times may be closely followed by the evidences of his existence and his crafts scattered along the highway of the ages. To tell the story, however, is much less impressive and far less convincing than is production of the proofs of scientific deductions and conclusions in the form of specimens of handiwork, and with this thoroughly understood the anthropological department of the Louisiana Purchase Exposition was made a museum of objects rather than a school dependent upon pictographic art for the elucidation of theory.

In pursuing the study of mankind's development one very important fact must be kept well in view, viz., that it is not possible to measure the growth of the world's civilization with that precision which may be applied in estimating the periods of geology, during which the processes of nature reduced the earth to a habitable condition. For it is well to consider that in different localities two or more ages, so to speak, have always co-existed. The mind of man is so constituted that each individual presents special characteristics, so that there is perpetual conflict in concept and endless antagonisms in conclusions. A superior mind may point the way to higher and better conditions, but it does not follow that his counsel will be obeyed; and it is equally probable that the voice of one least qualified to give advice will be heeded as that of a leader. Thus it happens with families, clans, tribes and nations, for which reason development may be advanced or retarded as circumstances favor or hinder. In our own day, acquainted with and enjoying a high degree of civilization, we know that there are other countries in which barbarism still exists; even in almost primitive savagery; such for example as the Terre del Fuegans, the Seri Indians, on the Gulf of California, and the Ainu, of the Kurile Islands, north of Japan. If such low types, of which there are many more examples than the three noted, can exist in an age distinguished for great achievements in industry, commerce, art, science, we must, in justice to previous ages, believe that disparities equally great characterized all other periods; that the stone age, bronze age, the iron age, co-existed, though divided by lines geographic, tribal, and national; that man's growth has been indigenous and adventitious, dependent upon conditions of mind, environment, and climate. For these reasons, to know the human race in its multiplied aspects, past and present, we must specialize, since generalization leads inevitably into a labyrinth of uncertainties respecting origin, distribution, and development of peoples.

It is to make the study of mankind at once interesting and clearly understandable that the anthropological department was established at the World's Fair, in the elaboration of which reliance was placed in specialization and objective demonstration; thus, early man was a cave dweller, whose weapons were flint and stone, and whose appearance bore hairy resemblance to the wild beasts with which he contended. This description presents an image to the reader, who constructs according to preconceived opinions, and the vividness of his imagination. Similarly mere descriptions, or even drawings, of people, implements, and utensils, convey no more than a general idea, which being unsubstantial soon vanishes, like a vision, leaving no permanent impression.

The Anthropological exhibit at the St. Louis Fair represented the sum of human knowledge respecting races, presented in a concrete form by the exhibition of actual objects recovered from the graves of centuries; resurrections from the tombs of long ago civilizations; exhumations from the cemeteries wherein were laid the bones and relics of primitive man as he existed in all countries. To this interesting showing many nations contributed the most rare and precious specimens which scientists, archaeologists, and explorers have discovered, bearing in any wise upon the subject of primitive, prehistoric, savage and strange peoples that have inhabited the earth. This department of the Fair was accordingly a world's museum of human relics, and a congress of living examples of various human types, brought from the most remote parts of the globe.

A general survey of the anthropological department revealed to the visitor the appearance, habits, surroundings and every day life of early man, such as lived in caves, burrowed like wild animals, dwelt in trees, and existed in the primal state of savagery more than ten thousand, aye, perhaps fifty thousand years ago. And in the showing the ancient Egyptian reappeared, out of the spiced and pitched cerements that wrapped his body in preservatives long before the time of Noah—even from millenniums when human hands fashioned the first mud hut that stood upon the banks of the Nile.

CHAPTER 4

JUSTIFYING
AMERICAN
IMPERIALISM:
THE LOUISIANA
PURCHASE
EXPOSITION,
1904

The Assyrian, earliest of the tribe of Asshur, was there, mute of lip for a period so great that hoary antiquity cannot measure it, to remind beholders of the first monarchy of history; and the Babylonian was present, out of the cradle of civilization, with specimens of his workmanship and evidences of his marked attainments in sculpture, architecture, literature, religion, 6500 years ago in the far away and now desert land where the Garden of Eden is supposed to have been planted. It was resurrection and revivification of the most antique races of the world, brought forth from sepulchers of the nameless past, to be reviewed by the living present that the secrets of existence in the unnumbered ages might be exposed.

In the procession of peoples, extinct and living, that represented all the periods of human life on our planet, there appeared examples from orient, occident, continent and island the wide world over; tree dwellers from New Guinea; lake dwellers from the Orinoco valley; head hunters from Borneo; cannibals from Africa; hairy men from the Kuriles; devil worshipers from Saghalien; giants from Patagonia; pygmies from Africa; Eskimos from Arctic regions; in short, the exhibition was a congress of typical peoples from every corner and part of the earth, and a museum of humanity so comprehensive that it was possible for the visitor to gain therefrom a perception and mental grasp of man as he appeared in all ages, conditions, and countries. The showing being thus complete it was made comparatively easy to trace man's progress from his earliest manifestation through all the pauses, periods, and epochs of his advance even to the heights of his accomplishments in the dawn of the twentieth century, in the culmination of effort, as illustrated in the greatest and latest of Expositions. . . .

❈ QUESTIONS TO CONSIDER ❈

As you examine the photographs, first look for the photographer's intent and biases in each image. What "message" is the photographer trying to communicate? How might that message be used as a justification for American imperialism in the Philippines? For example, examine Sources 1 through 3, which show some of the majestic buildings at the exposition. What reactions (awe, pride, and so on) did the fair's organizers hope visitors would have to the buildings in Sources 1 through 3? What impressions (amusement, awe, disgust) might viewers have had of these edifices? Now compare the structures in Sources 1 through 3 with those in Sources 6 through 9. What message do the photographers hope viewers will receive?

The original caption for the Types and Development of Man exhibit shown in Source 4 (from the official history of the Louisiana Purchase Exposition) reads in part, "The photogravure herewith is from an excellent specially prepared drawing which very accurately illustrates, as nearly as the science of ethnology is able to do, the characteristic types of mankind arranged in a progressive order of development from primitive or prehistoric man to the highest example of modern civilization." How does this photograph of a painting (which was on display at the exposition) help you assess the intent of all the photographers? To answer this question, review the Background section of this chapter, particularly the discussion of the "scientific" thinking of the time on ranking humans by race or ethnicity, or consult Stephen Jay Gould's informative book, *The Mismeasure of Man* (see footnote 6).

Sources 5 through 11 are photographs of posed Philippine men and women from the Negrito, Igorot, Tagalo, and Bontoc tribes. These groups were among the most "primitive" of all Filipinos. Why did U.S. government officials select these groups of people to appear at the St. Louis Exposition? How are the groups portrayed by photographers? How are they dressed? What are they doing? What impressions might exhibition visitors viewing the photographs have had of these people? When American visitors appear in the photographs, as in Sources 9 and 14, what are they doing? Why do you think the photographers include Americans in these pictures?

Sources 12 and 13 are photographs of Visayans, a group of people quite different from the Negritos, Igorots, Tagalos, and Bontocs. What seems different about them? How might you ac-

count for these differences?[14] How might American visitors to the village exhibit and viewers of these photographs have reacted differently to the Visayans than to the other Filipino peoples at the exposition? What impressions would the Visayans have made? How might the Visayans have been used to justify American imperialism in the Philippines?

Source 14 is a photograph depicting a replica of an American school for Filipinos in the Philippines. What is the purpose of the photograph? What is the photographer's message? What impressions might visitors or viewers have had?

Once you have examined the photographs individually, analyze them collectively. What is their collective message? How does that message relate to American actions in the Philippines from 1898 to the exposition in 1904? Could these photographs or word descriptions of them have been used to justify American imperialism in the Philippines? How? Refer to specific photographs to prove your points.

In Source 15, the excerpt from his essay on the fair's Anthropology Department, W. J. McGee boasts that, in addition to relics, the department has created "a congress of living examples of various human types, brought from the most remote parts of the globe." By 1904, nearly all scientists had accepted Darwin's theory of evolution. To McGee, however, how could the world of 1904 simultaneously be home

14. The Visayans were Roman Catholics, whereas all the other Filipinos brought to St. Louis practiced non-Western religions or held on to native Filipino religious customs. What does this tell you about the Visayans?

CHAPTER 4

JUSTIFYING
AMERICAN
IMPERIALISM:
THE LOUISIANA
PURCHASE
EXPOSITION,
1904

to "primitive savagery" and the Western "attainments that distinguish and aggrandize our times"? Was evolution a universal phenomenon that affected all subgroups of a species? If not, did the "fittest" (to use Spencer's word) owe anything to their "unfit" brethren? How could McGee's essay be used as a justification for imperialism?

✳ EPILOGUE ✳

At the Louisiana Purchase Exposition in 1904, American visitors saw countless exhibits that communicated very strong messages. Arranged and erected by the nation's corporate, intellectual, and political leaders, the exhibits nevertheless were what Americans wanted to see. These exhibits trumpeted America's own scientific, technological, and cultural prowess while at the same time offering living proof that it was the United States' economic, political, and moral duty to become a colonial power. In addition to the Filipino village exhibits, villages had been set up for Native Americans and Alaskan Eskimos, who, like the Filipinos, were wards of the United States. These exhibits were as powerful a visual justification for American imperialism as could possibly have been contrived.

Once the Philippine revolt was broken in 1902, the United States invested considerable time and energy in trying to Americanize the Filipinos, largely through education and giving Filipinos an increasing voice in their own affairs. In 1913, President Woodrow Wilson appointed Francis B. Harrison governor general of the Philippines, with the explicit instructions to prepare the Filipinos for their ultimate independence (a promise Congress gave its assent to in 1916, noting that independence would be granted "as soon as a stable government can be established"). Schools were set up throughout the islands, and by the 1930s, almost 50 percent of the population was literate. Gradually, American officials increased the percentage of Filipinos in the civil service, from 49 percent in 1903 to 94 percent in 1923. Elections were held for a Philippine legislature, although the real power remained in the hands of Americans.

In economic matters, the Americans' record in the Philippines was not so impressive. Economic power remained in the hands of a small, native Philippine landed elite, who, with the cooperation of Americans, continued to dominate the Philippine economy. Between 1900 and 1935, poverty became more widespread, real wages actually declined, and sharecropping (like that in the American South) doubled. This was the situation when the Japanese attacked the Philippine Islands on December 8, 1941. Emilio Aguinaldo, leader of the Philippine independence movement that the United States had crushed, sided with the Japanese.

With the defeat of Japan in 1945, the United States moved quickly to grant independence to the Philippines (which occurred on July 4, 1946), although America's economic and military presence in the new nation remained strong. Favorable leases on military and naval bases were negotiated, and the Central Intelligence Agency closely monitored Philippine elections and on occasion secretly backed candidates for office.

In 1965, campaigning against widespread government corruption and favoritism to the landed elite, Ferdinand Marcos was elected president of the Philippines. A much-lauded war hero, Marcos had entered politics in 1949, when he had become the youngest person ever elected to the Philippine Congress. As president, Marcos increased the power of his office to virtual one-man rule, largely by hobbling or eradicating the other branches of government and by a brutal policy of political repression, with more than fifty thousand political prisoners and numerous reported incidents of assassinations and torture. Even so, Marcos's rule was insecure. In the nation's economic expansion, profits went to a very few, usually Marcos's associates (in 1972, the poorest 20 percent of Filipinos received only 4.4 percent of the nation's income), and a population boom (2.5 percent per year) increased poverty and unemployment.

Things began coming apart for Marcos on August 21, 1983, when his principal political rival, Benigno Aquino, was shot and killed at the Manila airport as he was returning to the Philippines to lead an anti-Marcos political movement. Public opinion in both the Philippines and the United States was that Marcos had been responsible

for Aquino's death. By 1984, opinion polls in the Philippines showed a serious erosion of support for the Marcos government.

In 1986, Marcos was challenged for the presidency by Corazon Aquino, the widow of the killed opposition leader. The election results were clouded by charges of fraud, and both Marcos and Aquino claimed victory. By this time, the aging and ill Marcos had become increasingly isolated from the people, as he and his wife, Imelda, remained cloistered in the presidential palace. In February 1986, a general strike by Aquino supporters, the army's turning against the government, and the increasing displeasure of the Reagan administration finally toppled Marcos, who fled the Philippines for American protection in Hawaii. Corazon Aquino became president, only to face the nation's severe economic and political problems. Her term expired in 1992, and she did not seek reelection, having survived numerous coup attempts. She left a nation that was more democratic but still economically and politically unstable.

Filipinos were not the only people "displayed" at the St. Louis Exposition. Indeed, the same economic, political, and intellectual strains that supported America's overseas imperialism also were evident in the conquest and subjugation of Native Americans, the growing efforts to exclude certain immigrants (the Chinese Exclusion Act of 1882, for example), the rising tide of American nativism, and the successful legal and extralegal methods southern whites used to deprive African Americans of their economic and civil rights. Not surpris-

Source 16 from *The World's Fair, Comprising the Official Photographic Views,* p. 137. Photo: Library of Congress.

16. Sioux Men and Women, 1904.

ingly, both Geronimo and Chief Joseph were extremely popular "attractions" at the exposition, as were the Sioux men and women pictured in Source 16. What similarities do you see in Source 16 and the photographs of Filipinos? Undoubtedly, ethnologist McGee, head of the exposition's Anthropology Department, spoke for most white Americans when he remarked that "*white* and *strong* are synonymous terms."

In one sense, the Louisiana Purchase Exposition of 1904 marked the high point of Americans' interest in international expositions and world's fairs. As Americans became less provincial, especially after the introduction of modern communications media, attendance at such events declined. As a result, such expositions became smaller (whereas the St. Louis Exposition covered 1,272 acres, the 1982 World's Fair in Knoxville, Tennessee, was held on less than 70 acres). Moreover, the purpose of American expositions changed. Rather than a celebration of the nation's technological might or a justification for American imperialism, the world's fair came to be viewed by its backers as a massive urban renewal project, whereby the host city's government could come into possession of valuable acreage to be used for economic development. Such was the goal of the world's fairs in Portland, Knoxville, and New Orleans. Finally, increased costs and lower attendance figures meant that such expositions were not economical. The New Orleans World's Fair lost millions of dollars. As a result, Chicago, which had planned to host an international exposition in 1992, had second thoughts.

In 1904, however, millions of Americans came to St. Louis to visit the Louisiana Purchase Exposition, a massive reinforcement of their own ideas about American superiority and the rectitude of Euro-American world domination. At the same time, the ideas that spurred and justified imperialism similarly spurred and justified increasingly harsh treatment of Native Americans, African Americans, Hispanics, Asian Americans, and recent immigrants from southern and eastern Europe. In a nation and a world filled with opportunities, few Americans realized that their own ideology and attitudes not only did not carry them forward but in many ways actually held them back.

5

Homogenizing a Pluralistic Nation: Propaganda During World War I

✳ THE PROBLEM ✳

One week after Congress approved the war declaration that brought the United States into World War I,[1] President Woodrow Wilson signed Executive Order 2594, which created the Committee on Public Information, a government agency designed to mobilize public opinion behind the war effort. Wilson selected forty-one-year-old journalist and political ally George Creel to direct the committee's efforts. Creel immediately established voluntary press censorship, which essentially made the committee the overseer of all war and war-related news.

The Committee on Public Information also produced films, engaged

some seventy-five thousand lecturers (called "Four Minute Men") who delivered approximately 7.5 million talks (each of which was to last no longer than four minutes), commissioned posters intended to aid recruitment and sell war bonds (seven hundred poster designs were submitted to the committee and more than 9 million posters were printed in 1918 alone), and engaged in numerous other propaganda activities.

Why did the federal government believe that the Committee on Public Information was necessary? For one thing, there appears to have been considerable concern in the Wilson administration that American public opinion, which had supported the nation's neutrality and noninvolvement, would not support the war effort. More important, however, was the

---

1. Wilson delivered his war message on April 2, 1917. The Senate declared war on April 3 and the House of Representatives followed suit on April 6.

fear of many government officials that large ethnic blocs of Americans would not support the United States' entry into the conflict. In 1917, the Census Bureau had estimated that approximately 4.7 million people living in the United States had been born in Germany or in one of the other Central Powers.[2] It was also known that the nation contained a large number of Irish Americans, many of whom were vehemently anti-British and thus might be expected to side with the Central Powers.[3] Could such a heterogeneous society be persuaded to support the war effort voluntarily? Could Americans of the same ethnic stock as the enemies be rallied to the cause?

In this chapter, you will be examining and analyzing the propaganda techniques of a modern nation at war. The Evidence section contains material sponsored or commissioned by the Committee on Public Information (posters, newspaper advertisements, excerpts from speeches by Four Minute Men) as well as privately produced works (song lyrics and commercial film advertisements) that either were approved by the committee or tended to parallel its efforts. After examining the evidence, you will work to answer the following questions:

1. How did the government attempt to mobilize the opinion of a diverse American public in support of a united war effort?
2. What were the consequences—positive and negative—of this effort?

On a larger scale, you should be willing to ponder other questions as well, although they do not relate directly to the evidence you will examine. To begin with, is government-sponsored propaganda during wartime a good thing? When it comes into conflict with the First Amendment's guarantees of freedom of speech, which should prevail? Finally, is there a danger that government-sponsored propaganda can be carried too far? Why do you think that was (or was not) the case during World War I?

❋ BACKGROUND ❋

By the early twentieth century, the United States had worldwide economic interests and even had acquired a modest colonial empire, but many Americans wanted to believe that they were insulated from world affairs and impervious to world problems. Two great oceans seemed to protect the nation from overseas threats, and the enormity of the country and comparative weakness of its neighbors appeared to secure it against all dangers. Let other nations waste their people

2. The actual figure was closer to 4.27 million people. See U.S. Bureau of the Census, *Historical Statistics of the United States* (Washington, D.C.: U.S. Government Printing Office, 1975), pt. I, p. 117.
3. According to the U.S. census of 1920, there were 1.04 million Americans who had been born in Ireland and 3.12 million native-born Americans who had one or both parents of Irish birth.

CHAPTER 5

HOMOGENIZING
A PLURALISTIC
NATION:
PROPAGANDA
DURING WORLD
WAR I

and resources in petty wars over status and territory, Americans reasoned. The United States should stand above such greed or insanity, and certainly should not wade into foreign mud puddles.

To many Americans, European nations were especially suspect. For centuries, European nations had engaged in an almost ceaseless round of armed conflicts—wars for national unity, territory, or even religion or empire. Moreover, in the eyes of many Americans, these bloody wars appeared to have solved little or nothing, and the end of one war seemed to be but a prelude to the next. Ambitious kings and their plotting ministers seemed to make Europe the scene of almost constant uproar, an uproar that many Americans saw as devoid of reason and morality. Nor did it appear that the United States, as powerful as it was, could have any effect on the unstable European situation.

For this reason, most Americans greeted news of the outbreak of war in Europe in 1914 with equal measures of surprise and determination not to become involved. They applauded President Wilson's August 4 proclamation of neutrality, his statement (issued two weeks later) urging Americans to be impartial in thought as well as in deed, and his insistence that the United States continue neutral commerce with all the belligerents. Few Americans protested German violation of Belgian neutrality. Indeed, most Americans (naively, as it turned out) believed that the United States both should and could remain aloof from the conflict in Europe.

But many factors pulled the United States into the conflict that later be-

came known as World War I.[4] America's economic prosperity to a large extent rested on commercial ties with Europe. In 1914, U.S. trade with the Allies (England, France, Russia) exceeded $800 million, whereas trade with the Central Powers (Germany, Austria, Turkey) stood at approximately $170 million. Much of the trade with Great Britain and France was financed through loans from American banks, something President Wilson and Secretary of State William Jennings Bryan openly discouraged because both men believed that those economic interests might eventually draw the United States into the conflict. Indeed, Wilson and Bryan probably were correct. Nevertheless, American economic interests were closely tied to those of Great Britain and France. Thus a victory by the Central Powers might damage U.S. trade. As Wilson drifted to an acceptance of this fact, Bryan had to back down.

A second factor pulling the United States into the war was the deep-seated feelings of President Wilson himself. Formerly a constitutional historian (Wilson had been a college professor and university president before entering the political arena as a reform governor of New Jersey), Wilson had long admired the British people and their form of government. Although technically neutral, the president strongly, though privately, favored the Allies and viewed a German victory as unthinkable. Moreover, many of Wilson's key advisers and the people close to him were decidedly

4. Until the outbreak of what became known as World War II, World War I was referred to as the Great War.

pro-British. Such was the opinion of the president's friend and closest adviser, Colonel Edward House, as well as that of Robert Lansing (who replaced Bryan as secretary of state)[5] and Walter Hines Page (ambassador to England). These men and others helped strengthen Wilson's strong political opinions and influence the president's changing position toward the war in Europe. Hence, although Wilson asked Americans to be neutral in thought as well as in deed, in fact he and his principal advisers were neither. More than once, the president chose to ignore British violations of America's neutrality. Finally, when it appeared that the Central Powers might outlast their enemies, Wilson was determined to intercede. It was truly an agonizing decision for the president, who had worked so diligently to keep his nation out of war.

A third factor affecting the United States' neutrality was the strong ethnic ties of many Americans to the Old World. Many Americans had been born in Europe, and an even larger number were the sons and daughters of European immigrants. Although these people considered themselves to be, and were, Americans, some retained emotional ties to Europe that they sometimes carried into the political arena—ties that could influence America's foreign policy.

Finally, as the largest neutral commercial power in the world, the United States soon became caught in the middle of the commercial warfare of the belligerents. With the declaration of war, both Great Britain and Germany threw up naval blockades. Great Britain's blockade was designed to cut the Central Powers off from war materiel. American commercial vessels bound for Germany were stopped, searched, and often seized by the British navy. Wilson protested British policy many times, but to no effect. After all, giving in to Wilson's protests would have deprived Britain of its principal military asset: the British navy.

Germany's blockade was even more dangerous, partly because the vast majority of American trade was with England and France. In addition, however, Germany's chief method of blockading the Allies was the use of the submarine, a comparatively new weapon in 1914. Because of the nature of the submarine (lethal while underwater, not equal to other fighting vessels on the surface), it was difficult for the submarine to remain effective and at the same time adhere to international law, such as the requirement that sufficient warning be given before sinking an enemy ship.[6] In 1915, hoping to terrorize the British into making peace, Germany unleashed its submarines in the Atlantic with orders to sink all ships flying Allied flags. In March, a German submarine sank the British passenger ship *Falaba*. Then on May 7, 1915, the British liner *Lu-*

---

5. Bryan resigned in 1915, in protest over what he considered Wilson's too sharp note to Germany over the sinking of the passenger liner *Lusitania*. Wilson called the act "illegal and inhuman." Bryan sensed that the Wilson administration was tilting away from neutrality.

6. International laws governing warfare at sea, as well as neutral shipping during wartime, were written in the mid-eighteenth century, more than one hundred years before the submarine became a potent seagoing weapon.

CHAPTER 5

HOMOGENIZING
A PLURALISTIC
NATION:
PROPAGANDA
DURING WORLD
WAR I

sitania was sunk with a loss of more than 1,000 lives, 128 of them American. Although Germany had published warnings in American newspapers specifically cautioning Americans not to travel on the *Lusitania,* and although it was ultimately discovered that the *Lusitania* had gone down so fast (in only eighteen minutes) because the British were shipping ammunition in the hold of the passenger ship, Americans were shocked by the Germans' actions on the high seas. Most Americans, however, continued to believe that the United States should stay out of the war and approved of Wilson's statement, issued three days after the *Lusitania* sank to the bottom, that "there is such a thing as a man being too proud to fight."

Yet a combination of economic interests, German submarine warfare, and other events gradually pushed the United States toward involvement. In early February 1917, Germany announced a policy of unrestricted submarine warfare against all ships—belligerent and neutral alike. Ships would be sunk without warning if found to be in what Germany designated as forbidden waters. Later that month, the British intercepted a secret telegram intended for the German minister to Mexico, stationed in Mexico City. In that telegram, German Foreign Secretary Arthur Zimmermann offered Mexico a deal: Germany would help Mexico retrieve territory lost to the United States in the 1840s if Mexico would make a military alliance with Germany and declare war on the United States in the event that the United States declared war on

Germany. Knowing the impact that such a telegram would have on American public opinion, the British quickly handed the telegram over to Wilson, who released it to the press. From that point on, it was but a matter of time before the United States would become involved in World War I.

On March 20, 1917, President Wilson called his cabinet together at the White House to advise him on how to proceed in the deteriorating situation with Germany. Wilson's cabinet officers unanimously urged the president to call Congress into session immediately and ask for a declaration of war against Germany. When the last cabinet member had finished speaking, Wilson said, "Well, gentlemen, I think there is no doubt as to what your advice is. I thank you," and dismissed the meeting without informing the cabinet of his own intentions.

Yet even though Wilson had labored so arduously to keep the United States out of the war in Europe, by March 20 (or very soon after) his mind was made up: The United States must make war on Germany. Typing out his war message on his own Hammond portable typewriter, Wilson was out of sorts and complained often of headaches. The president, devoted to peace and Progressive reform, was drafting the document he had prayed he would never have to write.

On April 2, 1917, President Wilson appeared in person before a joint session of Congress to deliver his war message. Congress was ready. On April 4, the Senate approved a war declaration (the vote was 82–6). The House of Representatives followed suit two days later (by a vote of 373–50).[7]

As noted earlier, at the outset of the United States' entry into the war, the Wilson administration feared that the ethnically diverse American public might not unite in support of the nation's involvement in the Great War. Without a decisive event to prompt the war declaration (some Americans even suspected the Zimmermann telegram was a British hoax), would the American people support the war with sufficient unanimity? No firing on Fort Sumter or blowing up of the battleship *Maine* would force America's entrance into this war, nor would the *Lusitania* sinking, which had occurred two years before the 1917 war declaration. Without the obvious threat of having been attacked, would the American people rally to the colors to defeat a faraway enemy? Could isolationist and noninterventionist opinion, very strong as late as the presidential election of 1916, be overcome? Could an ethnically heterogeneous people stand together in time of war? To bind together a diverse people behind the war effort, President Wilson created the Committee on Public Information.

✳ THE METHOD ✳

For George Creel and the Committee on Public Information, the purposes of propaganda were very clear:

1. Unite a multiethnic, pluralistic society behind the war effort.
2. Attract a sufficient number of men to the armed services and elicit universal civilian support for those men.
3. Influence civilians to support the war effort by purchasing war bonds or by other actions (such as limiting personal consumption or rolling bandages).
4. Influence civilians to put pressure on other civilians to refrain from antiwar comments, strikes, antidraft activities, unwitting dispersal of information to spies, and other public acts that could hurt the war effort.

To achieve these ends, propaganda techniques had to be used with extreme care. For propaganda to be effective, it would have to contain one or more of the following features:

1. Portrayal of American and Allied servicemen in the best possible light.
2. Portrayal of the enemy in the worst possible light.

7. The fifty-six votes in the Senate and House against the declaration of war essentially came from three separate groups: senators and congressmen with strong German and Austrian constituencies, isolationists who believed the United States should not become involved on either side, and some Progressive reformers who maintained that the war would divert America's attention from political, economic, and social reforms.

CHAPTER 5

HOMOGENIZING
A PLURALISTIC
NATION:
PROPAGANDA
DURING WORLD
WAR I

3. Portrayal of the American and Allied cause as just and the enemy's cause as unjust.
4. Message to civilians that they were being involved in the war effort in important ways.
5. Communication of a sense of urgency to civilians.

In this chapter, you are given the following six types of World War I propaganda to analyze, some of it produced directly by the Committee on Public Information and some produced privately but examined and approved by the committee:

1. One popular song, perhaps the most famous to come out of World War I, performed in music halls and vaudeville houses (Source 1). Although the Committee on Public Information did not produce this kind of material, it could—and did—discourage performances of "unpatriotic" popular songs.
2. Three newspaper and magazine advertisements produced directly by the Committee on Public Information (Sources 2 through 4).
3. Nine posters either commissioned or approved by the committee and used for recruiting, advertising liberty loans,[8] and other purposes (Sources 5 through 13).
4. Two cartoons, one an editorial cartoon and the other a prize-winning cartoon in a contest sponsored by a U.S. Army camp publication (Sources 14 and 15).

8. Liberty loans were loans made by U.S. citizens to the government to finance the war effort. They were repaid with interest, and were similar to liberty bonds.

5. Two excerpts of speeches by Four Minute Men and one poem by a Four Minute Man. (Sources 16 through 18).
6. Material concerning American-made feature films, including suggestions to theater owners on how to advertise the film *Kultur* ("Culture"), two film advertisements, and one still photograph used in advertising a feature film (Sources 19 through 22).

As you examine the evidence, you will see that effective propaganda operates on two levels. On the surface, there is the logical appeal for support to help win the war. On another level, however, certain images and themes are used to excite the emotions of the people for whom the propaganda is designed. As you examine the evidence, ask yourself the following questions:

1. For whom was this piece of propaganda designed?
2. What was this piece of propaganda trying to get people to think? to do?
3. What logical appeals were being made?
4. What emotional appeals were being made?
5. What might have been the results —positive and negative—of these kinds of appeals?

In songs, speeches, advertisements, and film reviews, are there key words or important images? Where there are illustrations (advertisements, posters, cartoons), what facial expressions and images are used? Finally, are there any common logical and emotional themes running through the government-sponsored propaganda during World War I? How did the United States use propaganda to mobilize public opinion during World War I?

❊ THE EVIDENCE ❊

Source 1 is a popular song by George M. Cohan, 1917.

1. "Over There."

Johnnie, get your gun,
Get your gun, get your gun,
Take it on the run,
On the run, on the run.
Hear them calling you and me,
Every son of liberty.
Hurry right away,
No delay, no delay.
Make your daddy glad
To have had such a lad.
Tell your sweetheart not to pine,
To be proud her boy's in line.

Chorus (repeat chorus twice)
Over there, over there,
Send the word, send the word over there—
That the Yanks are coming,
The Yanks are coming,
The drums rum-tumming
Ev'rywhere.
So prepare, say a pray'r,
Send the word, send the word to beware.
We'll be over, we're coming over,
And we won't come back till it's over
Over there.

CHAPTER 5

HOMOGENIZING
A PLURALISTIC
NATION:
PROPAGANDA
DURING WORLD
WAR I

Sources 2 through 4 from James R. Mock and Cedric Larson, *Words That Won the War: The Story of the Committee on Public Information* (Princeton: Princeton University Press, 1939), pp. 64, 169, 184. Photos: The National Archives.

2. "Spies *and* Lies" Advertisement Urging Americans to Report the Enemy.

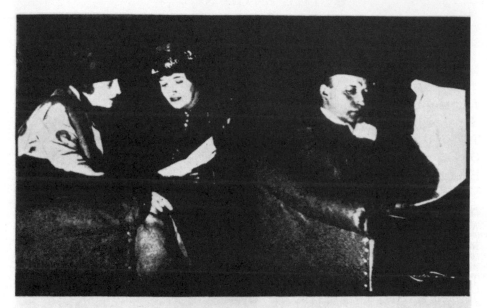

Spies *and* Lies

German agents are everywhere, eager to gather scraps of news about our men, our ships, our munitions. It is still possible to get such information through to Germany, where thousands of these fragments—often individually harmless—are patiently pieced together into a whole which spells death to American soldiers and danger to American homes.

But while the enemy is most industrious in trying to collect information, and his systems elaborate, he is *not* superhuman—indeed he is often very stupid, and would fail to get what he wants were it not deliberately handed to him by the carelessness of loyal Americans.

Do not discuss in public, or with strangers, any news of troop and transport movements, or bits of gossip as to our military preparations, which come into your possession.

Do not permit your friends in service to tell you—or write you—"inside" facts about where they are, what they are doing and seeing.

Do not become a tool of the Hun by passing on the malicious, disheartening rumors which he so eagerly sows. Remember he asks no better service than to have you spread his lies of disasters to our soldiers and sailors, gross scandals in the Red Cross, cruelties, neglect and wholesale executions in our camps, drunkenness and vice in the Expeditionary Force, and other tales certain to disturb American patriots and to bring anxiety and grief to American parents.

And do not wait until you catch someone putting a bomb under a factory. Report the man who spreads pessimistic stories, divulges—or seeks—confidential military information, cries for peace, or belittles our efforts to win the war.

Send the names of such persons, even if they are in uniform, to the Department of Justice, Washington. Give all the details you can, with names of witnesses if possible—show the Hun that we can beat him at his own game of collecting scattered information and putting it to work. The fact that you made the report will not become public.

You are in contact with the enemy today, just as truly as if you faced him across No Man's Land. In your hands are two powerful weapons with which to meet him—discretion and vigilance. *Use them.*

COMMITTEE ON PUBLIC INFORMATION

8 JACKSON PLACE, WASHINGTON, D. C.

George Creel, *Chairman*
The Secretary of State
The Secretary of War
The Secretary of the Navy

Contributed through Division of Advertising   *United States Gov't Comm. on Public Information*

3. "Bachelor of Atrocities" Advertisement for Fighting the Enemy by Buying Liberty Bonds.

Bachelor of Atrocities

IN the vicious guttural language of Kultur,[9] the degree A. B. means Bachelor of Atrocities. Are you going to let the Prussian Python strike at your Alma Mater, as it struck at the University of Louvain?[10]

The Hohenzollern[11] fang strikes at every element of decency and culture and taste that your college stands for. It leaves a track so terrible that only whispered fragments may be recounted. It has ripped all the world-old romance out of war, and reduced it to the dead, black depths of muck, and hate, and bitterness.

You may soon be called to fight. But you are called upon right now to buy Liberty Bonds. You are called upon to economize in every way. It is sometimes harder to live nobly than to die nobly. The supreme sacrifice of life may come easier than the petty sacrifices of comforts and luxuries. You are called to exercise stern self-discipline. Upon this the Allied Success depends.

Set aside every possible dollar for the purchase of Liberty Bonds. Do it relentlessly. Kill every wasteful impulse, that America may live. Every bond you buy fires point-blank at Prussian Terrorism.

BUY U. S. GOVERNMENT BONDS FOURTH LIBERTY LOAN

Contributed through Division of Advertising

United States Gov't Comm. on Public Information

This space contributed for the Winning of the War by
A. T SKERRY, '84, and CYRILLE CARREAU, '04.

Appeal to the Symbols of Education

Two Graduates of New York University Contributed the Space for This CPI Advertisement in Their "Alumni News"

9. Germans often asserted that they had *Kultur,* or a superior culture, in contrast to *civilization,* which they viewed as weak and effeminate.
10. The *University of Louvain,* in Belgium, was pillaged and partially destroyed by German troops. Some professors were beaten and others killed, and the library (containing 250,000 books and manuscripts, some irreplaceable) was totally destroyed. The students themselves were home for summer vacation.
11. *Hohenzollern* was the name of the German royal family since the nation's founding in 1871. It had been the Prussian royal family since 1525.

CHAPTER 5

HOMOGENIZING
A PLURALISTIC
NATION:
PROPAGANDA
DURING WORLD
WAR I

4. Advertisement Appealing to History Teachers, April 4, 1917.

The Committee on Public Information
Established by Order of the President, April 4, 1917

Distribute free *except as noted* the following publications:

I. Red, White and Blue Series:

No. 1. How the War Came to America (English, German, Polish, Bohemian, Italian, Spanish and Swedish).

No. 2. National Service Handbook (primarily for libraries, schools, Y. M. C. A.'s, Clubs, fraternal organizations, etc., as a guide and reference work on all forms of war activity, civil, charitable and military).

No. 3. The Battle Line of Democracy. Prose and Poetry of the Great War. Price 25 cent. Special price to teachers. Proceeds to the Red Cross. Other issues in preparation.

II. War Information Series:

No. 1. The War Message and Facts Behind it.

No. 2. The Nation in Arms, by Secretaries Lane and Baker.

No. 3. The Government of Germany, by Prof. Charles D. Hazen.

No. 4. The Great War from Spectator to Participant.

No. 5. A War of Self Defense, by Secretary Lansing and Assistant Secretary of Labor Louis F. Post.

No. 6. American Loyalty by Citizens of German Descent.

No. 7. Amerikanische Bürgertreue, a translation of No. 6.

Other issues will appear shortly.

III. Official Bulletin:

Accurate daily statement of what all agencies of government are doing in war times. Sent free to newspapers and postmasters (to be put on bulletin boards). Subscription price $5.00 per year.

Address Requests to

Committee on Public Information, Washington, D. C.

What Can History Teachers Do Now?

You can help the community realize what history should mean to it.

You can confute those who by selecting a few historic facts seek to establish some simple cure-all for humanity.

You can confute those who urge that mankind can wipe the past off the slate and lay new foundations for civilization.

You can encourage the sane use of experience in discussions of public questions.

You can help people understand what democracy is by pointing out the common principle in the ideas of Plato, Cromwell, Rousseau, Jefferson, Jackson and Washington.

You can help people understand what German autocracy has in common with the autocracy of the Grand Mogul.

You can help people understand that democracy is not inconsistent with law and efficient government.

You can help people understand that failure of the past to make the world safe for democracy does not mean that it can not be made safe in the future.

You can so teach your students that they will acquire "historical mindedness" and realize the connection of the past with the present.

You can not do these things unless you inform yourself, and think over your information.

You can help yourself by reading the following:
"History and the Great War" bulletin of Bureau of Education.

A series of articles published throughout the year in THE HISTORY TEACHER'S MAGAZINE.

You can obtain aid and advice by writing to
The National Board for Historical Service, 1133 Woodward Building, Washington, D. C.

United States Bureau of Education, Division of Civic Education, Washington, D. C.

Committee on Public Information, Division of Educational Co-operation, 10 Jackson Place, Washington, D. C.

The Committee on Patriotism through Education of the National Security League, 31 Pine Street, New York City.

Carnegie Endowment for International Peace, 2 Jackson Place, Washington, D. C.

National Committee of Patriotic and Defense Societies, Southern Building, Washington, D. C.

The World Peace Foundation, 40 Mount Vernon St., Boston, Mass.

American Association for International Conciliation, 407 West 117th Street, New York City.

The American Society for Judicial Settlement of International Disputes, Baltimore, Md.

The Editor, THE HISTORY TEACHER'S MAGAZINE, Philadelphia.

4

Source 5 from *The James Montgomery Flagg Poster Book,* introduction by Susan E. Meyer (New York: Watson-Guptill Publications, 1975). Courtesy of the Library of Congress.

5. The Famous Uncle Sam Poster.

CHAPTER 5

HOMOGENIZING
A PLURALISTIC
NATION:
PROPAGANDA
DURING WORLD
WAR I

Source 6 from Peter Stanley, *What Did You Do in the War, Daddy?* (Melbourne: Oxford University Press, 1983), p. 55. Photo: Imperial War Museum.

6. Poster Portraying Germany as a Raging Beast.

Source 7 from *The James Montgomery Flagg Poster Book.*

7. United States Marines Recruiting Poster.

CHAPTER 5

HOMOGENIZING
A PLURALISTIC
NATION:
PROPAGANDA
DURING WORLD
WAR I

Source 8 from Anthony Crawford, *Posters in the George C. Marshall Research Foundation* (Charlottesville: University of Virginia Press, 1939), p. 30. Photo: Culver Pictures.

8. "Women of America, Save Your Country" Poster.

Source 9 from Joseph Darracott, ed., *The First World War in Posters* (New York: Dover Publications, 1974), p. 30.

9. "Be Prepared" Poster: Columbia and a Boy Scout.

CHAPTER 5

HOMOGENIZING
A PLURALISTIC
NATION:
PROPAGANDA
DURING WORLD
WAR I

Source 10 from Walton Rawls, *Wake Up, America! World War I and the American Poster* (New York: Abbeville Press, 1988), p. 232.

10. "Americans All!" Poster.

Sources 11 and 12 from Special Collections, University of Tennessee.

11. "See Him Through" Poster, Knights of Columbus, 1918.

CHAPTER 5

HOMOGENIZING
A PLURALISTIC
NATION:
PROPAGANDA
DURING WORLD
WAR I

12. Jewish Welfare Board Poster, 1918.

Source 13 from private collection. Used with permission.

13. "Colored Man Is No Slacker" Poster.

CHAPTER 5

HOMOGENIZING
A PLURALISTIC
NATION:
PROPAGANDA
DURING WORLD
WAR I

Source 14 from John Higham, *Strangers in the Land: Patterns of American Nativism, 1860–1925* (New Brunswick, N.J.: Rutgers University Press, 1955), p. 210.

14. *New York Herald* Editorial Cartoon: German American Dr. Karl Muck, Conductor of the Boston Symphony Orchestra, Needed a Police Escort When He Conducted a Concert in March 1918 in New York City.

Source 15 from *New York Times,* January 6, 1918.

15. Hines's Prize-Winning Cartoon in the 1918 *Trench and Camp* Cartoon Contest.[12]

12. *Trench and Camp* was a weekly publication of the United States Army for its thirty-two training centers in the United States. For this prize-winning cartoon, Frank Hines won a wristwatch. In the cartoon, the American soldier is holding a *pickelhaube,* a German spiked helmet.

CHAPTER 5

HOMOGENIZING
A PLURALISTIC
NATION:
PROPAGANDA
DURING WORLD
WAR I

Sources 16 through 18 from Alfred E. Cornbise, *War as Advertised: The Four Minute Men and America's Crusade, 1917–1918* (Philadelphia: American Philosophical Society, 1984), pp. 72–73, 122, 60.

16. Excerpt of a Speech by a Four Minute Man.

Ladies and Gentlemen:

I have just received the information that there is a German spy among us—a German spy watching *us*.

He is around here somewhere, reporting upon you and me—sending reports about us to Berlin and telling the Germans just what we are doing with the Liberty Loan. From every section of the country these spies have been getting reports over to Potsdam[13]—not general reports but details— where the loan is going well and where its success seems weak, and what people are saying in each community.

For the German government is worried about our great loan. Those Junkers[14] fear its effect upon the German *morale*. They're raising a loan this month, too.

If the American people lend their billions now, one and all with a hip-hip-hurrah, it means that America is united and strong. While, if we lend our money half-heartedly, America seems weak and autocracy remains strong.

Money means everything now; it means quicker victory and therefore less bloodshed. We are *in* the war, and now Americans can have but *one* opinion, only *one* wish in the Liberty Loan.

Well, I hope these spies are getting their messages straight, letting Potsdam know that America is *hurling back* to the autocrats these answers:

For treachery here, attempted treachery in Mexico, treachery everywhere—*one billion*.

For murder of American women and children—*one billion more*.

For broken faith and promise to murder more Americans—*billions and billions more*.

And then we will add:

In the world fight for Liberty, our share—*billions and billions and billions and endless billions*.

Do not let the German spy hear and report that *you* are a slacker.

13. *Potsdam* (a suburb of Berlin) was where the Kaiser lived.
14. *Junkers* were the Prussian nobility.

17. Part of a Speech by a Four Minute Man.

German agents are telling the people of this . . . race[15] through the South that if they will not oppose the German Government, or help our Government, they will be rewarded with Ford automobiles when Germany is in control here. They are told that 10 negroes are being conscripted to 1 white man in order that the Negro race may be killed off; and that the reason Germany went into Belgium was to punish the people of that country for the cruel treatment of the negroes in the Congo.

18. "It's Duty Boy," a Poem Read by Four Minute Men.

My boy must never bring disgrace to his immortal sires—
At Valley Forge and Lexington they kindled freedom's fires,
John's father died at Gettysburg, mine fell at Chancellorsville;
While John himself was with the boys who charged up San Juan Hill.
And John, if he was living now, would surely say with me,
"No son of ours shall e'er disgrace our grand old family tree
By turning out a slacker when his country needs his aid."
It is not of such timber that America was made.
I'd rather you had died at birth or not been born at all,
Than know that I had raised a son who cannot hear the call
That freedom has sent round the world, its precious rights to save—
This call is meant for you, my boy, and I would have you brave;
And though my heart is breaking, boy, I bid you do your part,
And show the world no son of mine is cursed with craven heart;
And if, perchance, you ne'er return, my later days to cheer,
And I have only memories of my brave boy, so dear,
I'd rather have it so, my boy, and know you bravely died
Than have a living coward sit supinely by my side.
To save the world from sin, my boy, God gave his only son—
He's asking for MY boy, to-day, and may His will be done.

15. At the front lines in France, Germans barraged America's African American soldiers with leaflets urging them to desert (none did). One of those propaganda leaflets said, in part, "Do you enjoy the same rights as the white people do in America . . . or are you rather not treated over there as second-class citizens?" As to the charge of discrimination against African Americans by draft boards, there were numerous complaints that African Americans found it almost impossible to get exemptions from military service. In the end, about 31 percent of the African Americans who registered were called into service, as opposed to 26 percent of the registered whites. To counteract German propaganda, prominent African Americans were sent to France to lecture to the African American troops.

CHAPTER 5

HOMOGENIZING
A PLURALISTIC
NATION:
PROPAGANDA
DURING WORLD
WAR I

Source 19 from *The Moving Picture World,* September 28, 1918.

19. Promotional Tips to Theater Managers, 1918.

ADVERTISING AIDS FOR BUSY MANAGERS
"KULTUR."

William Fox Presents Gladys Brockwell in a Typical Example of the Brutality of the Wilhelmstrasse to Its Spy-slaves.

Cast.
Countess Griselda Von Arenburg,
                                  Gladys Brockwell
Eliska ....Georgia Woodthorpe
René de Bornay.................William Scott
Baron von Zeller ....Willard Louis
Archduke Franz Ferdinand ....Charles Clary
Danilo ....Nigel de Brullier
The Kaiser ....William Burress
Emperor Franz Josef..........Alfred Fremont

Directed by Edward J. Le Saint.

The Story: The Kaiser decides that the time is ripe for a declaration of war, and sends word to his vassal monarch of Austria. René de Bornay is sent by France to discover what is being planned. He meets the Countess, who falls in love with him. She sickens of the spy system and declares that she is done with it, but is warned that she cannot withdraw. She is told to secure René's undoing, but instead procures his escape and in her own boudoir is stood against the wall and shot for saving the man whom she loves better than her life.

Feature Gladys Brockwell as Countess Griselda Von Arenburg and William Scott as René de Bornay.

Program and Advertising Phrases: Gladys Brockwell, Star of Latest Picture, Exposing Hun Brutality and Satanic Intrigue.
How An Austrian Countess Gave Her All for Democracy.
She Was an Emperor's Favorite Yet She Died for World Freedom.
Story of an Emperor's Mistress and a Crime That Rocked the World.
Daring Exposure of Scandals and Crimes in Hun Court Circles.
Astonishing Revelations of Hun Plots to Rape Democracy.

Advertising Angles: Do not offer this as a propaganda story, but tell that it is one of the angles of the merciless Prussian spy system about which has been woven a real romance. Play up the spy angle heavily both in your newspaper work and through window cards with such lines as "even the spies themselves hate their degradation." Miss Brockwell wears some stunning and daring gowns in this play, and with these special appeal can be made to the women.

Source 20 from the National Archives.

20. Advertisement for the Feature Film *The Kaiser, the Beast of Berlin* (1918), Described by Some as the Most Famous "Hate Picture."

Source 21 from the Everett Collection.

21. Still Photograph from *The Kaiser, the Beast of Berlin* (1918). Used in Advertising.

Source 22 from Fox Film Corporation, 1918.

22. Advertising Poster for *The Prussian Cur* (1918).

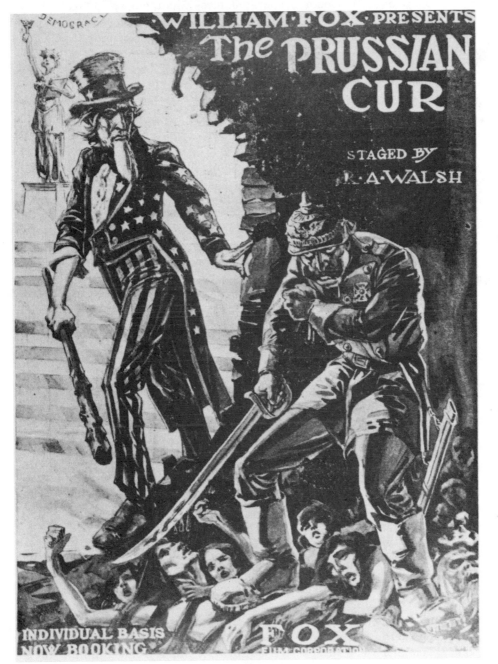

CHAPTER 5

HOMOGENIZING
A PLURALISTIC
NATION:
PROPAGANDA
DURING WORLD
WAR I

✳ QUESTIONS TO CONSIDER ✳

Source 1, George M. Cohan's enormously popular song, "Over There," was familiar to almost every American in 1917 to 1918 and has been since. What is the song urging young men to do? What emotions are the song's lyrics trying to arouse? How would you interpret the lines, "Make your daddy glad" and (speaking of sweethearts) "To be proud her boy's in line"? Recordings of the song "Over There" are readily available. As you listen to the song, how does it make you feel?

The advertisements shown in Sources 2 through 4 were produced by the Committee on Public Information. How are the Germans portrayed in the "Spies *and* Lies" ad (Source 2)? in the "Bachelor of Atrocities" ad (Source 3)? Source 4 is an appeal to history teachers. Did the Committee on Public Information ask history teachers to "tilt" their treatments of the past? If so, how? Were there any dangers inherent in the kinds of activities the committee was urging on patriotic Americans?

In some ways, poster art (Sources 5 through 13) is similar to editorial cartoon art (Sources 14 and 15), principally because the artist has only one canvas or frame on which to tell his or her story. Yet the poster must be more arresting than the cartoon, must convey its message rapidly, and must avoid ambiguities and confusion. Posters, commissioned or approved by the Committee on Public Information, were an extremely popular form of propaganda during World War I. Indeed, so popular were the posters of

James Montgomery Flagg (1877–1960) that he helped sell $1,000 of liberty bonds by performing (in his case, painting posters) in front of the New York Public Library.

Source 5, Flagg's Uncle Sam poster, probably is the most famous poster ever created. The idea was taken from a British poster by Alfred Leete, and Flagg was his own model for Uncle Sam. The poster is still used by the United States Army. What feeling did the poster seek to elicit?

Sources 6 and 7 are military recruiting posters, urging men to enlist in the armed services. What innuendoes are common to both posters? How are the Germans portrayed? What feelings are the posters intended to elicit? How are the appeals of these recruiting posters different from the appeals of the song in Source 1?

The posters in Sources 8 and 9 focus on women. How are women portrayed in each poster? In Source 9, what is the relationship between the Boy Scout and Miss Liberty? How might women have reacted to this poster?

Sources 10 through 13 are extremely interesting in light of the government's fears and the role President Wilson assigned to the Committee on Public Information. What emotion does the extraordinary "Americans All!" poster (Source 10) attempt to elicit? What is the poster's intended "message"? How do Sources 11 through 13 seek to bolster that message? If the goal of the committee was to *unite* Americans behind the war effort, why do you think it chose to target appeals to specific groups?

Speaking of cartoons, nineteenth-century New York political boss William Marcy ("Boss") Tweed once exclaimed, "Let's stop these damn pictures. I don't care so much what the papers say about me—my constituents can't read; but damn it, they can see the pictures!" The editorial cartoon from the *New York Herald* (Source 14) is fairly self-explanatory. What emotions does the cartoon seek to elicit? What actions, intended or unintended, might have resulted from those emotions? Karl Muck, incidentally, was deported. Frank Hines's prize-winning cartoon (Source 15) seeks to elicit very different emotions. Compare this cartoon with Cohan's lyrics (Source 1).

Sources 16 through 18, by the Four Minute Men, were also published in the Committee on Public Information's *Bulletin,* which was distributed to all volunteer speakers. Several of the Four Minute Men were women. Speakers received certificates from President Wilson after the war. What appeals are made in Source 16? How are appeals to African Americans (Source 17) the same or different? The poem in Source 18 is particularly painful to read. Why is that so? How can this poem be compared with Sources 1 and 15?

From 1917 to 1918, the American film industry and the Committee on Public Information produced over 180 feature films, 6 serials, 72 short subjects, 112 documentaries, 44 cartoons, and 37 liberty loan special films. Unfortunately, the vast majority of those motion pictures no longer are available, principally because the nitrate film stock on which the films were printed was extremely flammable and subject to decomposition.[16]

No sound films were produced in the United States before 1927. Until that time, a small orchestra or (more prevalent) a piano accompanied a film's showing. What dialogue there was—and there was not much—was given in subtitles.

The advertising tips for the film *Kultur* (Source 19) suggest a number of phrases and angles designed to attract audiences. What are the strongest appeals suggested to theater owners? Do those same appeals also appear in the song, advertisements, posters, cartoons, and speeches?

Sources 20 through 22 are advertisements for two films produced in 1918: *The Kaiser, the Beast of Berlin* (Sources 20 and 21) and *The Prussian Cur* (Source 22). What appeal is made to prospective viewers in Source 20? How are Germans depicted in Source 21? How can Source 21 be compared with Sources 6 and 7? How can Source 22 be compared with those sources as well?

You must now summarize your findings and return to the central questions: How did the United States use propaganda to mobilize public opinion in support of the nation's par-

---

16. In 1949, an improved safety-based stock was introduced. Those films that do survive, except in private collections, are in the Library of Congress; the American Film Institute Library in Beverly Hills, California; the Academy of Motion Picture Arts and Sciences in Los Angeles; the Museum of Modern Art in New York; the National Archives in Washington, D.C.; the New York Public Library; and the Wisconsin Center for Theater Research in Madison.

CHAPTER 5

HOMOGENIZING
A PLURALISTIC
NATION:
PROPAGANDA
DURING WORLD
WAR I

ticipation in World War I? What were the consequences—positive and negative—of the mobilization of public opinion?

❋ EPILOGUE ❋

The creation of the Committee on Public Information and its subsequent work show that the Wilson administration had serious doubts concerning whether the American people, multi-ethnic and pluralistic as they were, would support the war effort with unanimity. And, to be sure, there was opposition to American involvement in the war, not only from socialist Eugene Debs and the left but also from reformers Robert La Follette, Jane Addams, and others. As it turned out, however, the Wilson administration's worst fears proved groundless. Americans of all ethnic backgrounds overwhelmingly supported the war effort, sometimes rivaling each other in patriotic ardor. How much of this unanimity can be attributed to patriotism and how much to the propaganda efforts of the Committee on Public Information will never really be known. Yet, for whatever reason, it can be said that the war had a kind of unifying effect on the American people. Women sold liberty bonds, worked for agencies such as the Red Cross, rolled bandages, and cooperated in the government's effort to conserve food and fuel. Indeed, even African Americans sprang to the colors, reasoning, as did the president of Howard University, that service in the war might help them achieve long-withheld civil and political rights.

However, this homogenization was not without its price. Propaganda was so effective that it created a kind of national hysteria, sometimes with terrible results. Vigilante-type groups often shamefully persecuted German Americans, lynching one German American man of draft age for not being in uniform (the man was physically ineligible, having only one eye) and badgering German American children in and out of school. Many states forbade the teaching of German in schools, and a host of German words were purged from the language (sauerkraut became liberty cabbage, German measles became liberty measles, hamburgers became liberty steaks, frankfurters became hot dogs). The city of Cincinnati even banned pretzels from saloons. In such an atmosphere, many Americans lived in genuine fear of being accused of spying or of becoming victims of intimidation or violence. In a society intent upon homogenization, being different could be dangerous.

During such hysteria, one would expect the federal government in general and the Committee on Public Information in particular to have attempted to dampen the more extreme forms of vigilantism. However, it seemed as if the government had become the victim of its own propaganda. The postmaster general (Albert Burleson), empowered to censor the mail, looking for examples of treason, insurrection, or forcible resistance to laws, used his power to suppress all socialist publications, all anti-British and pro-Irish mail, and anything that he believed threatened the war effort. One movie producer, Robert Goldstein, was sentenced to ten years in prison for releasing his film *The Spirit of '76* (about the American Revolution) because it portrayed the British in an unfavorable light.[17] Socialist party leader Eugene Debs was given a similar sentence for criticizing the war in a speech in Canton, Ohio.[18] The left-wing Industrial Workers of the World (IWW) was broken. Freedom of speech, press, and assembly were violated countless times, and numerous lynchings, whippings, and tar-and-featherings occurred. Excesses by both government and private individuals were as effective in *forcing* homogeneity as were the voluntary efforts of American people of all backgrounds.

Once the hysteria had begun, it is doubtful whether even President Wilson could have stopped it. Yet Wilson showed no inclination to do so, even stating that dissent was not appreciated by the government. Without the president to reverse the process, the hysteria continued unabated.

Before the outbreak of World War I, anti-immigrant sentiment had been growing, although most Americans seem to have believed that the solution was to Americanize the immigrants rather than to restrict their entrance. But the drive toward homogenization that accompanied America's war hysteria acted to increase cries for restricting further immigration and to weaken champions of the "melting pot." As restriction advocate Madison Grant wrote in 1922, "The world has seen many such [racial] mixtures and the character of a mongrel race is only just beginning to be understood at its true value. . . . Whether we like to admit it or not, the result of the mixture of two races . . . gives us a race reverting to the more ancient, generalized and lower type." Labor leaders, journalists, and politicians called for immigration restrictions, and a general immigration restriction (called the National Origins Act) became law in 1924.

This insistence on homogenization also resulted in the Red Scare of 1919, during which Attorney General A. Mitchell Palmer violated many people's civil liberties in a series of raids, arrests, and deportations directed largely against recent immigrants. As seen, the efforts to homogenize a pluralistic nation could have an ugly side.

As Americans approached World War II, some called for a revival of the Committee on Public Information. Yet President Franklin Roosevelt rejected this sweeping approach. The Office of War Information was created, but its role was a restricted one. Even so, Japanese Americans were subjected to relocation and humiliation in one of the most shameful episodes of recent American history. And although propaganda techniques were sometimes more subtle, they nevertheless displayed features that would cause Americans to hate their enemies and want to destroy them. Japanese especially were portrayed as barbaric. A good example is Source 23. In general,

17. This gave rise to a court case with the improbable title *United States v. The Spirit of '76*.

18. Debs, indicted the day before he made his speech, spent three years in prison.

CHAPTER 5

HOMOGENIZING
A PLURALISTIC
NATION:
PROPAGANDA
DURING WORLD
WAR I

however, a different spirit pervaded the United States during World War II, a spirit generally more tolerant of American pluralism and less willing to stir Americans into an emotional frenzy.

And yet the possibility that propaganda will create mass hysteria and thus endanger the civil rights of some Americans is present in every national crisis, especially in wartime. In the "total wars" of the twentieth century, in which civilians played as crucial a role as fighting men (in factories, in training facilities for soldiers, and in shipping soldiers and materiel to the front), the mobilization of the home front was a necessity. But could that kind of mobilization be carried too far?

Source 23 from Library of Congress.

23. United States Army Poster from World War II.

6

The "New" Woman: Social Science Experts and the Redefinition of Women's Roles in the 1920s

❋ THE PROBLEM ❋

In 1920, the Nineteenth Amendment to the Constitution, granting women the right to vote, was finally ratified. "Few people live to see the actual and final realization of hopes to which they have devoted their lives," announced Carrie Chapman Catt to the two thousand women attending the National American Woman Suffrage Association (NAWSA). "That privilege is ours." After more than an hour of singing, parading, and waving banners, the delegates turned their attention to the business of converting the NAWSA into the League of Women Voters (LWV). After some initial uncertainty about its purpose, the LWV became a nonpartisan organization dedicated to educating voters about issues and candidates and encouraging citizens to get out and vote. "A dream has come true," exulted the new league president and former suffragist, Maude Wood Park.[1]

Little did these women realize what lay ahead. As the decade of the 1920s progressed, more and more of the former suffragists became discouraged and disillusioned. In spite of the passage of some important pieces of federal legislation for women, a succession of Republican presidents—Warren Harding, Calvin Coolidge, and Herbert Hoover—seemed to practice politics as usual, very much as things had been before women gained the right to vote. Nor did women vote as a bloc, although they did come to-

1. Barbara Stuhler (ed.), *For the Public Record: A Documentary History of the League of Women Voters* (Westport, CT: Greenwood Press, 2000), pp. 31, 43.

CHAPTER 6

THE "NEW"
WOMAN: SOCIAL
SCIENCE
EXPERTS AND
THE
REDEFINITION
OF WOMEN'S
ROLES IN THE
1920s

gether occasionally on certain issues of special interest to them. For most of the decade, however, women were divided by their party affiliations and by their support for or opposition to the Equal Rights Amendment.

Even more disappointing were the attitudes of the new generation of women who came of age during this era. These "new" women, the flappers and their imitators, refused to identify with serious-minded reform efforts, criticized feminism as old-fashioned, and rejected what they described as Victorian attitudes toward sex and sexuality. The "new" women also argued that they were already equal to men and that they would be the first generation of women to have it all: education, career, marriage, and children. For advice on how to gain personal fulfillment, they turned to the experts, primarily social scientists such as sociologists, psychologists, economists, political scientists, home economists, and anthropologists. However, creating real change in such institutions as colleges and universities, the family, and the economy proved extremely difficult, and the experts were not in agreement about *how* or even *whether* such changes should occur.

In this chapter, you will read several selections from some of the vast social science literature of the 1920s, in order to identify and understand the issues surrounding the redefinition of "new" (or modern) women's roles. What were these issues? What assumptions and recommendations did social scientists make?

❋ BACKGROUND ❋

The struggle for woman suffrage had, indeed, been very long and hard, beginning with the demand for the vote at the Seneca Falls Convention in 1848, and culminating in the exhausting, state-by-state ratification campaigns of 1920. Issues of race, class, and tactics had often badly divided the suffragists: Should they reach out to immigrant women? What role, if any, should working women have in the movement? And what about African American women? Wouldn't their inclusion in the suffrage movement alienate both southern white women and southern legislators? Should the suffragists focus on amending state constitutions, or should they work only for a federal amendment? Should they use aggressive protest tactics in Washington, D.C., to influence the president (as Alice Paul and the Constitutional Union had done), or should they try to persuade male legislators of both parties through more traditional lobbying techniques (as Catt and the NAWSA had done)?

In some northern industrial cities, suffragists did reach out to immigrants and working women. In a few of these cities, middle-class African American women were also included in suffrage activities through the affiliation of their clubs and the "colored" Young Women's Christian Association (YWCA). However, the national leaders were always aware of the "race question" and were willing to placate southerners on this issue. Suffragists worked both for state voting rights and, increasingly after 1910, for the federal woman suffrage amendment. The National American Woman Suffrage Association and the Congressional Union coexisted uneasily until the latter became the National Woman's Party (NWP) under Alice Paul's leadership. In general, it is fair to say that both the NAWSA and the NWP remained white, upper- and middle-class women's organizations dedicated to winning the vote for women like themselves.

Moreover, because the fight for suffrage had been so long and difficult, many women came to believe that the struggle for women's rights and the recognition of women's abilities were completed by the passage of the Nineteenth Amendment. The LWV's membership was much smaller than that of the NAWSA, and membership in women's reform organizations, such as the Consumer's League and the Women's Trade Union League, declined drastically during the 1920s.

Although women's reform initiatives were generally weaker in the 1920s than in the pre–World War I era, they did continue with some success throughout the decade. Passage of the federal Sheppard-Towner Maternity Act, in effect from 1921 to 1928, provided funding to states for improved maternal and infant health care measures. Another breakthrough came in the form of the Cable Act (1930), which allowed American women who married foreign citizens to retain their own U.S. citizenship, rather than losing it as they had previously. Many women were also politically active on the municipal and state levels, as well

as working to create female networks and a "place" for themselves within national party politics. But in a discouraging setback, the effort to pass a federal amendment outlawing child labor failed in the 1920s, in spite of the combined support and diligent work of several women's organizations.

Furthermore, former suffragists who remained politically active during the 1920s were badly divided. Shocked at the remaining civil inequalities of women, the National Woman's Party proposed an Equal Rights Amendment (ERA) to the Constitution in 1923. The proposed amendment declared that "men and women shall have equal rights throughout the United States and every place subject to its jurisdiction." The NWP argued that the ERA would eliminate laws that discriminated against women, such as those that granted automatic guardianship of children to husbands, established different grounds for divorce for men and women, excluded women from certain occupations, barred them from running for certain political offices and serving on juries, and sanctioned different pay scales for men and women. The Equal Rights Amendment, the NWP feminists argued, would complete the legal equalization of men and women.

The League of Women Voters—and most other women's groups of the 1920s—opposed the ERA. The amendment was so broad, they maintained, that it would remove certain essential, hard-earned protections that women already had in the law. Although there was some concern about alimony and service in the armed forces, the real problem lay in protective labor laws for women in the various states. These

[167]

CHAPTER 6

THE "NEW"
WOMAN: SOCIAL
SCIENCE
EXPERTS AND
THE
REDEFINITION
OF WOMEN'S
ROLES IN THE
1920s

laws were based on women's physical differences from men, especially their reproductive functions. Such laws kept women out of dangerous trades or job situations, restricted the amount of weight that women were expected to lift, required seats or rest periods for women on the job, limited the number of hours and shifts that women could work, and so forth. Whereas the NWP saw such laws as *restrictive* of women's rights, the LWV viewed them as *protective* of women's special nature. Thus, the former suffragists battled each other over the Equal Rights Amendment throughout the decade.

Suffrage was only one of women's many interlinked reform activities during the Progressive era, most of which had been supported by innovative approaches to studying society. Beginning in the late nineteenth century as a response to massive immigration, rapid industrialization, and widespread urbanization, researchers began investigating and documenting the problems associated with these social changes. Borrowing some of their methods from natural science and taking their general field of study as society, new social scientists began to emerge in the universities and government service. Sociologist Thorstein Veblen wrote *The Theory of the Leisure Class* (1899) while teaching at the University of Chicago; Richard Ely was head of the Economics Department at the University of Wisconsin when he wrote *Monopolies and Trusts* (1900). Both men were interested in the analysis of the formation and functions of great wealth during the period. In contrast, anthropologist Elsie Clews Parsons was teaching part time

at Columbia University when she wrote *The Family* (1906), followed by five other books during the next ten years in which she compared contemporary American social attitudes and conventions to those of other, preindustrial cultures.

Progressive reformers were generally optimistic, believing that people were basically good. If Americans were properly educated about social problems, reformers believed, they could and would find solutions to the problems. The new social sciences—especially sociology, political science, psychology, economics, and home economics—fit into this orientation very well. Gathering data, interviewing individuals, and compiling statistics provided the material with which reformers could work to educate people, formulate social policy, and convince government officials of the need for corrective ordinances or laws. In this era, there seemed to be little personal conflict for most social scientists between the need for objectivity in their research and the reformist convictions that guided their choice of subject matter and methodology. In the natural sciences, well-known sociologist Robert Lynd pointed out, one might be motivated by pure curiosity, but it was "the *interested* desire to know in order to do something about problems that has predominantly motivated social science. . . ."[2] In other words, social scientists saw themselves as practical researchers and writers whose work could form the basis for important social and economic reforms.

2. Robert S. Lynd, *Knowledge for What? The Place of Social Science in American Culture* (Princeton: Princeton University Press, 1939), pp. 114–115.

During World War I, social scientists gained even more prestige as they cooperated with the government in a series of studies of the backgrounds, intelligence, and physical health of army recruits. The dramatic changes of the postwar decade, nearly all of which had their origins in pre–World War I America, provided a fertile field of study for the new social scientists. Widely accepted as experts in their specialized fields, they published their research findings and recommendations in popular middle-class books and magazines as well as in scholarly journals during the 1920s. For the first half of the decade, political scientists were very interested in the impact of the newly enfranchised women voters. That interest waned, however, as the decade progressed, and political questions were replaced by questions about women's roles in the work force and the family.

To most economists, the 1920s appeared to be a time of enormous prosperity. There were, nevertheless, some troubling trends: the growth of consumer debt fueled by the new advertising, the increase in corporate mergers, the development of a kind of corporate paternalism to counteract labor unionism, and the gross inflation of the unregulated stock market. In addition, farming, mining, and some other sectors of the economy were not sharing in the economic good times at all. Home economists were especially aware of the rates at which women were entering high schools and universities, preparing for professions, and entering the work force, especially in the expanding service sector. Although the typical woman worker was single, there was a definite increase in married women (and married women with children) in the work force. As more women pursued jobs and careers, the role of homemaker seemed to become less important. This in turn raised important questions about women's traditional roles in the home and family, questions that home economists, psychologists, and sociologists all tried to answer.

There is no doubt that this decade was characterized by serious social and cultural strains. Anti-immigrant sentiment increased, culminating in a new quota system that drastically limited immigration from southern and eastern Europe. The decade also saw the rise of a new Ku Klux Klan, for the first time popular in urban areas and outside the South, dedicated to "100 percent Americanism" and devoted to enforcing the values of nineteenth-century rural America. Two famous trials of the decade—the Sacco and Vanzetti case against Italian anarchists convicted of committing a murder during a payroll robbery, and the Scopes case involving a teacher found guilty of breaking state law by teaching about evolution—highlighted the social and cultural strains inherent in the conflict between the older values of rural and small-town America and the newer values of twentieth-century modernism.

These were especially difficult times for African Americans. A series of race riots occurred immediately after World War I, followed by episodes of lynching throughout the South. The migration to northern cities had already begun, Garveyism promoted pride in the African heritage for northern migrants, and the Harlem Renaissance showcased black writers,

CHAPTER 6

THE "NEW"
WOMAN: SOCIAL
SCIENCE
EXPERTS AND
THE
REDEFINITION
OF WOMEN'S
ROLES IN THE
1920s

artists, and intellectuals. But racial ghetto formation was also well under way in northern cities, and most blacks still lived in abject poverty in the rural South. White sociologists studied immigrants far more frequently than they studied African Americans. Although sociologist W. E. B. Du Bois had written about the effects of racial oppression in the pre–World War I era, other famous African American sociologists E. Franklin Frazier and Charles S. Johnson were still studying and doing research during the 1920s, and thus they did not publish their major studies of the African American community and family until the 1930s and 1940s.

Perhaps nowhere were the cultural and social strains of the decade more evident than in the confusion and debates about the proper place and roles of white women. There was no doubt in the minds of contemporary observers that women's experiences were changing, and there was a great deal of public concern about the modern or "new" women. Fashions in clothing and hairstyles had altered dramatically, and the movies, department stores, and mail-order catalogues made this "new look" available to women across the country. Smoking and drinking in public, dating casually, and dancing all night to the new jazz music, the young women known as flappers embodied the most extreme, sometimes shocking, changes in behavior. But many other women were also affected by these new standards. What impact would these changes have on the home and family, long considered the basis of American society?

In this chapter, you will read some selections from the social science literature of the 1920s about the roles of modern women in order to answer several questions: What did these researchers identify as the major social and economic issues surrounding the roles of modern women? What ethnic groups and social classes most concerned researchers? What assumptions did the social scientists make? What were their recommendations, and to what degree did they suggest redefining women's roles?

❋ THE METHOD ❋

Historians who use evidence such as social science literature from the early twentieth century do so with caution. Although these writers and researchers believed themselves truly to be objective (unbiased) "scientists," they were influenced by who they were and the times in which they lived. The great majority of these social scientists were from middle- or upper-class backgrounds; most were also Protestants whose families had lived in the United States for many generations. Most of them were white and—an important point to note—most of them had been directly or indirectly involved in various urban reform activities.

The obvious problems of the 1920s were related to the major impacts of the immigration, industrialization, and urbanization that had begun in the late nineteenth century. However, the social scientists themselves *chose* which problems they would study. As noted earlier in the Background section, most social scientists of this decade chose to study the "problems" of the immigrants, rather than African American ghettos, lynchings, or segregation, for example. Thus, we certainly cannot say that the social science literature of this era was really objective.

However, this does not mean that such evidence is worthless to the historian. In fact, much, perhaps most, of the evidence relied on by historians is imperfect or "tainted." Because of this, historians avoid taking any evidence literally or at face value; rather, they approach their evidence critically, aware of its imperfections and limits in answering historical questions.

In analyzing the social science literature presented in the Evidence section, you should focus on three specific tasks:

1. Briefly summarize the *message* of each excerpt. What does it describe, criticize or praise, and/or recommend? What issues are revealed?
2. Identify the underlying *assumptions* of the author. Does the writer assume readers are male or female? of a working- or middle-class background? Does the writer seem to have fixed or flexible beliefs about women's roles? How do these assumptions affect the author's message?
3. What does this piece of evidence reveal about the *dilemmas* surrounding the redefinition of women's roles during the 1920s?

Of course, social science literature is only one of several types of evidence that help us understand the degree to which women's roles were being redefined in the 1920s. We need to be very cautious about making generalizations based on such limited evidence. Nevertheless, an analysis of the social science literature can give us insight into an important part of the story.

❋ THE EVIDENCE ❋

SEX AND SEXUALITY

Source 1 from W. I. Thomas, *The Unadjusted Girl* (New York: Harper, 1967 [1923]), pp. 98, 230, 231.

1. W. I. Thomas on Changing Standards of Morality.

The rôle which a girl is expected to play in life is first of all indicated to her by her family in a series of æsthetic-moral definitions of the situation. Civilized societies, more especially, have endowed the young girl with a character of social sacredness. . . .

[171]

CHAPTER 6

THE "NEW"
WOMAN: SOCIAL
SCIENCE
EXPERTS AND
THE
REDEFINITION
OF WOMEN'S
ROLES IN THE
1920s

But we must understand that this sublimation of life is an investment. It requires . . . incessant attention and effort . . . and goes on best when life is economically secure. And there are families and whole strata of society where life affords no investments. There is little to gain and little to lose. Social workers report that sometimes overburdened mothers with large families complain that they have no "graveyard luck"—all the children live. In cases of great neglect the girl cannot be said to fall, because she has never risen. She is not immoral, because this implies the loss of morality, but a-moral—never having had a moral code. . . .

Source 2 from Alyse Gregory, "The Changing Morality of Women," *Current History* 19 (1923): 298, 299.

2. Alyse Gregory on Sex and the New Woman.

Girls' New Habits

Then suddenly all was changed again. The war [World War I] was over and women were admonished to hurry once more home and give the men back their jobs. It was too late. The old discipline had vanished in the night. There was neither an avenging God nor an avenging father to coerce women back into their old places at the family board. They took flats or studios and went on earning their livings. They filled executive offices, they became organizers, editors, copywriters, efficiency managers, artists, writers, real estate agents, and even in rare instances brokers. . . . However unwilling one may be to acknowledge it, girls began to sow their wild oats. Women of the aristocratic upper classes and the poorest women had never followed too rigidly the cast-iron rules of respectability because in neither instance had they anything to lose by digressing. But for the first time in the memory of man, girls from well-bred, respectable middle-class families broke through those invisible chains of custom and asserted their right to a nonchalant, self-sustaining life of their own with a cigarette after every meal and a lover in the evening to wander about with and lend color to life. If the relationship became more intimate than such relationships are supposed to be, there was nothing to be lost that a girl could not well dispense with. Her employer asked no questions as to her life outside the office. She had her own salary at the end of the month and asked no other recompense from her lover but his love and companionship. Into the privacy of her own snug and pleasant rooms not even her mother or her oldest brother could penetrate, for she and she alone, unless perhaps one other, carried the only key that would fit the lock.

Profoundly shocking as such a state of affairs may seem to large numbers of people, there is no use pretending that it does not exist. There are too many signs abroad to prove that it does. Ministers may extol chastity for women from pulpit rostrums and quote passages from the Old and New Testaments to prove that purity and fidelity are still her most precious assets, but this new woman only shrugs her shoulders and smiles a slow, penetrating, secret smile. . . .

Source 3 from Ernest Groves, *Personality and Social Adjustment* (New York: Longman, Green, 1925), pp. 204, 213, 214.

3. Ernest Groves on the Psychological Development of Girls.

The development of the girl's affection is not so simple as that of the boy's. It also has greater opportunities for emotional disturbances. The girl begins, as does the boy, with a fixation upon the mother. But this in the case of the girl is a homosexual experience and thus at the very start of the evolution of affection of the girl there is satisfaction in a relationship which does not require cognizance of sex differences. It is easier therefore for the girl to continue the expression of affection upon members of her own sex straight through childhood into the adult period. Even if the boy has only the dimmest of ideas of the differences between his mother and himself he nevertheless has some slight understanding that he belongs to the class to which his father belongs and not to that of his mother.

It is fortunate that most girls, as if by instinct, tend as they pass the first years of the infantile period to turn their affection to their fathers. . . .

The period that covers the daughter's greatest need of her father's help is necessarily brief. She normally passes quickly on to the next adventure in affection and her impulses turn all the deep interests of her life toward men of her own age. Her emotions and her thought are concentrated upon her new experiences in heterosexual association. It is easy for the adult to forget how tremendous these reactions are in the average girl. What she wears, where she goes, what she does, all her behavior is primarily related to "man." Her feeble efforts to conceal this fact frequently make it all the more noticeable. She is like an actress playing a part with her consciousness fixed upon her audience.

CHAPTER 6

THE "NEW"
WOMAN: SOCIAL
SCIENCE
EXPERTS AND
THE
REDEFINITION
OF WOMEN'S
ROLES IN THE
1920s

If her new attention to men receives a favorable response her emotional life is wont to flow smoothly. She may still err, to be sure, in her judgment and may consequently make an unwise choice for a life-mate, but she has at least passed through all the various phases of the love experience that precedes adulthood. . . .

Source 4 from Elaine Showalter, ed., *These Modern Women* (New York: Feminist Press, 1978 [1926]), pp. 142, 143.

4. John Watson on the Sex Adjustment of Modern Women.

. . . These women were too modern to seek happiness; they sought what? Freedom. So many hundreds of women I have talked to have sought freedom. I have tried to find out diplomatically but behavioristically what they mean. Is it to wear trousers? Is it to vote—to hold office—to work at men's trades—to take men's jobs away from them—to get men's salaries? Does their demand for this mystical thing called freedom imply a resentment against child-bearing—a resentment against the fact that men's sex behavior is different from women's (but not so much any more)? I rarely arrive at a reasonable answer. . . . When a woman is a militant suffragist the chances are, shall we say, a hundred to one that her sex life is not well adjusted? Marriage as such brings adjustment in only approximately 20 per cent of all cases, so poorly have men and women been taught about sex. Among the 20 per cent who find adjustment I find no militant women, I find no women shouting about their rights to some fanciful career that men—the brutes—have robbed them of. They work—they work like a man (than which nothing better can be said about work)—they often quietly achieve careers. Most of the terrible women one must meet, women with the blatant views and voices, women who have to be noticed, who shoulder one about, who can't take life quietly, belong to this large percentage of women who have never made a sex adjustment. . . .

WOMEN'S WORK INSIDE AND OUTSIDE THE HOME

Source 5 from Gwendolyn Hughes, *Mothers in Industry* (New York: New Republic, 1925), pp.1, 149, 180–181.

5. Gwendolyn Hughes on Working Mothers.

When the mother of young children leaves her traditional place in the home to earn money in a factory she becomes the subject of heated controversy.

By some sincere observers she is regarded as a menace to the race and held accountable for the falling birthrate, declining parental responsibility and decadence in home and family life. To others, equally in earnest, her action is entirely commendable and she is regarded as a champion of woman's rights, establishing the greater personal freedom and financial independence of women. . . .

Most of the mothers are working full time in industry. . . . The most common weekly schedule is nine and one-fourth hours or nine and three-fourths hours a day with five and one-fourth hours on Saturday, a total of 52½ or 54 hours. . . .

. . . Although most of these homes have running water in the kitchen, there are no stationary tubs, no washing machines, no mangles,[1] no electric irons. The wage-earning mother does not have the means to purchase these household appliances and must do the washing under conditions which most increase her two great disabilities, exhaustion and lack of time. . . .

On Saturday afternoon and Sunday these mothers who work full time clean house, scrub the steps, wash and iron, bathe the children and do the extra cooking. Practically without exception, they maintain that they give their families home cooking; some of them even bake bread. . . .

Source 6 from Christine Frederick, *Efficient Housekeeping, or Household Engineering: Scientific Management in the Home* (Chicago: American School of Home Economics, 1925), pp. 17, 70, 384, 385.

6. Christine Frederick on Efficient Housekeeping.

I want you who take this course to feel that you are *not working alone* in your own home kitchen. I want you to feel that when you discover new methods of housework and better ways of management that you can receive the same recognition that a scientist or business investigator receives. Do not think you are working out the problem for your own home only. You are helping solve the problems of countless other women and homes, and *what you do will be passed on,* and help build up a great mass of proved knowledge on housekeeping. . . .

1. Machines for pressing fabrics by means of heated rollers.

CHAPTER 6

THE "NEW"
WOMAN: SOCIAL
SCIENCE
EXPERTS AND
THE
REDEFINITION
OF WOMEN'S
ROLES IN THE
1920s

[Sample] Schedule for Family of Five

Monday

6:00– 6:30	Rise and dress; start water heater
6:30– 7:00	Prepare breakfast
7:00– 7:30	BREAKFAST
7:30– 8:30	Wash dishes; straighten kitchen; inspect icebox; plan meals for Monday and Tuesday
8:30– 9:00	Prepare towards lunch
9:00–10:00	Bedrooms, bath and hall cleaned; sort and prepare soiled linen and laundry
10:00–11:00	Thorough downstairs cleaning
11:00–11:30	*Rest period*
11:30–12:00	Serve lunch
12:00– 1:00	LUNCH
1:00– 3:00	Lunch dishes; prepare cooking for Monday and Tuesday; mop kitchen
3:00– 4:00	Sewing and mending
4:00– 4:30	Soak clothes and prepare for next day's washing
4:30– 5:30	*Rest period;* play with children; walk, recreation or market
5:30– 6:00	Prepare supper
6:00– 7:00	SUPPER
7:00– 7:30	Wash dishes

Tuesday

6:00– 6:30	Rise and dress; put on boiler [tub in which to boil dirty clothes]
6:30– 7:00	Prepare breakfast
7:00– 7:30	BREAKFAST
7:30– 8:00	Stack dishes; make beds
8:00–11:30	Washing
11:30–12:00	*Rest period*
12:00– 1:00	LUNCH (prepared day before)
1:00– 2:30	Wash breakfast and lunch dishes; clear up laundry
2:30– 4:00	Take in clothes; fold, sprinkle [dampen clothes before ironing], lay away
4:00– 5:30	*Rest period*
5:30– 6:00	Prepare supper
6:00– 7:00	SUPPER
7:00– 7:30	Wash dishes

In some households where there is no permanent worker, it often happens that the homemaker looks to the husband as a kind of nursemaid, choreman or kitchen assistant. The author's feeling is very much against this view,—that the moment a man comes into the house he should be asked to carry out the slops, hold the baby or wash the dishes. If the father works hard and faithfully at his task of earning money during his work day, it is not more fair to ask him to turn choreman as soon as he comes home, than it would be to ask the woman who has cooked and cleaned all day to turn around and do office or business work after five o'clock. It is not fair to put on a father any housework duties; his hours at home should be hours of recuperation, or so that he can study *his own work,* become more proficient, and thus secure advancement or a better economic position.

There comes to mind the case of a gifted man starting a profession, who, because of his wife's poor management, spent his time after office hours caring for the children and doing chores. He never seemed to "get on" as far as people had expected. Would it not have been better to use his spare time studying and improving in his own profession and thus be eventually able to pay for more service to help his wife, than to neglect his own opportunities by doing the housework? . . .

Source 7 from Lillian M. Gilbreth, *The Homemaker and Her Job* (New York: Appleton-Century, 1927), pp. vii, 50, 51.

7. Lillian M. Gilbreth on Making Housework Satisfying.

Home-making is the finest job in the world, and it is the aim of this book to make it as interesting and satisfying as it is important.

Waste of energy is the cause of drudgery in work of any kind. In industry the engineer and the psychologist, working together, have devised means of getting more done with less effort and fatigue and of making everything that is done more interesting. The worker not only spends his working hours more effectively and with more satisfaction, but has more time and more energy freed for other things.

This book applies to the home the methods of eliminating waste that have been successful in industry. To the home-maker it offers a philosophy that will make her work satisfying, a technic that will make it easy, and a method of approach that will make it interesting. . . .

CHAPTER 6

THE "NEW"
WOMAN: SOCIAL
SCIENCE
EXPERTS AND
THE
REDEFINITION
OF WOMEN'S
ROLES IN THE
1920s

Source 8 from Alice Rogers Hager, "Occupations and Earnings of Women in Industry," in *The Annals: Women in the Modern World* (Philadelphia: American Academy of Political and Social Science, 1929), p. 72.

8. Alice Rogers Hager on Men's and Women's Factory Pay in the Mid-1920s.

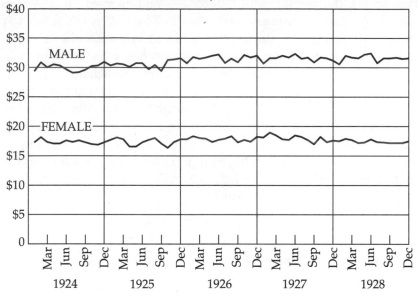

WEEK'S EARNINGS OF MALES AND OF FEMALES IN FACTORIES.
ILLINOIS, 1924 TO 1928

Source 9 from Benjamin R. Andrews, "The Home Woman as Buyer and Controller of Consumption," in *The Annals: Women in the Modern World* (Philadelphia: American Academy of Political and Social Science, 1929), pp. 47, 48.

9. Benjamin R. Andrews on Ethical Duties of the Home Buyer.

What ethical duties has the private buyer? Some standards the buyer is recognizing as a code, and these, with other techniques, the new household buyer will be taught. She will not seek her personal advantage, when it means a loss to the dealer. This is the standard that she would demand of him, not to seek his advantage at her loss, and it is only fair that she practice it herself. She will not hold goods unnecessarily on approval and cause losses that have to be made up by higher prices. She will not take unnecessary time in examining goods in stores. She is willing to pay for all the services that she demands. She returns goods promptly, and in perfect condition. She does not abuse her credit privileges, or seek unusual advantages as a credit customer. She remembers that courtesy is equally binding upon customer and salesperson. . . .

The home buyer must realize that, to her family, she is the guardian of the treasury, and that her watch over expenditures makes, or mars, the quality of life which they achieve. She must seek the best that her income makes possible, and she is finding that controlled and planned spending pays. . . .

Source 10 from Caroline Manning, *The Immigrant Woman and Her Job* (Washington, D.C.: U.S. Government Printing Office, 1930), pp. 40, 50, 59.

10. Caroline Manning on Immigrant Women Workers.

Care during mother's absence.—The families were large, the children young, and life was especially strenuous for the 500 employed mothers whose youngest child was less than 6. It was not customary for children to begin school before they were 6, and in more than half of the families with five, six, and seven or more children the youngest child was not yet 4 years old. . . .

The opinion was general among the families visited that children of 7 who were in school part of the time certainly knew enough to get something to eat at noon and to take care of themselves when not in school, and that children as old as 12 were quite able to care not only for themselves but for younger children; in fact, the care of a 12-year-old presented few problems. . . .

To the question as to why the women had returned to work after marriage there was repetition in the answers: "Times weren't so good." "Expenses so high." "We were getting behind in everything." "The men were laid off and we needed a slice of bread." "Never know when sickness comes how much it cost." "To pay for my home some day." All "needed to help a little out"—husbands ill, husbands out of work or on part time, rent to pay, and children to feed were indeed common to all. . . .

. . . Yet the conversation often drifted into channels that revealed deeper hopes and ambitions. Though the women did not give such desires as their definite reasons for working, they constituted perhaps the impelling force

CHAPTER 6

THE "NEW"
WOMAN: SOCIAL
SCIENCE
EXPERTS AND
THE
REDEFINITION
OF WOMEN'S
ROLES IN THE
1920s

that directed the lives of these wage earners. At least 700 mothers referred to the plans they had for their children and the problems arising in regard to their education and the kinds of work in which they should be trained. Their comments speak for themselves: "I am still a greenhorn. My little girl must be smart." "She must not do stripping like me." "My boys must go to high school if they have good heads." "He must not work in the mill but be an American." The children of an ambitious woman who was spending her days at the polishing wheel took music lessons. Another mother, recalling her days of "slavery" in the mill, was helping her daughter through a business college.

Women feeling the pinch of hard times were ready to make sacrifices: "We do by our children in school what we can afford." The goal of a widow who worked 10 hours a day was to see her daughter a graduate of the normal school: "I no care how long I work if she can teach in a school." . . .

MARRIAGE AND THE FAMILY

Source 11 from W. I. Thomas, *The Unadjusted Girl* (New York: Harper, 1967 [1923]), pp. 72, 73.

11. W. I. Thomas, Case 37: A Married Woman's Despair.

My husband's career, upon which I spent the best years of my life, is established favorably; our children are a joy to me as a mother; nor can I complain about our material circumstances. But I am dissatisfied with myself. My love for my children, be it ever so great, cannot destroy myself. A human being is not created like a bee which dies after accomplishing its only task. . . .

Desires, long latent, have been aroused in me and become more aggressive the more obstacles they encounter. . . . I now have the desire to go about and see and hear everything. I wish to take part in everything—to dance, skate, play the piano, sing, go to the theatre, opera, lectures and generally mingle in society. As you see, I am no idler whose purpose is to chase all sorts of foolish things, as a result of loose ways. This is not the case.

My present unrest is a natural result following a long period of hunger and thirst for non-satisfied desires in every field of human experience. It is the dread of losing that which never can be recovered—youth and time which do not stand still—an impulse to catch up with the things I have missed. . . . If it were not for my maternal feeling I would go away into the wide world. . . .

Source 12 from Elaine Showalter, ed., *These Modern Women* (New York: Feminist Press, 1978 [1926]), pp. 143, 144.

12. John Watson on Married Women and Careers.

I have never believed that there were any unsuperable difficulties which keep women from succeeding. They have strength enough to paint, yet there has never been a great woman painter. They have strength enough to play the violin and yet there has never been a great woman violinist. They have endurance and strength enough to become great scientists and yet one can count on fewer than the fingers of one hand the women scientists who have achieved real greatness. During the past thirty years thousands of women have taken the degree of Ph.D. and yet scarcely a dozen have come to the front. . . .

Not being trained from infancy to the tradition of incessant manipulative work they drop out of the race as soon as they get comfortable. Marriage is usually the shady spot that causes them to lie down and rest. And when they fail in that, as 80 per cent do, restlessness again sets in, but now it is too late to go back and take up the threads of the old career. Most women who had aspirations for a career have tried to eat their cake and have it too. A career is a jealous all-consuming taskmaster.

Marriage as such should be no barrier to a career. Apartment hotels, which can be found in every town where a woman would have a career, have freed married women without children almost completely. The having of children is almost an insuperable barrier to a career. The rearing of children and the running of a home for them is a profession second to none in its demands for technique. . . .

Source 13 from Ernest Groves and Gladys Hoagland Groves, *Wholesome Marriage* (Boston: Houghton Mifflin, 1927), pp. 100, 101, 206–209, 214.

13. Ernest and Gladys H. Groves on How to Have a Happy Marriage.

LIFE PARTNERSHIP. What is the secret of those marriages in which the wedding day seems to be a turning-point that brings the man to the straightaway leading to business success? It would be well to know, if the knowledge could be used to help those for whom the marriage ceremony is but a milestone in a long, slow, uphill climb to financial security.

The answer lies in the reactions of the newly married couple to their new relationship. Normally the man is very proud of his responsibility for the

CHAPTER 6

THE "NEW"
WOMAN: SOCIAL
SCIENCE
EXPERTS AND
THE
REDEFINITION
OF WOMEN'S
ROLES IN THE
1920s

welfare of his family. He takes his business much more seriously than he did before, for now he has two mouths to feed instead of one. It would never do to lose his job, or even to miss an expected promotion.

The young husband "settles down" to his work, determined to make good if it is in him. He is somewhat helped in the settling-down process by the strange, new fact that he is no longer in constant fear of losing his sweetheart. She is his "for keeps" now, and his only anxiety is to be able to do his part well in the establishment of the home life they are entering upon.

This means money, a steady stream of it that can be depended on and promises to grow larger in time. So the young man throws himself into his work whole-heartedly, and the stuff he is made of shows. That is his side of the story. . . .

Of course the wife who helps her husband on to success makes the home life restful and refreshing. Dissatisfaction finds no quarters within the four walls of the house, be it two-room flat or rambling country homestead. Good housekeeping is not enough to turn the trick, but it is an indispensable card. Singleness of purpose, alertness of mind, and a broad outlook on life are all needed.

Then the wife does not put her embroidery, bridge, and tea parties above her husband's peace of mind. She does her best to keep the home life pleasant, that her man may be in tip-top condition for his work outside. Turning and twisting to save a penny, she sees to it that the family lives within its income, so that her husband will not be worried by unpaid bills, when he is trying to increase his earning capacity. Above all she has faith in her husband's ability to better his condition. . . .

Source 14 from Lorine Pruette, "The Married Woman and the Part-Time Job," in *The Annals: Women in the Modern World* (Philadelphia: American Academy of Political and Social Science, 1929), pp. 302, 303, 306.

14. Lorine Pruette on the Demoralizing Influence of the Home.

The worst thing that can be said for the American home is that it ruins so many of its members. It is a disheartening and disillusioning business to survey the middle-aged married women of the country. They have been permanently damaged as persons by the disintegrating influences of the modern home and family life. Conversely, they contribute to the further disintegration of the institution to which they have given their lives.

It is only the rare woman who can pass without deterioration through many years of uninterrupted domesticity. . . . Schemes for coördination and coöperation in women's activities appear predicated on the idea that wives, when freed from minor household responsibilities, will find their satisfactions in helping their husbands get ahead in their vocations. This implies a subordination of self unfashionable in an age where the emphasis is on self-expression and uncommon among the individualistic American women of today. . . .

Not only does part-time employment of the married woman offer the opportunity for the development of a new home life, it lessens or destroys the appalling economic risk taken by every woman who today marries and devotes herself to the traditional rôle of wife. There is no security in domesticity. It is heart-breaking to see the middle-aged woman, trained for nothing except the duties of the home, venture out into the industrial world. Divorce, death or loss of money may put her in this position, where she has so little to offer organized industry and so much to suffer. The married woman who lets herself go upon the easy tide of domesticity is offering herself as a victim in a future tragedy. . . .

Source 15 from Willystine Goodsell, *Problems of the Family* (New York: Century Company, 1928), pp. 281, 282.

15. Willystine Goodsell on the Frustration of Educated Wives.

Perhaps a concrete instance of the situation in which the trained woman often finds herself after marriage may serve to make the problem more real in the minds of the indifferent or the unsympathetic. In one of the issues of the *Journal of the Association of Collegiate Alumnae,* there appeared a few years ago a brief article entitled "Reflections of a Professor's Wife." With her husband, the writer had spent several years in the graduate school of a university where both had earned their doctors' degrees. Then the equality in work and the delightful companionship ceased. The man was appointed assistant professor in a state university at a small salary; and the woman, who had eagerly looked forward to a similar appointment in the same institution, was brought face to face with the ruling, by no means uncommon, which prohibited wives of faculty members from teaching in the university. The comments of the professor's wife, after years spent in housekeeping, are worth quoting, for they reflect the feelings of many other women caught in a similar net of circumstance:

"After an expenditure of several thousand dollars and the devotion of some of the best years of my life to special study, I was cut off from any

CHAPTER 6

THE "NEW"
WOMAN: SOCIAL
SCIENCE
EXPERTS AND
THE
REDEFINITION
OF WOMEN'S
ROLES IN THE
1920s

opportunity to utilize this training. And unless I could earn enough money to pay some one else to do the housework, I was doomed to spend a large part of my time in tasks which a woman with practically no education could do. However, accepting the situation, I put on my apron and went into the kitchen, where for six years I have cooked a professor's meals and pondered over the policy of our university. Can it be in the divine order of things that one Ph.D. should wash dishes a whole life time for another Ph.D. just because one is a woman and the other a man?" . . .

Source 16 from Ernest Mowrer, *Domestic Discord* (Chicago: University of Chicago Press, 1928), pp. 160, 169.

16. Ernest Mowrer, Notes from Two Social Workers' Visits with Two Immigrant Families, 1928.

"Visited home. Mr. M and children at home. House and children very dirty and the babies half dressed. Mr. M said Mrs. M is working. Goes early in the morning and works ten hours. . . .

"Told him that if he would leave drink alone and work regularly that Mrs. M wouldn't have to work. Compared the neatness and cleanliness of the children when Mrs. M was home and the filth and dirt now. He said she wanted to work. I told him that was because she couldn't see the children without clothes and food."

Then four months later:

"I told the interpreter to explain very carefully to Mr. M that Mrs. M should not be working. That it was her job to stay at home and take care of the children. It is his job to support them, and if he does not do it, we will have to send him to the Bridewell [correctional institution]. . . . I am going to check up his pay every two weeks, and if he does not come up to the standard he will have to give me satisfactory reason, or we will have to bring him into court. . . ."

"Visited the B home. The house was in a terrible condition, the bed was unmade, everything was dusty and dirty, and the children were dirty and half-dressed.

Mrs. B still wishes to leave her husband as she feels that there will never be any harmony between them. She proposes to leave the two oldest children with Mr. B and take the baby with her. She knows that Mr. B is a dutiful father and will not abuse them. She states "she is still young and can make a living for herself at any time."

Mrs. B is selfish and is always thinking of her own comfort and pleasure. She has permitted her jealousy to overrule her and is constantly doubting her husband's fidelity. Also finding fault in the unimportant things.

Worker tried to make Mrs. B realize her responsibility as a wife and mother. Advised her that she ought to keep her house and children clean if she wishes to command the respect of her husband. Also advised her to have her husband's meals ready on time when he comes home from a hard day's work." . . .

❈ QUESTIONS TO CONSIDER ❈

The Evidence is grouped into three broad categories—*sex and sexuality, women's work inside and outside the home,* and *marriage and the family*—with some unavoidable overlap among them. In the section on sex and sexuality, a variety of social scientists comment on the changing standards. W. I. Thomas (Source 1) was one of the pioneers of social psychology and the sociological case study. Alyse Gregory (Source 2) was a feminist, a statistical researcher for the Carnegie Educational Foundation, and a "new" woman herself. Ernest Groves (Source 3), deeply affected by Freudian psychology, was a professor of social science and the author of numerous college textbooks on child and family studies. Psychologist John Watson (Source 4), in contrast, was the founder of American behaviorism, a school of thought that maintained that human behavior was conditioned by the environment and training of the individual. What is the *message* of each piece of evidence? What *assumptions* does each author reveal? How were *attitudes* about women's sexuality

changing? What *difficulties* were involved in these changes?

The section on women's work inside and outside the home also includes an assortment of writings by social scientists in various fields. Dr. Gwendolyn Hughes (Source 5) was a social research fellow at Bryn Mawr College for Women when she prepared *Mothers in Industry,* a massive research project involving twelve thousand households of wage-earning women in Philadelphia. As participants in the scientific management movement of the early twentieth century, both Christine Frederick (Source 6), an educator, and Dr. Lillian M. Gilbreth (Source 7), a consulting engineer, sought to apply the standards of industrial efficiency to housekeeping. Alice Rogers Hager (Source 8) and Caroline Manning (Source 10) were researchers and writers for the Women's Bureau of the U.S. Department of Labor. Dr. Benjamin R. Andrews (Source 9) was a professor of economics at Columbia University. When looking for the *message, assumptions,* and *issues* in this section,

CHAPTER 6

THE "NEW"
WOMAN: SOCIAL
SCIENCE
EXPERTS AND
THE
REDEFINITION
OF WOMEN'S
ROLES IN THE
1920s

be especially aware of which women—immigrants, native born, highly educated professionals, or ordinary homemakers—are the subjects of each piece of evidence. In what ways are the situations of all classes of women similar? In what ways are they different? What recommendations do the social scientists make? Do these apply to all classes of women? Why or why not? This section is especially useful for considering the *difficulties* involved in redefining modern women's roles.

The final section of the evidence focuses on women's roles in marriage and the family. W. I. Thomas (Source 11), John Watson (Source 12), and Ernest and Gladys H. Groves (Source 13) are identified earlier. Although they are all psychologists, you should note the major differences in their ideas about married women's roles and hap-

piness. Dr. Lorine Pruette (Source 14) was an economist whose dissertation, *Women and Leisure,* was published in 1924. Married and divorced twice, Pruette became a freelance consultant in order to try to adapt to her husbands' academic career moves. The last two selections are from books by sociology professors: Dr. Willystine Goodsell (Source 15) taught at Teachers College, Columbia University, and Dr. Ernest Mowrer (Source 16) taught at Northwestern University. Apply the same methodology to this section that you used for the other two sections. Finally, try to pull all the material together in order to understand the degree to which women's roles (sexual, economic, and as wives and mothers) were—or were not—being redefined by social scientists in the 1920s.

❋ EPILOGUE ❋

During the depression of the 1930s, social scientists eagerly enlisted in New Deal experiments, such as efforts to help the unemployed, create model communities in rural areas, and devise programs for families in trouble. African American sociologists began publishing studies of southern black family and community experiences during this era, although very little was done to alleviate the problems of black poverty. For all practical purposes, the stock market crash of 1929 and the deep depression that lasted throughout the 1930s ended the fascination with the "new woman" and replaced it with sympathy and concern

for the "forgotten man." Women who worked, especially married women, were perceived as taking jobs away from unemployed men who desperately needed to support their families. In hard times, people clung to traditional male and female roles: Men should be the breadwinners, and women should stay home and take care of the family. Women's fashions changed just as dramatically. Clothing became more feminine, hemlines dropped, and hairstyles were no longer short and boyish.

Yet women, including married women, continued to move into paid employment throughout the 1930s, and with the United States' entry into World War II, millions of women who had never held paying jobs before went to work in factories and shipyards, motivated by patriotism and a desire to aid the war effort. By the 1950s, women workers, having been replaced by returning veterans, were once again being urged to stay at home and fulfill their destinies as wives and mothers. Women's educational achievements and age at marriage dropped, while the white middle-class birthrate nearly doubled. Women were still entering the work force, but in feminized clerical and retail jobs and in professions such as elementary school teaching and nursing. Fashions changed from knee-length tailored suits and dresses and "Rosie the Riveter" slacks to puff-sleeved, tiny-waisted, full-skirted, ankle-length dresses.

The discomfort about changes in women's roles, so prominent in the 1920s, was also present in the 1960s and 1970s. Unisex fashions, the development and widespread use of the birth control pill, the availability of legal abortions, the rise of women's athletics, and the influx of young women into graduate and professional programs all seemed to threaten both women's traditional roles in marriage and the family and men's traditional role as breadwinners. In this era, there was also a new awareness about the importance of socioeconomic class, race, and ethnicity—as well as about their impact on women's options. Old assumptions about heterosexuality and homosexuality were questioned and, in many cases, rejected. A new, broader-based women's movement led to the formation of new feminist organizations, and a revised version of the ERA was passed but not ratified by the states. By the 1980s, a conservative backlash against these changes was well under way, yet today the roles of women and girls continue to change and are still being redefined.

7

Documenting the Depression: The FSA Photographers and Rural Poverty

✳ **THE PROBLEM** ✳

On a cold, rainy afternoon in the spring of 1936, Dorothea Lange was driving home from a month-long field trip to central California. One of several young photographers hired by the Historical Section of the Farm Security Administration (FSA), Lange had been talking with migrant laborers and taking photographs of the migrants' camps.

After passing a hand-lettered road sign that read PEA PICKERS CAMP, Lange drove on another twenty miles. Then she stopped, turned around, and went back to the migrant camp. The pea crop had frozen, and there was no work for the pickers, but several families were still camped there. Lange approached a woman and her daughters, talked with them briefly, asked to take a few pictures, and left ten minutes later. The result was one of the most

famous images of the Great Depression, *Migrant Mother* (see Source 8).

On the opening day in 1938, over seven thousand visitors attended the first International Exposition of Photography in New York City. The FSA's exhibit was a very small part of the three thousand photographs displayed, yet it drew shocked comments from many viewers. "Wake up, smug America," read one response card. "It makes you think of tomorrow and what it will bring," another viewer reflected after seeing the powerful images of rural poverty, dislocation, and suffering. "It brings home to me some of the things in our country that we need to do something about," a third viewer wrote.[1] These photographs

1. James Curtis, *Mind's Eye, Mind's Truth: FSA Photography Reconsidered* (Philadelphia: Temple University Press, 1990), pp. 5–6.

moved Americans deeply and helped to create support for New Deal legislation and programs to aid migrant workers, sharecroppers, tenant farmers, and small-scale farmers.

In this chapter, you will be analyzing documentary photographs from the FSA to determine how and why they were so effective in creating support for New Deal legislation to aid rural Americans.

✵ BACKGROUND ✵

In 1930, President Herbert Hoover was at first bewildered and then defensive about the rapid downward spiral of the nation's economy. Hoover, like many other Americans, believed in the basic soundness of capitalism, advocated the values of individualism, and maintained that the role of the federal government should be limited. Nevertheless, Hoover was a compassionate man. As private relief sources dried up, he authorized public works projects and some institutional loans, at the same time vetoing other relief bills and trying to convince the nation that prosperity would return soon. The media, especially newspapers and middle-class magazines, followed Hoover's lead.

Americans turned out at the polls in record numbers for the election of 1932—and voted for the Democratic candidate, Franklin D. Roosevelt, in equally record numbers. As unemployment increased dramatically along with bank and business failures, Congress reacted by rapidly passing an assortment of programs collectively known as the New Deal. Calling together a group of experts (mainly professors and lawyers) to form a "brain trust," the newly elected president acted quickly to try to restore the nation's confidence. In his fireside radio chats, as well as in his other speeches, Roosevelt consistently reassured the American public that the country's economic institutions were sound.

Like her husband, First Lady Eleanor Roosevelt was tireless in her efforts to mitigate the effects of the depression. With boundless energy, she traveled throughout the country, observing conditions firsthand and reporting back to her husband. One of the few New Dealers deeply committed to civil rights for African Americans, she championed both individuals and the civil rights movement whenever she could. Although she was criticized and ridiculed for her nontraditional behavior as first lady, to millions of Americans, Eleanor Roosevelt was the heart of the New Deal. In fact, during the depression, more than 15 million Americans wrote directly to the president and first lady about their personal troubles and economic difficulties.

In an emergency session early in 1933, Congress began the complicated process of providing immediate relief for the needy and legislation for longer-term recovery and reform. Banking, business, the stock market, unemployed workers, farmers, and young people were targets of this early New Deal legislation.

CHAPTER 7

DOCUMENTING
THE
DEPRESSION:
THE FSA
PHOTOGRAPHERS
AND RURAL
POVERTY

The New Deal administration soon realized that the problems of farmers were going to be especially difficult to alleviate. To meet the unusual European demand for farm products during World War I, many American farmers had overexpanded. They had mortgaged their farms and borrowed money to buy expensive new farm equipment, but most had not shared in the profits of the so-called prosperous decade of the 1920s.

Unfortunately, the New Deal's Agricultural Adjustment Act benefited only relatively large, prosperous farmers. Intended to reduce farm production and thus improve the prices farmers received for their goods, the act unintentionally encouraged large farmers to accept payment for reducing their crops, use the money to buy machinery, and evict the sharecroppers and tenants who had been farming part of their land. Explaining to Dorothea Lange why his family was traveling to California, one farmer simply said they had been "tractored out." With no land of their own to farm, sharecroppers and tenants packed their few belongings and families into old trucks and cars and took to the road looking for seasonal agricultural work in planting, tending, or picking produce.

In so doing, they joined thousands of other American farm families who lived in the Dust Bowl—the plains and prairie states where unwise agricultural practices and a long drought had combined to create terrifying dust storms that blotted out the sun, blew away the topsoil, and actually buried some farms in dust. These Dust Bowl refugees, along with former tenants and sharecroppers, joined Mexican Americans already working as migrant laborers in California. For those left behind, especially in the poverty-stricken areas of the rural Midwest and South, conditions were almost as terrible as in the migrant camps.

It was to aid these displaced farmers that President Roosevelt created the Resettlement Administration (RA), which two years later became the Farm Security Administration. The RA was headed by Rexford Tugwell, an economics professor from Columbia University. A former Progressive, Tugwell was an optimist who believed that if the public was educated about social and economic problems, Americans would support legislation to correct whatever was wrong. To accomplish this task, Tugwell hired his former graduate student, Roy Stryker, to direct the Historical Section of the agency.

Stryker in turn hired a small group of photographers to travel around the country and take photos illustrating the difficulties faced by small farmers, tenants, and sharecroppers and, to a lesser extent, the FSA projects intended to ameliorate these problems. Hoping to mobilize public opinion in support of FSA-funded projects such as model migrant camps, rural cooperatives, health clinics, and federal relief for the poorest families, Stryker made the photographs widely available to national middle-class magazines and local newspapers. The Historical Section also organized traveling exhibits and encouraged authors to use the photographs in their books.

These photographic images were intended to elicit emotional responses from viewers. What kinds of subjects did the photographs portray? In what ways did the impact of the depression, as visualized in the photographs, seem to endanger traditional American values and deeply held beliefs? In other words, why were these images so effective in creating support for New Deal legislation to help rural Americans?

❋ THE METHOD ❋

By the end of the nineteenth century, technological advances had made using cameras and developing photographs easier, but both the equipment and the developing methods were still cumbersome and primitive by today's standards. Nevertheless, people were fascinated by photography, and many talented amateurs, such as E. Alice Austen, spent hours taking pictures of their families, friends, and homes. Indeed, these photographs are an important source of evidence for social historians trying to reconstruct how Americans lived in the past.

Documentary photography, however, has a different purpose: reform. During the Progressive era of the late nineteenth and early twentieth centuries, middle-class Americans increasingly became concerned about the growing number of poor families who depended on the labor of their children to supplement their meager standard of living. First Jacob Riis, the author of *How the Other Half Lives* (1890), and then Lewis Hine, in his work for the National Child Labor Committee, photographed the living and working conditions of young children and documented the ill effects of child labor. These photographs were used to persuade the public to support the strict regulation or abolition of child labor.

Roy Stryker was impressed by the power of such photographs and had used many of Hine's images to illustrate Rexford Tugwell's reform-oriented economics textbook in the 1920s. The dozen or so talented photographers whom Stryker hired to work for the Historical Section of the FSA were relatively young (most were in their twenties or thirties) and came from a variety of backgrounds. Most of the photographers, including Dorothea Lange, Walker Evans, Jack Delano, Carl Mydans, John Collier, Marion Post Wolcott, and Theodor Jung, were already either established professionals or serious amateurs. Others took their first professional photographs for the Historical Section: Ben Shahn and Russell Lee had been painters, and Arthur Rothstein and John Vachon were unemployed college students. All the photographers were white, except Gordon Parks, a twenty-nine-year-old African American fashion photographer who joined the Historical Section in 1941. Parks never photographed farmers while at the FSA; instead, he sensitively documented the lives of African Americans and racial discrimination in Washington, D.C.

The documentary tradition in American photography was never based on neutrality or objectivity—in fact, complete objectivity would be im-

CHAPTER 7

DOCUMENTING
THE
DEPRESSION:
THE FSA
PHOTOGRAPHERS
AND RURAL
POVERTY

possible even if it were desirable. As soon as a photographer frames a picture in the camera's viewfinder, poses subjects, or rearranges things in any way, elements of manipulation and interpretation enter the image-making process. Further personal interpretation may be introduced in the cropping and printing of a photograph as well as in the selection of one image over another of the same subject. In order to encourage child labor reforms, Progressive-era photographers such as Lewis Hine often posed their subjects in ways that emphasized their dirtiness and poverty. Similarly, in an effort to educate viewers about depression conditions in rural America, the FSA photographers sought to document the suffering and poverty of their subjects—farmers and sharecroppers—in images that also portrayed the dignity and will to survive of these rural Americans.

To create an effective photograph, for example, Arthur Rothstein moved the steer skull (shown in Source 3) from parched soil in South Dakota to a location where he could photograph it against a background of overgrazed scrub vegetation (thereby creating a variation on Source 3). For the photograph in Source 4, an image of a man and his children running from an approaching dust storm, Rothstein darkened the sky to re-create what it looked like during the dust storm (since he obviously could not photograph the actual storm). Dorothea Lange, who had been a successful portrait photographer before she joined the FSA, took six photos of a migrant mother and the four of her seven children who were present at the time.

Lange posed the woman and her children and kept moving in closer and closer until she captured the image that she thought best portrayed both the plight of the migrants and the nobility of the mother. The resulting image (Source 8) came to be considered an archetypal work of art and is now in the Museum of Modern Art.

Perhaps the most extreme manipulation of photographic images is seen in the work of Walker Evans, who worked briefly for the FSA. When he and James Agee were in Alabama photographing tenant farmers for their book *Let Us Now Praise Famous Men* (1941), Evans rearranged furniture, posed and reposed people, and cleaned up what he thought was clutter. Working with a huge eight-by-ten view camera, Evans considered himself an artist who saw the potential for beauty in the poverty and hard lives of the tenant farmers. Evans may also have thought middle-class viewers would react more sympathetically to his somewhat romantic vision of the rural poor than to the actual realities of their poverty.

Stryker himself was not a photographer but an able administrator who planned the field trips, developed background reading lists for the photographers, and wrote "shooting scripts" to guide them once they were in the field. "As you are driving through the agricultural areas . . . ," Stryker wrote to Dorothea Lange in California, "would you take a few shots of various types of farm activities such as your picture showing the lettuce workers?" But beyond these kinds of general suggestions, Stryker gave his photographers remarkable freedom while he concentrated on co-ordinating their activities, selecting images for the files, promoting the wide use of their photos, and defending the Historical Section against congressional criticism and budget cuts.

When analyzing these pictures, then, you must remember that documentary photographs are not intended to present a balanced or an unbiased view. Instead, these photo-graphs are intended to appeal to viewers' emotions and motivate viewers to work for and support change. As a student looking at these photographs, you will need to be specific about *what* is portrayed, *what* you feel, and *why* the photograph makes you feel that way. Finally, try to make some connections between the photographs and the federal programs to aid the rural poor.

CHAPTER 7

DOCUMENTING
THE
DEPRESSION:
THE FSA
PHOTOGRAPHERS
AND RURAL
POVERTY

❋ THE EVIDENCE ❋

Sources 1 through 17 from United States Farm Security Administration, Historical Division, Library of Congress, Washington, D.C.

1. Abandoned Farm Home, Ward County, North Dakota, 1940 (John Vachon).

2. "Tractored-out" Farm, Hall County, Texas, 1938 (Dorothea Lange).

3. Skull, South Dakota Badlands, 1936 (Arthur Rothstein).

CHAPTER 7

DOCUMENTING
THE
DEPRESSION:
THE FSA
PHOTOGRAPHERS
AND RURAL
POVERTY

4. Farmer and Sons in Dust Storm, Cimarron County, Oklahoma, 1936 (Arthur Rothstein).

5. Family Moving to Krebs, Oklahoma, from Idabel, Oklahoma, 1939 (Dorothea Lange).

6. Migrant Family Living in a Shack Built on an Abandoned Truck Bed, Highway 70, Tennessee, 1936 (Carl Mydans).

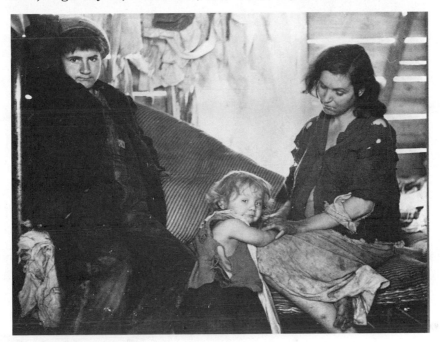

7. Migrants from Oklahoma, Blyth, California, 1936 (Dorothea Lange).

CHAPTER 7

DOCUMENTING
THE
DEPRESSION:
THE FSA
PHOTOGRAPHERS
AND RURAL
POVERTY

8. Migrant Mother, Nipomo, California, 1936 (Dorothea Lange).

9. Mexican Migrant Worker's Home, Imperial Valley, California, 1937 (Dorothea Lange).

10. Living Quarters of Fruit-Packing House Workers, Berrien, Michigan, 1940 (John Vachon).

11. Plantation Owner and Field Hands, Clarksdale, Mississippi, 1936 (Dorothea Lange).

CHAPTER 7

DOCUMENTING
THE
DEPRESSION:
THE FSA
PHOTOGRAPHERS
AND RURAL
POVERTY

12. Cotton Pickers, Pulaski County, Arkansas, 1935 (Ben Shahn).

13. Owner of the General Store, Bank, and Cotton Gin, Wendell, North Carolina, 1939 (Marion Post Wolcott).

14. FSA Client and His Family, Beaufort, South Carolina, 1936 (Carl Mydans).

15. Mule Dealer, Creedmoor, North Carolina, 1940 (Arthur Rothstein).

CHAPTER 7

DOCUMENTING
THE
DEPRESSION:
THE FSA
PHOTOGRAPHERS
AND RURAL
POVERTY

16. Bud Fields and His Family, Tenant Farmers, Hale County, Alabama, 1936 (Walker Evans).

17. Christmas Dinner, Tenant Farmer's Home, Southeastern Iowa, 1936 (Russell Lee).

❋ QUESTIONS TO CONSIDER ❋

The photographs in Sources 1 through 4 illustrate what happened to the once-fertile farmlands of the plains and prairies. How would you describe these pictures to someone who could not see them? What happened to the land? What was the impact on people who lived there?

Sources 5 through 8 show photographs of farm families who were on the road. They had left or been evicted from the farms where they had lived and were looking for jobs as migrant workers. How would middle-class Americans have felt when they saw these pictures? Which photograph do you think is the most effective? Why?

Sources 9, 10, 12, 14, 16, and 17 show the living and working conditions at migrant camps and for the tenant and sharecropper families who did not leave their homes. What do you notice most when you look at these photographs? What do these images reveal about women? children? family? In contrast, the images in Sources 11, 13, and 15 are of men who were relatively well off during the depression. How are they portrayed? What characteristics do they seem to have? What is your reaction to these images?

During an interview conducted many years after his work in Georgia as an FSA photographer, Jack Delano remarked that "you couldn't work down there very long without becoming acutely aware of the race problem. . . ."[2] Reexamine Sources 11 through 15. What do these images tell you about the living conditions of rural blacks in the South? About the economic and social relationships between blacks and property-owning whites? Compare the images of black and white tenant farmers depicted in Sources 14 and 16.

Finally, think about the photographs as a whole. What messages did they send to the middle-class Americans who saw them in newspapers, magazines, books, or traveling exhibits? What major problems did the photographs portray, and what kinds of programs did the FSA propose to try to aid poor farmers? Why do you think these documentary photographs were so effective in creating sympathy and support for aid to these farmers?

❋ EPILOGUE ❋

By 1941, the FSA photographs were well known to millions of Americans, and the Historical Section had justified its existence. That year also saw the publication of the classic book *Let Us Now Praise Famous Men: Three Tenant Families,* written by James Agee and illustrated with photos by FSA photographer Walker Evans. After the Japanese attack on Pearl Harbor in December 1941 and

2. Louis Schmeir and Denise Montgomery, "The Other Depression: The Black Experience in Georgia Through an FSA Photographer's Lens," *Georgia Historical Quarterly* 78 (1994): 135.

CHAPTER 7

DOCUMENTING
THE
DEPRESSION:
THE FSA
PHOTOGRAPHERS
AND RURAL
POVERTY

the United States' subsequent entry into World War II, the direction of the Historical Section changed. The buildup of defense industries and the effects of the war on everyday Americans dominated the photographers' assignments. Eventually, the Historical Section was moved to the Office of War Information, and in 1943, after transferring more than 130,000 FSA photographs to the Library of Congress, Roy Stryker resigned from government service.

America's participation in World War II finally brought an end to the Great Depression—and an end to the New Deal as well. Stryker spent the next decade working for Standard Oil of New Jersey, and most of the former FSA photographers did freelance work, taught courses, or found permanent jobs in photojournalism with magazines such as *Life* and *Look*. Ben Shahn went back to his first love, painting, and became a well-known artist. Marion Post Wolcott got married and raised a family, returning to photography only when she was in her sixties. The plight of the rural poor was once again forgotten, and middle-class materialism and conformity dominated the cold war years of the 1950s.

Yet a whole new generation was soon to rediscover the work of the FSA photographers. In 1962, Edward Steichen, head of the photography department at the New York Museum of Modern Art and a photographer himself, mounted a major exhibition of the FSA images called "The Bitter Years, 1935–1941." By the end of the 1960s, young Americans also had rediscovered some of the same problems the New Deal photographers had captured in their pictures: rural poverty, racial discrimination, and social injustice. Once again, Americans demanded reform, especially during the presidencies of John F. Kennedy and Lyndon Johnson.

8

Presidential Leadership, Public Opinion, and the Coming of World War II: The USS *Greer* Incident, September 4, 1941

❋ THE PROBLEM ❋

At 11:50 A.M. on Thursday, September 4, 1941, crewmen aboard the destroyer USS *Greer* sighted the track of a torpedo that had been fired at the ship, ultimately passing about two hundred yards astern of the United States naval vessel. The *Greer* counterattacked, dropping eight depth charges in an effort to destroy the submarine. At 11:58, a second torpedo track was sighted; this torpedo also missed the ship. For the next six hours, the *Greer* chased the submarine, dropping eleven more depth charges, apparently to no effect. At 6:40 P.M., the American destroyer gave up the search and proceeded to Iceland, its original destination.[1]

On September 11, President Franklin D. Roosevelt went on the radio in one of his famous "fireside chats."[2] Characterizing Germany's submarines as the "rattlesnakes of the Atlantic," the president told listeners that the *Greer* had been attacked without warning while the destroyer was "proceeding on a legitimate mission" and said that thenceforth he would order American ships to shoot on sight any German submarines; moreover, American ships would protect merchant ships of all nations that were

1. The USS *Greer* was approximately 125 miles southwest of Reykjavik, Iceland, when the incident took place. The ship was carrying mail to United States Marines stationed in Iceland. The ship, built in 1918, was relegated

to the "bone yard" of the Philadelphia Navy Yard sometime after World War I but was recommissioned in 1940. It was named for Rear Admiral James A. Greer (1833–1904), a Civil War veteran (Union) and commander of the European Squadron from 1887 to 1889.
2. The fireside chat was scheduled to be delivered earlier but was postponed when the president's mother died over the weekend.

CHAPTER 8

PRESIDENTIAL
LEADERSHIP,
PUBLIC OPINION,
AND THE
COMING OF
WORLD WAR II:
THE USS *GREER*
INCIDENT,
SEPTEMBER 4,
1941

carrying cargoes to Germany's enemies. At the end of Roosevelt's address, the radio network played a recording of the national anthem, and all the people in the diplomatic reception room of the White House (except the president) rose emotionally to their feet.

About two weeks later, a Gallup public opinion poll showed that 56 percent of those surveyed agreed with Roosevelt's "shoot on sight" order,[3] even though it seemed clear that such a step would make war with Germany almost unavoidable. This result was in marked contrast to an October 26–31, 1939, poll, which reported that 96 percent of Americans opposed war against Germany. Yet whether President Roosevelt was using his powers to shape public opinion toward a more belligerent stand against the Axis Powers (Germany, Italy, and Japan), or whether the president was carefully following public opinion as he moved the United States closer to war is a question that still elicits considerable debate.

This chapter concentrates on one incident, the attack on the USS *Greer* by a German submarine on September 4, 1941. Your task in this chapter is two-fold. To begin, you must arrange the evidence. Unlike the evidence in other chapters of this book, the evidence in this chapter has not been arranged for you but instead has been set down in no particular order—the way in which historians actually find evidence. Arrange the evidence in order to answer the following two questions (the second part of the task): (1) What *actually happened* in the *Greer* incident? and (2) Was President Roosevelt shaping public opinion or following it (or a combination of both)?

The causes of the United States' involvement in World War II are exceedingly complex and would require analyses of literally hundreds of events that took place between the mid-1930s and December 7, 1941, the date of the Japanese attack on Pearl Harbor, which brought the United States into the war in both Europe and the Pacific. You will not be able to determine those causes through an examination and analysis of one single event, albeit a pivotal one. You will, however, be able to gain some important clues regarding President Franklin Roosevelt's attitudes and behavior and their relation to American public opinion.

❋ BACKGROUND ❋

On September 1, 1939, German chancellor Adolf Hitler's armies attacked Poland. Two days later, France and Great Britain declared war on Germany. Ever since March 1935, when Hitler announced that he would defy the Treaty of Versailles and rearm

---

3. The poll was taken between September 19 and 24, 1941. Of those surveyed, 34 percent disagreed with Roosevelt's policy, and 10 percent expressed no opinion. See George H. Gallup, *The Gallup Poll: Public Opinion, 1935–1971* (New York: Random House, 1972), Vol. I, p. 299.

Germany, France and Great Britain had watched with increasing alarm as Germany reoccupied the Rhineland in March 1936, seized and annexed Austria in March 1938, and demanded the Sudetenland (the German-speaking part of Czechoslovakia). At a conference in Munich that took place on September 29–30, 1938, Hitler promised that the Sudetenland was "the last territorial claim which I have to make in Europe." Naively believing that Hitler's appetite had been satiated, Britain's prime minister, Neville Chamberlain, announced that the Munich Conference had brought "peace in our time." But in March 1939, Hitler absorbed the rest of Czechoslovakia. Realizing their error, France and Great Britain declared war when Germany invaded Poland.

Less than two weeks after the attack on Poland, President Roosevelt called Congress into special session to lift the United States' embargo on arms trade with countries at war. The Neutrality Act of 1939 lifted the embargo but mandated that such trade could be carried out only on a cash-and-carry basis (thereby prohibiting any loans to the belligerents, believing that such loans had been a principal cause of America's involvement in World War I)[4] and forbid American troops to enter danger zones in the Atlantic.

The outbreak of war in Europe presented the American people with a dilemma. On the one hand, an overwhelming majority wanted the United States to stay out of the war. Disillusioned by the dashing of their World War I idealism, both the American people and their government had been staunchly isolationist throughout the 1920s and much of the 1930s. On the other hand, most Americans were decidedly unneutral, hoping that the Allied Powers would be able to defeat Germany, Italy, and the Soviet Union.[5] This was especially true after the German blitzkrieg (lightning war) in the spring of 1940. In six weeks, German armies overran Denmark, Norway, Belgium, the Netherlands, Luxembourg, and France (which capitulated on June 22, 1940), leaving Great Britain to stand alone against the German military might. In the summer and fall of 1940, Hitler unleashed the Luftwaffe (the German air force) against Britain in hopes that massive bombing of civilian targets would force the British to surrender. Tens of thousands of British civilians were killed or wounded, the city of Coventry was completely destroyed, and large parts of London lay in ruins (with twenty thousand killed in that city alone), but the British tenaciously hung on. "We will never surrender," promised Prime Minister Winston Churchill. Gradually the Royal Air Force gained control of the skies over Great Britain.

In late June 1940, 86 percent of Americans surveyed believed the United States should stay out of the war, but the bombing of Britain had a

---

4. In late October 1939, 68 percent of Americans surveyed believed that it had been a mistake for the United States to have entered World War I. See Gallup, *Gallup Poll*, Vol. I, p. 189.

5. Prior to his attack on Poland, Hitler had signed the Non-Aggression Pact with the Soviet Union. While Germany was smashing the Polish army, the Soviet Union gobbled up eastern Poland.

CHAPTER 8

PRESIDENTIAL
LEADERSHIP,
PUBLIC OPINION,
AND THE
COMING OF
WORLD WAR II:
THE USS *GREER*
INCIDENT,
SEPTEMBER 4,
1941

profound effect on American public opinion. Asked in early September whether it was more important for the United States to keep out of the war or to help England, a bare majority (52 percent) preferred to help England. Taking advantage of that apparent shift in public opinion, Roosevelt concluded an executive agreement with Churchill to trade fifty World War I vintage American destroyers in exchange for leases on British military bases in the Western Hemisphere (especially in Newfoundland, Bermuda, and Trinidad), which the president claimed was for the purpose of bolstering American defenses. In October 1940, Congress authorized the first peacetime draft of men for military service. But when the *New York Daily News* claimed that the United States "has one foot in the war and the other on a banana peel," Roosevelt retorted, "Your president says this country is not going to war."

Having won reelection by defeating Republican challenger Wendell Willkie, in January 1941 Roosevelt proposed to Congress a sweeping revision of the Neutrality Act that would repeal the cash-and-carry provision and authorize the president to lend or lease war material to Great Britain. Although polls showed that 88 percent of Americans still wanted the United States to stay out of war, at the same time, 54 percent favored the Lend-Lease bill. Congress passed the bill in March 1941, by votes of 317–71 in the House of Representatives and 60–31 in the Senate. Interestingly, the bill in the House was numbered HR1776.

Not all Americans were happy with what appeared to be a trend toward greater and greater involvement in the war in Europe. Germany had approximately thirty submarines (U-boats) in the Atlantic, which were inflicting a terrible toll on British shipping. Isolationists warned that the United States ultimately would have to escort vessels carrying Lend-Lease goods or use American ships, either of which would bring Americans into direct conflict with German U-boats and inevitably into war. For his part, columnist Walter Lippmann attacked Roosevelt himself:

> In this tremendous time the American people must look to the President for leadership. They are not getting leadership from the President. They are not being treated as they deserve to be treated and as they have a right to be treated. They are not being treated as men and women but as if they were inquisitive children. They are not being dealt with seriously, truthfully, responsibly, and nobly. They are being dealt with cleverly, indirectly, even condescendingly and nervously.[6]

Although Roosevelt scoffed at the isolationists and insisted that his actions were meant to keep the nation out of war, not enter it, the isolationists had made a telling point. Between January and June 1941, the British lost 756 merchant ships, with an additional 1,450 damaged. With this loss of ships at the rate of 500,000 tons per month, it was obvious that a large proportion of Lend-Lease goods were ending up on the bottom of the Atlantic. Admiral Harold R. Stark wrote, "The situation is obviously critical in the Atlantic. In my opinion it is hopeless

6. Lippmann, quoted in T. R. Fehrenbach, *F.D.R.'s Undeclared War, 1939 to 1941* (New York: David McKay Co., 1967), p. 218.

except as we take strong measures to save it."[7]

As it had been in the past, public opinion was contradictory. In May 1941, 79 percent of those surveyed believed the United States should stay out of the war, yet in that same poll, 52 percent said that the United States Navy should guard ships carrying war materiel to Britain. Prior to the poll's being taken, Roosevelt ordered Admiral Ernest King to patrol waters as far as longitude 25 degrees west and inform British convoys of lurking German submarines.[8] Then in June 1941, Roosevelt ordered Admiral Stark to send United States Marines to occupy Iceland, a possession of Denmark that had been occupied by British troops when Denmark was swallowed in Hitler's blitzkrieg.[9] Thus the United States Navy in essence was escorting British convoys to an island well within the war zone. With the navy short of officers, the United States Naval Academy had graduated its 1941 class six months early. Lieutenant Commander Laurence H. Frost had been on the USS *Greer* thirty-five days when the incident with the German submarine took place.

As a reminder, your task in this chapter is to arrange the randomly sorted evidence in order to answer the following two questions:

1. What *actually happened* in the *Greer* incident of September 4, 1941?
2. Was President Roosevelt *shaping* public opinion, *following* it, or doing a combination of both?

✳ THE METHOD ✳

In most cases, historians find it best to arrange the evidence at their disposal in chronological order. This is especially true when a historian is combining a series of events to tell a story (a narrative history) or is writing a biography of an individual (a biographical history). At first glance, then, it would seem most appropriate to arrange your evidence chronologically.

And yet, at second glance, certain interesting problems arise. For example, the deck log of the USS *Greer* (Source 12) was written by United States Navy Lieutenant T. H. Copeman on the same day on which the incident took place, or very soon after. U-boat 652's report (Source 13) also was written on September 4, 1941. The speech by Senator Robert A. Taft (Source 23), however, was delivered to the Senate on October 28, 1941. And Roosevelt's fireside chat of September 11, 1941 (Source 20), and Secretary of the Navy Frank Knox's address to the American Legion on September 15, 1941 (Source 21), were delivered sev-

---

7. Stark to Admiral Husband S. Kimmel, April 4, 1941, quoted in Patrick Abbazia, *Mr. Roosevelt's Navy: The Private War of the U.S. Atlantic Fleet, 1939–1942* (Annapolis: Naval Institute Press, 1975), p. 153.
8. One joke Admiral King's men told about him was that "while [King] did not yet think he was God, God thought that he was Admiral King." Ibid., p. 134.
9. Iceland's prime minister, Hermann Jonasson, was not informed of the United States' impending occupation until the marines were already at sea.

CHAPTER 8

PRESIDENTIAL
LEADERSHIP,
PUBLIC OPINION,
AND THE
COMING OF
WORLD WAR II:
THE USS *GREER*
INCIDENT,
SEPTEMBER 4,
1941

eral days after the *Greer* incident took place. Yet because all of these other pieces of evidence deal with the events of September 4, they must be placed with the *Greer*'s deck log. Similarly, the Gallup poll data (Sources 1 through 11) often was published weeks after the actual polls were taken. Public opinion can shift very rapidly, so you must use the dates on which those polls *actually were taken,* not the dates on which they were released.

Once having arranged your evidence, you must then subject it to the test of believability. The deck log of the USS *Greer* and the log of U-652 (the German submarine) are reports to superior officers in Washington and Berlin, respectively, of what actually took place. Are these two reports, the only ones written by eyewitnesses, accurate? How accurate are the *New York Times*'s reports of the incident (Sources 14 and 15) and of the German disclaimer (Source 18)? Similarly, is President Roosevelt's account of the incident in his September 5 news conference (Source 19) and his September 11 fireside chat (Source 20) an accurate one? If not, why do you think this was so? Admiral Stark was requested to report to the Senate Naval Affairs Committee, and he did so in writing, thereby avoiding a face-to-face confrontation (Source 22). How believable is Stark? Finally, Senator Robert A. Taft (Source 23) was a political opponent of Roosevelt, a fact you should keep in mind as you read his excerpted remarks. How would you assess Taft's speech? Is he believable?

Very quickly you will see that certain pieces of evidence will help you in answering one question but will not be relevant in answering the other. For example, the Gallup polls tell you nothing about what really happened off the coast of Iceland on September 4, 1941, but those same polls will be invaluable in determining President Roosevelt's relations to public opinion. Be precise in matching the polls to Roosevelt's actions. Was he ahead of public opinion, behind it, or step by step with it? What does that say about the nature of his presidential leadership? FDR clearly did not tell the full story of the *Greer* incident to the American people, in either his press conference (Source 19) or his fireside chat (Source 20). Why do you think this was so?

Because the evidence has not been arranged for you, you will have to take detailed notes on each source. You might want to use a separate sheet of paper or note card for each piece of evidence, so you can rearrange the evidence as you rearrange your notes. Be sure to write down your impressions of each source as to its accuracy and believability, as well as any reasons you think the particular piece of evidence is or is not accurate or believable.

The Gallup poll results (Sources 1 through 11) are grouped together, but obviously they will have to be inserted in their proper places in the rest of the evidence (which includes speeches, newspaper accounts, and the like).

❋ THE EVIDENCE ❋

Sources 1 through 11 from George H. Gallup, *The Gallup Poll: Public Opinion, 1935–1971* (New York: Random House, 1972), Vol. I, pp. 270, 275–276, 279–280, 291, 296, 299–302.

1. Gallup Poll, Released March 21, 1941.

EUROPEAN WAR

Interviewing Date 3/9–14/41
Survey #232-K

If you were asked to vote on the question of the United States entering the war against Germany and Italy, how would you vote—to go into the war, or to stay out of the war?

Go in	17%
Stay out	83

The Southern states show the highest vote for war, 20%, and the West Central states the lowest, 14%.

2. Gallup Poll, Released April 23, 1941.

EUROPEAN WAR

Interviewing Date 4/10–15/41
Survey #234-K

Should the United States navy be used to guard ships carrying war materials to Britain?

Yes	41%
No	50
No opinion	9

3. Gallup Poll, Released May 16, 1941.

EUROPEAN WAR

Interviewing Date 5/8–13/41
Survey #236-K

If you were asked to vote today on the question of the United States entering the war against Germany and Italy, how would you vote—to go into the war or to stay out of the war?

Go in	21%
Stay out	79

Five per cent expressed no opinion.

[211]

CHAPTER 8

PRESIDENTIAL
LEADERSHIP,
PUBLIC OPINION,
AND THE
COMING OF
WORLD WAR II:
THE USS *GREER*
INCIDENT,
SEPTEMBER 4,
1941

By State

	Go In	Stay Out		Go In	Stay Out
Wisconsin	14%	86%	New Mexico	24%	76%
Minnesota	15	85	Nevada	24	76
Iowa	15	85	Delaware	25	75
Indiana	15	85	Oklahoma	25	75
Ohio	15	85	Louisiana	26	74
Massachusetts	17	83	Tennessee	26	74
New Hampshire	17	83	Montana	26	74
Illinois	17	83	Utah	26	74
Michigan	18	82	Maryland	27	73
Nebraska	18	82	West Virginia	27	73
South Dakota	18	82	Kentucky	27	73
Connecticut	19	81	Idaho	27	73
Kansas	20	80	Oregon	27	73
North Dakota	21	79	Georgia	28	72
Maine	21	79	Arkansas	28	72
Rhode Island	22	78	Virginia	28	72
Pennsylvania	22	78	Mississippi	28	72
Washington	22	78	Colorado	28	72
Vermont	23	77	North Carolina	29	71
New Jersey	23	77	Alabama	29	71
Missouri	23	77	Texas	29	71
South Carolina	23	77	Wyoming	29	71
California	23	77	Arizona	33	67
New York	24	76	Florida	35	65

4. Gallup Poll, Released May 21, 1941.

EUROPEAN WAR

Interviewing Date 5/8–13/41
Survey #236-K

Should the United States navy be used to guard ships carrying war materials to Britain?

Yes	52%
No	41
No opinion	7

5. Gallup Poll, Released July 25, 1941.

ICELAND

Interviewing Date 7/11–16/41
Survey #241-K

Do you approve or disapprove of the Government's action in taking over the defense of Iceland?

Approve	61%
Disapprove	17
No opinion	22

6. Gallup Poll, Released September 23, 1941.

EUROPEAN WAR

Interviewing Date 8/21–26/41
Survey #245-K

Do you think the American navy should be used to convoy ships carrying war materials to England?

Yes	52%
No	39
No opinion	9

7. Gallup Poll, Released September 26, 1941.

EUROPEAN WAR

Interviewing Date 9/19–24/41
Survey #248-K

Do you approve or disapprove of having the United States shoot at German submarines or warships on sight?

Approve	56%
Disapprove	34

CHAPTER 8

PRESIDENTIAL
LEADERSHIP,
PUBLIC OPINION,
AND THE
COMING OF
WORLD WAR II:
THE USS *GREER*
INCIDENT,
SEPTEMBER 4,
1941

8. Gallup Poll, Released October 1, 1941.

NEUTRALITY

Interviewing Date 9/19–24/41
Survey #248-K

Should the Neutrality Act be changed to permit American merchant ships with American crews to carry war materials to Britain?

Yes	46%
No	40
No opinion	14

By Political Affiliation

Democrats

Yes	51%
No	33
No opinion	16

Republicans

Yes	42%
No	48
No opinion	10

9. Gallup Poll, Released October 5, 1941.

EUROPEAN WAR

Interviewing Date 9/19–24/41
Survey #248-K

Which of these two things do you think is the more important—that this country keep out of war or that Germany be defeated?

Keep out of war	30%
Germany be defeated	70

10. Gallup Poll, Released October 8, 1941.

PRESIDENT ROOSEVELT

Interviewing Date 9/19–24/41
Survey #248-K

So far as you personally are concerned, do you think President Roosevelt has gone too far in his policies of helping Britain, or not far enough?

Too far	27%
About right	57
Not far enough	16

11. Gallup Poll, Released October 19, 1941.

NEUTRALITY

Interviewing Date 10/9–14/41
Survey #250-K

Should the Neutrality Act be changed to permit American ships to be armed?

Yes	72%
No	21
No opinion	7

Should the Neutrality Act be changed to permit American merchant ships with American crews to carry war materials to England?

Yes	46%
No	40
No opinion	14

Source 12 from National Archives, Record Group 45, p. 528.

12. Deck Log, Lieutenant T. H. Copeman, USS *Greer,* September 4, 1941.

4 to 8. 0400[10] Changed course to 056 T, 057 PGC, 092 PSC at standard speed 17.5 knots. 0430 Went to General Quarters.[11] 0503 Secured from General Quarters. 0538 Shifted steering control to after steering station.

10. The armed services mark the time of day from 0001 hours (1 minute after midnight) to 2359 hours (1 minute until midnight), not repeating the hours (1, 2, 3, and so on) after noon. Therefore, 0400 is 4:00 A.M., and 1535 (below) is 3:35 P.M.
11. *General Quarters* refers to a full battle alert.

CHAPTER 8

PRESIDENTIAL
LEADERSHIP,
PUBLIC OPINION,
AND THE
COMING OF
WORLD WAR II:
THE USS *GREER*
INCIDENT,
SEPTEMBER 4,
1941

0545 Shifted control back to bridge. 0740 Sighted British plane ULA. 0747 Plane reported U-boat had submerged bearing 057 T, distance 10 miles. Commenced zigzagging in accordance with zigzag plan # 1. Went to General Quarters.

8 to 12. Steaming as before on zigzag courses. 0801 Changed course to 045 T. 0815 Changed speed to 10 knots and started sound search. 0820 Made contact with underwater sound gear and maneuvered on various courses and speeds maintaining contact. 0932 British plane ULA attacked submarine releasing four depth charges. 0952 Plane departed. 1030 Heard submarine propellers on sound gear. 1100 Sighted British plane UAK. 1140 Submarine appeared to be changing course to right approaching ship. Changed course to the right. Bearing changed rapidly aft to starboard and distance closed to about 50 yards. Lost sound contact at 150 yards on starboard bow. Track of submarine sighted. 1144 Sighted firingbubble abeam to starboard opposite bridge distant 25 yards. At time of sighting bubble submarine wake indicated she was then on port quarter. CDD 61 ordered attack. Went ahead flank speed and changed course 180 to the right. 1150 Sighted torpedo track broad on starboard beam distance 1000 yards which passed 200 yards astern. 1156 Attacked dropping 8 depth charges. 1158 Sighted torpedo track 10 degrees on starboard bow and changed course to right to avoid torpedo. Torpedo passed about 100 yards on port beam. Recommenced search of area immediately.

12 to 16. Steaming as before on various courses at various speeds conducting sound search for submarine. 1315 Sighted British destroyer I26. 1316 Discontinued search and set course 059 T, 060 PGC, 099 PSC standard speed 15 knots for Reykjavik, Iceland. Secured from General Quarters, set condition III. 1333 On orders from Commander Destroyer Division 61 changed course to 330 T, 329 PGC, 002 PSC to continue search. 1407 Made sound contact with submarine bearing 10 degrees on starboard bow distance 900 yards. Sounded General Quarters and proceeded to attack submarine. 1412 Attacked submarine dropping eleven depth charges. 1413 Changed course to 250 T, at flank speed. 1414 Changed course to 270 T and slowed to 15 knots. 1415 Slowed to 5 knots continuing on sound search. 1431 Changed course to 095 T and went ahead at 10 knots. 1535 Changed course to 090 T, 089 PGC, 059 PSC. Secured from General Quarters and set condition III.

Approved: [signed]   *Examined:* [signed]
L. H. FROST,   T. H. COPEMAN,
Lt. Comdr. U.S. Navy,   Lieutenant.
Commanding.

Source 13 from National Archives, Record Item T1022, Rolls 3387–3388. Translated by Christiane M. Hunley.

13. Report of U-652 (German submarine), September 4, 1941.[12]

Time	Occurrences
445	Remained Stopped
445–725	Diving Test
909	Diving alert because of aircraft in 80 degrees, has 2 motors, very high, but close
	Because the crew is tired from the night before, and I do not wish to be surprised once again (the Warrant Officer is of the opinion that we are still undiscovered), I remain underwater
1200	I made the mistake and did not go on a different course
1230	I want to go to periscope depth, but when I have reached 28 meters [from the surface] suddenly at 1230 there fall 3 bombs. I
1300	remain at first at a depth of 25 meters and then go to periscope depth. Perhaps I have an oil trace and, therefore, I want to get away as soon as possible.
1322	Without being heard, a destroyer with 4 chimneys lies in a distance of 1200 meters. Position bow to the right 5-10, apparently stopped.
1328	Course 200 degrees, depth 30 meters. Destroyer is of the same type as in the convoy on 8/25 and 8/26/1941, one of the 50 American vessels that are now sailing for England.
1417	Thus, this is in fact the destroyer which released what were in fact [the three] water bombs at 1230.
	However, I still cannot explain its silent approach. I want to distance myself as soon as possible from this sinister companion.
1420	Have gone to periscope depth. Nothing heard on the hydrophone. The enemy should be at the elapsed distance, if he had remained stopped and stayed at his old location. Instead, he is in a position directly behind me. . . . I can now only believe that I can be heard exactly in his hydrophone and that he follows me with the most frugal turns in such a way that I cannot hear him in the aft sector. Even his backup machines cannot be heard. A plane is flying in the lowest altitude over the destroyer, apparently a large plane. I now must assume that the plane did see me this morning and that it has ordered the destroyer to this location. However, I still do not understand his tentative behavior. I must assume that he wants to slowly starve me [of oxygen], because I cannot count on surfacing unnoticed in the clear visibility of night. Also, he probably can keep this distance, if he succeeded so far.

12. At the conclusion of World War II, all German U-boat records fell into Allied hands and were deposited in the National Archives in Washington, D.C.

CHAPTER 8

PRESIDENTIAL
LEADERSHIP,
PUBLIC OPINION,
AND THE
COMING OF
WORLD WAR II:
THE USS *GREER*
INCIDENT,
SEPTEMBER 4,
1941

Time	Occurrences
1425	Since I must assume that I am being pursued and in order to avoid further attacks as well, or feint attacks, I am now changing to an underwater attack. . . . I can clearly see the enemy: no flag, no name or insignia, caps on the 4 chimneys—an old tin can. [Torpedo fired]
1439	*Bad shot.* Course of attack was incorrectly calculated. The enemy's course was mistakenly assumed to be 230 degrees, although before it was clearly 180 degrees. A quick movement at the time of the shot causes us to conclude that opponent's speed was accelerated, which was not recognized in the periscope as the closeness forced us to use the periscope sparingly. The enemy has either seen me while firing, because he knew I was [close], or heard me, because he must have had me exactly on his instrument. But I only thought later about the fact that for these reasons the unnoticed shot was not successful. [Second torpedo fired]
1447	I shot with true position from approximately 120 degrees, but did not manage to achieve the calculated course of attack. . . .
1505–1740	Five water bombs [depth charges], still somewhat spread. Damage only in the diesel room (light bulbs). Moving further to the north, turning several times, going to counter course as the destroyer still often comes close.
2050	Moving slowly in the general direction of NW with a depth of 50 meters. In the E-room the bilge is filling because of the leaking portside sternpost bushing, cannot be pulled along. Either the destroyer already has lost me or follows me. . . .
2324	Two airplanes circle in the destroyer's vicinity, one of which comes awfully close to me. . . . One water bomb [depth charge], further away. . . .

Source 14 from *New York Times*, September 5, 1941.

14. News Report of the *Greer* Incident, 1941.

WASHINGTON, Sept. 4—A submarine of undetermined nationality attacked the United States destroyer Greer this morning in the Atlantic on the way to Iceland, the Navy Department stated tonight. Torpedoes were fired at the vessel.

The Greer, which was not damaged, counter-attacked by dropping depth charges, the announcement said.

President Roosevelt, it was learned, was at once apprised of the incident, but there was no immediate comment from the White House. A spokesman for the State Department said that it was a question for the Navy and that he was not authorized to make any statement.

The Navy reported the attack as follows:

"The U. S. S. Destroyer Greer, en route to Iceland with mail, reported this morning that a submarine had attacked her by firing torpedoes which missed their mark.

"The Greer immediately counter-attacked with depth charges. Results are not known."

The attacking submarine was assumed to be German.

The destroyer was operating as a part of the Atlantic patrol which was established by President Roosevelt early in the Summer. At that time the White House stated that the duties of the patrol were to report to the Navy Department the presence of any potentially hostile craft.

In addition to being the first attack on an American warship in the European war the incident is the first of a warlike nature since American forces took over occupation of Iceland at the invitation of the Icelandic government early in the Summer. . . .

Source 15 from *New York Times*, September 6, 1941.

15. Additional News Concerning the *Greer* Incident, 1941.

REYKJAVIK, Iceland, Sept. 5—The men of the United States destroyer Greer, which was attacked by a submarine on the way to Iceland, said on their arrival here today that the Greer's depth charges might well have sunk the undersea vessel.

The incident was described here as a German attack.

The Greer's officers and crew expressed the conviction that they had at least damaged the submarine, for their instruments indicated that they were directly above her when they dropped their bombs.

The destroyer was in very deep water at the time, they added, and thus the submarine may have been sunk without trace.

The American warship was assisted in repelling the attack by British aircraft, they said. Those in the vicinity cooperated in reconnaissance. . . .

CHAPTER 8

PRESIDENTIAL
LEADERSHIP,
PUBLIC OPINION,
AND THE
COMING OF
WORLD WAR II:
THE USS *GREER*
INCIDENT,
SEPTEMBER 4,
1941

Sources 16 and 17 from Patrick Abbazia, *Mr. Roosevelt's Navy: The Private War of the U.S. Atlantic Fleet, 1939–1942* (Annapolis: Naval Institute Press, 1975), pp. 52, 176.

16. Wehrmacht[13] Command Memorandum, September 1939.

The American Neutrality Law is a shackle for the most war-loving of American Presidents, one which presumably cannot be shaken off so long as we do not provide him with the excuse to breach this shackle. . . . Even if we are convinced that, should the war be of long duration, the USA will enter it in any case . . . it must be our object to delay this event so long that American help would come too late.

17. Hitler to Admiral Raeder, Führer Conference, May 22, 1941.

Weapons are not to be used. Even if American vessels conduct themselves in a definitely unneutral manner . . . weapons are to be used *only if US ships fire the first shot.*

Source 18 from *New York Times,* September 7, 1941.

18. German Communiqué, September 6, 1941.

On the fourth of September a German submarine was attacked with depth bombs and continuously pursued in the German blockade zone at a point charted at Lat. 62 degrees 31 minutes N. and Long. 27 degrees 6 minutes W. The German submarine was unable to establish the nationality of the attacking destroyer.

In justified defense against the attack, the submarine thereupon at 14:39 o'clock fired two torpedoes at the destroyer, both of which missed aim. The destroyer continued its pursuit and attacks with depth bombs until midnight, then abandoned them.

If official American quarters, namely the Navy Department, assert the attack was initiated by the German submarine, such charge can only have the purpose of giving the attack of an American destroyer on a German submarine which was undertaken in complete violation of neutrality a semblance of legality. This attack is evidence that President Roosevelt despite his previous assertions to the contrary has commanded American

13. *Wehrmacht* is the German military.

destroyers not only to report the location of German U-Boats and other German craft as violating neutrality but also to proceed to attack them.

Roosevelt there is endeavoring with all the means at his disposal to provoke incidents for the purpose of baiting the American people into the war.

Source 19 from Samuel I. Rosenman, *The Public Papers and Addresses of Franklin D. Roosevelt* (New York: Harper & Brothers, 1950), Vol. X, pp. 374–377.

19. FDR Press Conference, September 5, 1941.[14]

THE PRESIDENT. You will all be asking about the attack of yesterday, so we might as well clear that up first.

There is nothing to add, except that there was more than one attack, and that it occurred in daylight, and it occurred definitely on the American side of the ocean. This time there is nothing more to add except two thoughts I have. I heard one or two broadcasters this morning, and I read a few things that have been said by people in Washington, which reminded me of a—perhaps we might call it an allegory.

Once upon a time, at a place where I was living, there were some school children living out in the country who were on their way to school, and somebody undisclosed fired a number of shots at them from the bushes. The father of the children took the position that there wasn't anything to do about it—search the bushes, and take any other steps—because the children hadn't been hit. I don't think that's a bad illustration, in regard to the position of some people this morning.

The destroyer—it is a very, very fortunate thing that the destroyer was not hit in these attacks. And I think that is all that can be said on the subject today.

Q. Mr. President, there is one thing that occurred to me, and I wondered if you could clear that up: Was the identification of our ship solely by that little flag astern, or were there other ships going with this destroyer? Were there larger ships that made identification much easier?

THE PRESIDENT. She was alone at the time, clearly marked. Of course an identification number was on her, plus the flag. And the fact remains that, as I said before, there was more than one attack.

Q. Mr. President, does that mean more than one torpedo, or—

14. Roosevelt delighted in holding press conferences, and this was his 767th since taking office in March 1933. He averaged about two per week.

CHAPTER 8

PRESIDENTIAL
LEADERSHIP,
PUBLIC OPINION,
AND THE
COMING OF
WORLD WAR II:
THE USS *GREER*
INCIDENT,
SEPTEMBER 4,
1941

THE PRESIDENT. *(interposing)* More than one attack.

Q. On the same ship, Mr. President?

THE PRESIDENT. On the same ship. . . .

Q. What did you say, sir, about being on the—you said on the American side of the ocean?

THE PRESIDENT. Yes.

Q. Plainly on the American side?

THE PRESIDENT. Yes, yes. . . .

Q. Mr. President, how would you class this incident with regard to a shooting war?

THE PRESIDENT. Oh, well, those are hypothetical questions. I said that was all there was to be said about it.

Q. As another landlubber, I would like to ask a question here. Is it possible for a destroyer to be on the American side of the Atlantic, and still be within the zone delineated by Mr. Hitler as a belligerent zone?

THE PRESIDENT. Such a zone—of course, in the first place, we have never been notified of it, and in the second place it was said to be a blockade. Well, of course, everybody knows that a blockade is never recognized unless it is effective. . . .

Source 20 from Russell D. Buhite and David W. Levy, eds., *F.D.R.'s Fireside Chats* (Norman: University of Oklahoma Press, 1992), pp. 189–196.

20. FDR's Fireside Chat, September 11, 1941.

My fellow Americans. The Navy Department of the United States has reported to me that on the morning of September 4, the United States destroyer *Greer*, proceeding in full daylight toward Iceland, had reached a point southeast of Greenland. She was carrying American mail to Iceland. She was flying the American flag. Her identity as an American ship was unmistakable.

She was then and there attacked by a submarine. Germany admits that it was a German submarine. The submarine deliberately fired a torpedo at the *Greer*, followed later by another torpedo attack. In spite of what Hitler's propaganda bureau has invented, and in spite of what any American obstructionist organization may prefer to believe, I tell you the blunt fact that the German submarine fired first upon this American destroyer without warning, and with deliberate design to sink her.

Our destroyer, at the time, was in waters which the government of the United States had declared to be waters of self-defense—surrounding outposts of American protection in the Atlantic. . . .

The United States destroyer, when attacked, was proceeding on a legitimate mission.

If the destroyer was visible to the submarine when the torpedo was fired, then the attack was a deliberate attempt by the Nazis to sink a clearly identified American warship. On the other hand, if the submarine was beneath the surface of the sea and, with the aid of its listening devices, fired in the direction of the sound of the American destroyer without even taking the trouble to learn its identity—as the official German communiqué would indicate—then the attack was even more outrageous. For it indicates a policy of indiscriminate violence against any vessel sailing the seas—belligerent or nonbelligerent.

This was piracy—piracy legally and morally. It was not the first nor the last act of piracy which the Nazi government has committed against the American flag in this war. For attack has followed attack. . . .

[Here Roosevelt listed other attacks and threats, including the sinking of the three U.S. merchant ships, one of them flying the Panamanian flag.]

It would be unworthy of a great nation to exaggerate an isolated incident, or to become inflamed by some one act of violence. But it would be inexcusable folly to minimize such incidents in the face of evidence which makes it clear that the incident is not isolated, but is part of a general plan.

The important truth is that these acts of international lawlessness are a manifestation of a design, a design that has been made clear to the American people for a long time. It is the Nazi design to abolish the freedom of the seas, and to acquire absolute control and domination of these seas for themselves.

For with control of the seas in their own hands, the way can obviously become clear for their next step—domination of the United States, domination of the Western Hemisphere by force of arms. Under Nazi control of the seas, no merchant ship of the United States or of any other American republic would be free to carry on any peaceful commerce, except by the condescending grace of this foreign and tyrannical power. The Atlantic Ocean which has been, and which should always be, a free and friendly highway for us would then become a deadly menace to the commerce of the United States, to the coasts of the United States, and even to the inland cities of the United States.

CHAPTER 8

PRESIDENTIAL
LEADERSHIP,
PUBLIC OPINION,
AND THE
COMING OF
WORLD WAR II:
THE USS *GREER*
INCIDENT,
SEPTEMBER 4,
1941

The Hitler government, in defiance of the laws of the sea, in defiance of the recognized rights of all other nations, has presumed to declare, on paper, that great areas of the seas—even including a vast expanse lying in the Western Hemisphere—are to be closed, and that no ships may enter them for any purpose, except at peril of being sunk. Actually they are sinking ships at will and without warning in widely separated areas both within and far outside of these far-flung pretended zones.

This Nazi attempt to seize control of the oceans is but a counterpart of the Nazi plots now being carried on throughout the Western Hemisphere— all designed toward the same end. For Hitler's advance guards—not only his avowed agents but also, also his dupes among us—have sought to make ready for him footholds, bridgeheads in the New World, to be used as soon as he has gained control of the oceans. . . .

To be ultimately successful in world mastery, Hitler knows that he must get control of the seas. He must first destroy the bridge of ships which we are building across the Atlantic and over which we shall continue to roll the implements of war to help destroy him, to destroy all his works in the end. He must wipe out our patrol on sea and in the air if he is to do it. . . .

[*Here Roosevelt warned that if Britain were to fall, the Western Hemisphere would be left standing alone against Hitler. Calling Naziism "an enemy of all law, all liberty, all morality, all religion," the president stated that the United States would not make the mistake of other nations that had "refused to look the Nazi danger squarely in the eye until it actually had them by the throat."*]

These Nazi submarines and raiders are the rattlesnakes of the Atlantic. They are a menace to the free pathways of the high seas. They are a challenge to our own sovereignty. They hammer at our most precious rights when they attack ships of the American flag—symbols of our independence, our freedom, our very life. . . .

If submarines or raiders attack in distant waters, they can attack equally well within sight of our own shores. Their very presence in any waters which America deems vital to its defense constitutes an attack.

In the waters which we deem necessary for our defense, American naval vessels and American planes will no longer wait until Axis submarines lurking under the water, or Axis raiders on the surface of the sea, strike their deadly blow—first.

Upon our naval and air patrol—now operating in large number over a vast expanse of the Atlantic Ocean—falls the duty of maintaining the American policy of freedom of the seas—now. That means, very simply, very clearly, that our patrolling vessels and planes will protect all merchant ships—not only American ships but ships of any flag—engaged in commerce in our defensive waters. They will protect them from submarines; they will protect them from surface raiders. . . .

My obligation as president is historic; it is clear. Yes, it is inescapable.

It is no act of war on our part when we decide to protect the seas that are vital to American defense. The aggression is not ours. Ours is solely defense.

But let this warning be clear. From now on, if German or Italian vessels of war enter the waters, the protection of which is necessary for American defense, they do so at their own peril.

The orders which I have given as commander in chief of the United States Army and Navy are to carry out that policy—at once.

The sole responsibility rests upon Germany. There will be no shooting unless Germany continues to seek it.

That is my obvious duty in this crisis. That is the clear right of this sovereign nation. This is the only step possible, if we would keep tight the wall of defense which we are pledged to maintain around this Western Hemisphere.

I have no illusions about the gravity of this step. I have not taken it hurriedly or lightly. It is the result of months and months of constant thought and anxiety and prayer. In the protection of your nation and mine it cannot be avoided.

The American people have faced other grave crises in their history—with American courage, with American resolution. They will do no less today.

They know the actualities of the attacks upon us. They know the necessities of a bold defense against these attacks. They know that the times call for clear heads and fearless hearts.

And with that inner strength that comes to a free people conscious of their duty, conscious of the righteousness of what they do, they will—with divine help and guidance—stand their ground against this latest assault upon their democracy, their sovereignty, and their freedom.

Source 21 from *New York Times,* September 16, 1941.

21. Excerpts from a Speech by Secretary of the Navy Frank Knox to the American Legion Convention, September 15, 1941.

. . . A German submarine encountered an American destroyer engaged in carrying mail to our outpost on Iceland. The encounter came in broad

CHAPTER 8

PRESIDENTIAL
LEADERSHIP,
PUBLIC OPINION,
AND THE
COMING OF
WORLD WAR II:
THE USS *GREER*
INCIDENT,
SEPTEMBER 4,
1941

daylight and the American destroyer carried identification marks which left no possible room for doubt as to its nationality.

At close range the submarine discharged three torpedoes aimed at the American destroyer. The Greer evaded them and promptly attacked the submarine with depth charges. After the second depth-charge attack all contact with the submarine was lost by the destroyer.

Immediately upon receipt of this news, the Navy Department gave the public every fact in its possession, based upon the dispatch direct from the commander of the American destroyer. The German Government countered by saying that the American destroyer had fired the first shot.

The whole issue is far too broad to make the question of who fired first of great importance. I allude to it chiefly because it offered a chance for that curious organization known as "the America First Committee"[15] to tell the American public that, in its judgment, it was more likely the German U-boat commander was telling the truth than the American naval officer who commanded the Greer.

That is an important fact for the American public to digest: that we have in our midst an organization of American citizens who, on a question of veracity, declared publicly that they prefer to accept the word of a piratical murderer of women and children on the high seas, engaged in a type of warfare denounced by every civilized nation in the world, rather than accept the word of an American commander of an American warship. . . .

Source 22 from Leland M. Goodrich, ed., *Documents on American Foreign Relations* (Boston: World Peace Foundation, 1942), Vol. IV, pp. 95–99.

22. Written Statement of Admiral Harold R. Stark to the Senate Naval Affairs Committee, Undated (committee sent the request for a statement to Stark on September 5, 1941).

On September 4, 1941, at 08:40 G. C. T., the U.S.S. *Greer,* while en route to Iceland with United States mail and passengers and some freight, was informed by a British plane of the presence of a submerged submarine, distance about 10 miles directly ahead.

This British plane continued in the vicinity of the submarine until 10:52 when she departed. Prior to her departure, at 10:32, she dropped four depth charges in the vicinity of the submarine.

15. The *America First Committee,* formed in September 1940, was a group that sought to mobilize American public opinion against intervention in the war. At its peak, the group had over eight hundred thousand members.

Acting on the information from the British plane the *Greer* proceeded to search for the submarine and at 09:20 she located the submarine directly ahead by her underwater sound equipment. The *Greer* proceeded then to trail the submarine and broadcasted the submarine's position. This action taken by the *Greer* was in accordance with her orders, that is, to give out information but not to attack.

The *Greer* maintained this contact until about 12:48. During this period (3 hours 28 minutes) the *Greer* maneuvered so as to keep the submarine ahead.

At 12:40 the submarine changed course and closed the *Greer*.

The disturbance of the surface and the change in color of the water marking the passage of the submarine was clearly distinguished by the *Greer*.

At 12:48 an impulse bubble (indicating the discharge of a torpedo by the submarine) was sighted close aboard the *Greer*.

At 12:49 a torpedo track was sighted crossing the wake of the ship from starboard to port, distant about 100 yards astern.

At 12:56 the *Greer* attacked the submarine with a pattern of eight depth charges.

At 12:58 a second torpedo track was sighted on the starboard bow of the *Greer*, distant about 500 yards. The *Greer* avoided this torpedo.

At this time the *Greer* lost sound contact with the submarine.

At 13:00 the *Greer* started searching for the submarine and at 15:12 in latitude 62–43 N., longitude 27–22 W., the *Greer* made underwater contact with a submarine. The *Greer* attacked immediately with depth charges.

In neither of the *Greer*'s attacks did she observe any results which would indicate that the attacks on the submarine had been effective.

The *Greer* continued search until 18:40, at which time she again proceeded toward her destination, Iceland.

From the above it is clearly evident that the *Greer*, though continuously in contact with the submarine for 3 hours 28 minutes, did not attack the submarine although the *Greer* herself was exposed to attack.

At no time did the *Greer* sight the submarine's periscope.

The weather was good.

The commander-in-chief of the Atlantic Fleet corroborates the above report in detail and further states that the action taken by the *Greer* was correct in every particular in accordance with her existing orders.

H. R. Stark

CHAPTER 8

PRESIDENTIAL
LEADERSHIP,
PUBLIC OPINION,
AND THE
COMING OF
WORLD WAR II:
THE USS *GREER*
INCIDENT,
SEPTEMBER 4,
1941

Questions Addressed to the Secretary of the Navy, by the Chairman of the Senate Naval Affairs Committee, and Proposed Answers Thereto, in Connection with the "Greer" Incident

QUESTION 1. Did the incident take place in an area declared to be blockaded by the German Government?

ANSWER. The *Greer* incident took place in an area approximately 175 miles southwest of Iceland, and directly in the path of communication between American ports and Iceland. This area was within the zone of operations announced by the German Government on March 26, 1941, as a zone within which vessels entering exposed themselves "to the danger of destruction."

QUESTION 2. Did the *Greer* have orders from the Department to proceed through this area?

ANSWER. The *Greer* had orders from the commander-in-chief of the Atlantic Fleet to proceed through the area. The Navy Department had full knowledge of this.

QUESTION 3. Were any other ships in company with, or in sight of, the *Greer* just before or at any time during the encounter? If so, (*a*) what were the names and nationality of these vessels, and (*b*) did any of these ships take part in the encounter either directly or indirectly?

ANSWER. A British destroyer was in sight about 5 miles distant from the *Greer* when the *Greer* made a depth bomb attack at 15:12. This British destroyer had arrived on the scene at 14:15 and had asked the *Greer* if she (the *Greer*) desired to conduct a coordinated search for the submarine. To this question, the *Greer* replied "No." The British destroyer stood through the area and disappeared to the southward.

QUESTION 4. Were any airplanes in sight of, or in communication with, the *Greer* just before or during the encounter? If so, (*a*) what were the nationality of these planes, and (*b*) did any of these planes furnish any information to the *Greer* or take part either directly or indirectly in the encounter?

ANSWER. Yes. At 08:40, a British plane approached the U.S.S. *Greer* and signaled that a submarine had submerged about 10 miles directly ahead of the *Greer.* The plane furnished no further assistance to the *Greer.* At 10:32, this plane dropped four depth charges in the vicinity of the submarine and, at 10:52, the plane departed from the area. It should be particularly noted that this plane left the area at 10:52 and did not return, and that the *Greer* fired no guns or torpedoes or dropped any depth charges until 12:56—some 8 minutes after the submarine fired a torpedo at the *Greer*—or, in other words, over 2 hours after the British plane had left the scene.

QUESTION 5. Was the commanding officer of the *Greer* informed that a submarine was operating in this vicinity before his vessel was attacked or before the submarine or her periscope was seen? If so, when and from whom did he receive this information?

ANSWER. Yes. See answer to preceding question. The periscope of the submarine was not seen at any time by the *Greer.*

QUESTION 6. If he had information from an outside source that there was a submarine in the vicinity, (*a*) did he change his course and speed and start a search for the submarine; (*b*) how long did he search for the submarine before he was fired upon; and (*c*) did other vessels or planes assist in this search?

ANSWER. As soon as information was received by the *Greer* from the British plane that a submarine was directly ahead of her, the *Greer* increased speed, started zigzagging, and commenced a search for the submarine. Five minutes after the search began, namely, at 09:20, the *Greer* located the submarine by her underwater sound equipment; she held this contact until 12:48, namely, 3 hours 28 minutes before the submarine made her attack. No assistance by either planes or ships was given to the *Greer* during this period.

QUESTION 7. If he first learned of the presence of the submarine from his submarine detection device or from sighting it, (*a*) did he change his course to search for or head for the submarine; or (*b*) would he have been out of range of the submarine's torpedoes if he had continued on his course?

ANSWER. The first part of this question is answered by the answer to the preceding question. As to the second part of this question, the answer is problematical. No person can predict what the submarine's course would have been. The answer, therefore, might be "Yes" or it might be "No."

QUESTION 8. How many torpedoes were fired at the *Greer* and at what intervals were they fired? How long was it after the submarine was sighted or first heard that the first torpedoes were fired? How near did the torpedoes come to hitting the ship?

ANSWER. Two torpedoes were fired at the *Greer.* The firing of the first one was indicated by the sighting of the impulse bubble at 12:48, just 3 hours and 28 minutes after the *Greer* first detected the submarine by means of her sound equipment. At 12:49 the wake of this torpedo was observed about 100 yards astern. At 12:58 the wake of a second torpedo was observed 500 yards distant on the starboard bow. The *Greer* avoided it, the torpedo passing about 300 yards clear of the ship.

QUESTION 9. How many depth charges were dropped by the *Greer* and at what intervals?

CHAPTER 8

PRESIDENTIAL
LEADERSHIP,
PUBLIC OPINION,
AND THE
COMING OF
WORLD WAR II:
THE USS *GREER*
INCIDENT,
SEPTEMBER 4,
1941

ANSWER. U.S.S. *Greer* dropped 8 depth charges, commencing at 12:56; 11 depth charges were dropped, commencing at 15:12. All these depth charges were dropped after the first torpedo had been fired at the *Greer.*

QUESTION 10. Has anything been seen or heard from this submarine since the last depth charges were dropped by the *Greer*?

ANSWER. Not by the U.S.S. *Greer,* nor has the Department any word.

[*The remainder of the questions concerned the deck log of the* Greer *(which Stark refused to make public) and whether the German embassy had issued any official explanation of the incident (it had not).*]

Source 23 from *Congressional Record—Senate,* 77th Congress, 1st sess., pp. 8283–8284.

23. Excerpt from a Speech by Senator Robert A. Taft (Rep., Ohio) to the Senate, October 28, 1941.

Mr. President the whole approach of the administration today seems to be one of war. I think it is fair to say—at least, the impression given from the newspapers is—that the administration welcomes every incident which may possibly lead to war. Those incidents are not reported in the usual way. They are announced by the President at a press conference. They are sent out to the whole world as something by which, on the whole, the government is delighted. The story of the *Greer* was told by the President, it seems to me, in such a way as deliberately to incite more feeling than was justified by the actual event which occurred. He said, for instance: "Our destroyer at the time was in waters which the government of the United States had declared to be waters of self-defense, surrounding outposts of American protection in the Atlantic. The United States destroyer, when attacked, was proceeding on a legitimate mission."

As a matter of fact, the facts which came out much later before a committee, when the public had forgotten the *Greer,* show that it was in the neighborhood of a submarine of which it was told by a British destroyer which was also there; that after it had located the submarine a British plane came and dropped four depth bombs; and that the *Greer* then turned off its course and chased the submarine for three hours and twenty minutes, zigzagging in the way that a vessel would zigzag if it were going to attack a submarine. Whether or not the submarine was justified in finally shooting a torpedo, whether or not it thought this was a joint British-American attack, certainly the President's report of the incident was made in such a way as deliberately to incite the American people. No man who sincerely desired peace would have failed to state the actual circumstances. . . .

Mr. President, I may say that convoying was proposed last spring, but there was so much opposition to convoys that authority to convoy never was specifically presented to Congress. Apparently without such presentation we now have the United States engaging in convoying. But the point I wanted to make is that the whole intention of the administration, every indication that a reasonable man can draw from its acts, is that it intends to go into war; and certainly, if we pass this resolution, and the administration has such an intention, we are going very shortly to become involved in war.

There is no argument made today that, after all, we are already at war, and therefore we should not hesitate to go on and vote authority to conduct war. The power to declare war rests solely in the United States Congress. If the President can declare or create an undeclared naval war beyond our power to act upon, the Constitution might just as well be abolished. The Constitution deliberately gave to the representatives of the people the power to declare war, to pass on the question of war and peace, because that was something which kings had always done, which they had done against the interests of the people themselves, and which the founders of the Constitution thought the people ought to determine. It is true there have been one or two acts of war; but if Congress will refuse to repeal the Neutrality Act, I do not believe those acts of war can be continued. . . .

✳ QUESTIONS TO CONSIDER ✳

Almost immediately you will see that you will have to rearrange the evidence *twice:* once to answer the first question (What *actually happened* in the *Greer* incident of September 4, 1941?) and a second time to answer the second question (What was the relationship between President Roosevelt's actions and American public opinion?). Although at first you may feel that rearranging the evidence twice will be too time-consuming, in fact it should save you a great amount of time, principally because several pieces of evidence may be set aside when answering either of the two questions (for example, Sources 1 through 11 are of no use in answering the first question).

To determine what actually happened in the *Greer* incident, Sources 12 through 23 all have a bearing. And yet a number of these accounts are at serious variance with one another. Lieutenant T. H. Copeman, who composed the *Greer*'s deck log, and the author of U-652's report obviously were the two sources closest to the incident itself. Do those two accounts (Sources 12 and 13) vary in any sig-

CHAPTER 8
PRESIDENTIAL
LEADERSHIP,
PUBLIC OPINION,
AND THE
COMING OF
WORLD WAR II:
THE USS *GREER*
INCIDENT,
SEPTEMBER 4,
1941

nificant way? Are there any reasons that they should not be judged the most believable accounts? Since he was the only other source presented to you who actually saw the *Greer*'s deck log, does Admiral Stark's account (Source 22) differ in any important way with the deck log itself? How do the three German sources (Sources 16 through 18) corroborate or fail to corroborate the two eyewitness accounts in Sources 12 and 13 (Sources 16 and 17, obviously, by inference, since these two sources were written long before the incident itself)?

The *New York Times*'s reports on the incident (Sources 14 and 15) contain some significant errors. What are those errors? Why do you think this was so? What were the *Times*'s sources?

The accounts by President Roosevelt (Sources 19 and 20) and by Secretary of the Navy Frank Knox (Source 21) also appear to contain some important inaccuracies. What are they? Do you think that FDR and Knox were misinformed? Did they know what actually had occurred? If they did, what possible motivation might they have had for not being truthful?

Taft (Source 23) was a fierce Republican opponent of the president. Moreover, he was against American intervention in the war in Europe. What point does Taft make regarding the *Greer* incident? With what does he charge Roosevelt? How believable are those charges?

After examining and analyzing each source (especially as to any motivation behind each source's account), you should be able to answer the first question: What *actually happened* in the *Greer* incident?

In order to answer the second question, you will have to make use of George Gallup's polling data (Sources 1 through 11). You are looking for any changes or shifts in public opinion. For example, Gallup's poll taken April 10–15, 1941 (Source 2), revealed that 50 percent of those surveyed did not think the United States Navy should guard ships carrying war materiel to Britain. Yet by the time that question was next asked (on May 8–13, 1941, Source 4), fully 52 percent thought that the navy should do so—and only 41 percent opposed. How might Roosevelt have interpreted that shift?

Keep in mind the complexities of using polling data as historical evidence. For instance, you will want to differentiate between when a particular public opinion poll *was taken* and when its results *were released*. Although Source 6 shows the results of a Gallup poll that *was released* to the press on September 23, 1941, nineteen days after the *Greer* incident, that poll actually *was taken* on August 21–26, a week or more before the incident took place.

You will also want to establish whether any significant events took place from the time one poll was taken to the time another poll took place. The *Greer* incident, for example, occurred on September 4, 1941, after the poll in Source 6 was taken but before the results in Source 7 were summarized. Therefore, you will need to fill in the important events between the Gallup polls. Consult the Background section of this chapter and other sources. An examination of the 1941 volume of the printed index of the *New York Times* (almost surely in the reference section of your library or a nearby library) will prove helpful.

Finally, it is important to know when the results of a poll were released as well as when that particular poll was taken because respondents often are influenced by what other people think regarding a particular issue or question. They might actually change their minds once they see the results of an earlier poll.

As you examine and analyze the principal events of 1941 and know how they might have been reflected in the public opinion polls, pay special attention to President Roosevelt's actions and speeches. Can you establish whether Roosevelt was shaping public opinion (therefore ahead of it), was waiting for shifts in public opinion before taking action, or both—sometimes leading and sometimes following? How were his remarks about the *Greer* incident (Sources 19 and 20) perhaps intended to shape public opinion? Or did the polls (especially Sources 4 through 6) allow the president to detect an important shift in public opinion that would make his policy shift announced in the September 11 fireside chat acceptable to Americans? See Source 7, a poll taken after the fireside chat. Was Roosevelt shaping public opinion, following it, or doing both?

❋ EPILOGUE ❋

President Roosevelt's policy shift of September 11, 1941 (escorting convoys of Lend-Lease goods and shooting on sight German submarines), clearly put the United States on a collision course with the Third Reich. It was only a matter of time before a United States naval vessel would be hit by a U-boat torpedo. On October 16–17, 1941, the USS *Kearny,* speeding to the aid of a convoy that was under attack, dropped depth charges into the water and almost immediately was hit by a German torpedo. The *Kearny* limped to port under escort. Then, on the night of October 30–31, 1941, the USS *Reuben James* was sunk by a torpedo while escorting a convoy west of Iceland, with a loss of 115 American sailors. Americans were outraged, and public opinion decidedly shifted against Germany. Congress amended the Neutrality Act to allow American ships to take Lend-Lease supplies to Britain. Clearly the United States had abandoned its neutral posture. And yet, because the vote in the House of Representatives to extend the draft had passed by only one vote and because Hitler wanted no diversions from his life-and-death struggle against the Soviet Union,[16] no actual declaration of war came from either side. Nevertheless, a shooting war had begun in the Atlantic.

And yet as Americans concentrated their attention on the nation's slipping into war in Europe, it was United States–Japanese relations that ultimately brought the United States into

16. After signing the Non-Aggression Pact with Stalin, on June 22, 1941, Hitler attacked the Soviet Union in what was known as Operation Barbarossa.

CHAPTER 8

PRESIDENTIAL
LEADERSHIP,
PUBLIC OPINION,
AND THE
COMING OF
WORLD WAR II:
THE USS *GREER*
INCIDENT,
SEPTEMBER 4,
1941

World War II. Relations between the two countries had been testy since the National Origins Act of 1929 almost completely banned the immigration of all Asians, a move that Japan considered a racial slap in the face. When Japan invaded Manchuria in September 1931, the United States refused to recognize Japan's conquests or its puppet government in Manchuria and sided with China against Japan. On September 27, 1940, Japan signed the Tripartite Pact with Germany and Italy, promising that if the United States joined Great Britain in the Atlantic war, then Japan would attack the United States in the Pacific, whereas if the United States declared war on Japan, then Germany and Italy would declare war on the United States. Relations went from bad to worse as the United States, increasingly committed to China as well as to blocking Japanese expansion, moved to freeze all Japanese assets in the United States, cut off petroleum exports to Japan, and ultimately clamp a total trade embargo on Japan. On December 7, 1941, Japanese dive bombers and torpedo planes attacked Pearl Harbor in Hawaii. On December 8, Congress declared war on Japan, and on December 11, the German Reichstag declared war on the "half Judaized and the other half Negrified" American people. After nearly two years of slipping precariously toward

conflict, the United States at last was a combatant in World War II.

One of Franklin Roosevelt's biographers, James MacGregor Burns, described him as a lion and a fox. British prime minister Winston Churchill and many historians have concluded that Roosevelt had made up his mind to enter the war in Europe as early as January 1941, when the British and American military staffs held secret talks in Washington on a "broad design for the joint defense of the Atlantic Ocean" and on preparations for joint convoys of Lend-Lease goods.[17] Yet Roosevelt did not believe that the American public would support a war against Germany in January 1941. Instead, he would have to wait for public opinion to shift—or he would have to shape that opinion. The *Greer* incident may have been a pivotal event on the road to war.

U-652 escaped the *Greer*'s depth charges and went on to sink two British destroyers on March 20 and 26, 1942. The submarine was severely damaged by an air attack in the Aegean Sea in June 1942, and was sunk by U-81 after the crew had been recovered.

The USS *Greer* served throughout the war and was decommissioned on July 19, 1945. The destroyer was sold for scrap to the Boston Metal Salvage Company of Baltimore, Maryland, on November 30, 1945.

17. Winston S. Churchill, *The Grand Alliance,* Vol. III of *The Second World War* (Boston: Houghton Mifflin Co., 1950), pp. 137–138.

9

Separate but Equal?
African American Educational
Opportunities and the
Brown Decision

❋ THE PROBLEM ❋

In the mid-1890s, Homer Plessy took his seat in a passenger coach on a Louisiana train. Plessy's racial heritage was seven-eighths European American and one-eighth African American, and the railroad compartment in which he was sitting was reserved for whites. Asked to vacate his seat and move to the compartment reserved for blacks, Plessy refused and was arrested. He had violated an 1890 Louisiana law that required separate railroad accommodations for African Americans and for whites. People who broke the law by sitting in the wrong compartment or coach were fined twenty-five dollars or, if they could not pay, had to serve twenty days in jail. Plessy's action was actually part of a strategy planned by a group of Creole men in New Orleans to test the new race-based law.

After his arrest, Plessy sued, and the case eventually reached the U.S. Supreme Court on appeal. The majority opinion in *Plessy v. Ferguson* was that the Louisiana law was constitutional.[1] Because it provided for "separate but equal" accommodations, the law had not violated any rights guaranteed by the Fourteenth Amendment. In other words, states could legally segregate blacks and whites as long as they provided "separate but equal" facilities for African Americans. In an impassioned dissent, Justice John Marshall Harlan disagreed. "Our Constitution is color-blind," he argued, "and neither knows nor tolerates classes among citizens." But Har-

1. Seven justices agreed with the majority opinion, one abstained, and one (Harlan) dissented.

CHAPTER 9

SEPARATE
BUT EQUAL?
AFRICAN
AMERICAN
EDUCATIONAL
OPPORTUNITIES
AND THE
BROWN DECISION

lan's opinion was not supported by other judges or by the general public.

In fact, for almost sixty years *Plessy v. Ferguson* provided a powerful basis for other judicial decisions upholding segregation laws. Finally, in *Brown v. Board of Education of Topeka* (1954), the Supreme Court unanimously de-

clared that separate but equal schools were unconstitutional. Why did the Court reverse itself after so many years? In this chapter, you will be asked to identify some of the major arguments that finally caused the Supreme Court to change its thinking.

✳ BACKGROUND ✳

In the aftermath of the Civil War, much of the South was in economic and political chaos. Struggles between President Andrew Johnson and the Radical Republicans over who should control Reconstruction meant delay and confusion in readmitting the former Confederate states to the Union and providing economic relief where it was most needed. After nearly removing President Johnson from office, however, the Radicals were able to implement their plans in Congress.

Perhaps no other question of the Reconstruction era was more troublesome and divisive than that of the role of the newly freed slaves. Three amendments to the United States Constitution were intended to settle the legal questions: the Thirteenth Amendment that freed the slaves, the Fourteenth Amendment that defined citizenship and extended the protection of the Bill of Rights to citizens of the separate states, and the Fifteenth Amendment that gave African American men the vote. Would the freed slaves have full political rights? Should they be given land to farm? Could they be protected against discrimination and violence? Although

African Americans briefly enjoyed some political rights and protection, by the late nineteenth century all these questions had been answered negatively. The South had returned to white political control, the Ku Klux Klan and other vigilante groups had limited African American opportunities, and the sharecropping, tenant farming, and crop lien systems had impoverished poor whites and blacks alike. Furthermore, the Union army had withdrawn, and the federal Civil Rights Act of 1875 had been declared unconstitutional. As ordinary people in the North and West turned their attention to their own problems, African Americans in the South were left to fend for themselves.

In 1900, approximately 7 million of the nation's 10 million African Americans lived in the rural South, although more and more younger African Americans were leaving the grinding poverty of the farms and moving to nearby cities and towns seeking better opportunities. The black codes of the Redemption era had evolved into Jim Crow laws that segregated everything from schools and parks to hospitals and cemeteries, while lynching took the lives of seventy-five to one hundred African American men each year. The trickle of African Americans moving North was accelerated by World War I; almost half a million southern blacks moved to northern cities such as Chicago, Cleveland, and Philadelphia to obtain jobs during the war.

By 1920, there were a million and a half African Americans in northern cities. Although rarely segregated by law and permitted to vote, nevertheless they usually faced pervasive discrimination in their search for housing and jobs. Membership in the National Association for the Advancement of Colored People (NAACP) grew steadily as a new black middle class increasingly identified with the civil rights program of W. E. B. Du Bois rather than the accommodationist message of Booker T. Washington.

In the 1920s, a section of New York City called Harlem became the center for a ferment of African American cultural creativity, the Harlem Renaissance. Poets, novelists, artists, actors, dancers, and musicians all explored ways to express their African American experience. Well-to-do whites often supported such efforts and patronized Harlem night spots such as the Cotton Club. Harlem was also badly overcrowded, with decaying housing, epidemic disease, widespread unemployment, and a rising crime rate. The Harlem Renaissance had little meaning for many poor blacks who had recently emigrated from the South. For these newcomers, Jamaican-born Marcus Garvey and his Universal Negro Improvement Association seemed to offer a more practical alternative. Glorifying black cultural roots and sponsoring cooperative business ventures, Garvey also called on African Americans to return to Africa to found a new nation.

Garvey was convicted of fraud, imprisoned, and finally deported in the late 1920s, and the Harlem Renaissance was submerged by the stock market crash of 1929 and the ensuing depression. Both urban and rural blacks suffered extreme hardships during the Great Depression. New Deal urban relief programs were administered locally, and generally African Americans were among the last to receive aid. In the rural South, the New Deal agricultural policies had the unintended result of causing the eviction of sharecroppers and tenant farmers. Violence against African Americans also increased during the depression.

Not until the 1940s did the situation of African Americans begin to improve. In many ways, World War II was a turning point. From the beginning, black leaders declared a "Double V" campaign: a fight against fascism abroad and a fight against racism at home. The NAACP, with a half million members by the end of the war, was joined by the newly formed Congress of Racial Equality (CORE). While the NAACP pursued a strategy of boycotts and legal challenges, CORE began to experiment with nonviolent protests against racial discrimination during the 1940s. Full war production opened up new economic opportunities, nearly a million more African Americans continued the exodus from the South to northern cities, and almost a million blacks served in the armed forces. In spite of some serious race

CHAPTER 9

SEPARATE
BUT EQUAL?
AFRICAN
AMERICAN
EDUCATIONAL
OPPORTUNITIES
AND THE
BROWN DECISION

riots during 1943, African Americans entered the postwar era with rising expectations of equality.

Nowhere were these demands for equality more insistent or pressing than in education. For more than a decade, NAACP lawyers had been involved in cases testing the validity of state segregation laws. By the early 1950s, the Supreme Court had begun strictly scrutinizing separate but equal education to determine whether it really was equal. In 1938, the Court heard a case where a young African American college graduate and Missourian, Lloyd Gaines, had been denied entry into the University of Missouri Law School because he was black.[2] There was no black law school in Missouri, so the state had offered to pay his tuition to any law school in a neighboring state that would accept him. Gaines had been denied equal protection of the laws, the Supreme Court ruled, because Missouri had not provided the same opportunities to black students as it had to white students. Ten years later, a similar case, involving a young woman, Ada Sipuel, who was refused admission to the law school of the University of Oklahoma because of her race, was decided the same way.[3]

In two cases decided in 1950, the Supreme Court expanded the understanding of separate but equal. A black graduate student, George McLaurin, had been admitted to the University of Oklahoma, but was forced to sit at special tables in the cafeteria and in the library and to sit in a separate row in his classes. This was *not* equal treatment, the Court declared.[4] In the second case, *Sweatt v. Painter*, a black student was denied admission to the University of Texas Law School.[5] The state then built two new law schools for African Americans. When the Supreme Court justices compared the faculties, curricula, and libraries of the black and white schools, however, they found substantial inequalities. The opinion went even further, noting that intangible factors such as alumni networks, traditions, and prestige were also superior at the University of Texas Law School. Finally, the Court noted that no student could really learn to practice law at a school that was isolated from 85 percent of the population of the state.

All of these cases involved graduate or professional training and were decided on the question of the *equality* of the facilities. The plaintiffs won these cases because their educational facilities or opportunities were unequal to those provided for whites. In each case, then, *Plessy v. Ferguson* and the doctrine of separate but equal still formed the basis for the decision. Furthermore, the Supreme Court had clearly stated its reluctance to decide any broad constitutional issues, preferring instead to focus on specific questions raised by specific cases. "We have frequently reiterated that this Court will decide constitutional questions only when necessary to the disposition of the case at hand," wrote Chief Justice Fred Vinson in *Sweatt v. Painter* (1950), "and that such deci-

2. *Missouri ex rel. Gaines v. Canada,* 305 U.S. 337 (1938).
3. *Sipuel v. Board of Regents of the University of Oklahoma,* 332 U.S. 631 (1948).

4. *McLaurin v. Oklahoma State Regents,* 339 U.S. 637 (1950).
5. *Sweatt v. Painter,* 339 U.S. 629 (1950).

sions will be drawn as narrowly as possible."

In spite of the cautious stance of the Supreme Court, significant trends and events during the late 1940s and early 1950s were creating a climate more supportive of African American civil rights. The Nazi Holocaust that killed 6 million Jews and the cold war confrontations with the Soviet Union made Americans more aware of the democratic ideals of the United States. In his widely read book, *The American Dilemma,* sociologist Gunnar Myrdal had pointed out America's shortcomings with regard to race relations, and many whites began to feel guilty about the typical treatment of African Americans in the United States.

An outpouring of social science literature also focused on inequality and its effects. Popularized through paperback books, middle-class magazines, and television, much of this research seems relatively unsophisticated by our standards today, although it was pioneering in its time period. For example, Professor Kenneth Clark of City College of New York did research to determine the effects of racial segregation on young African American children. After giving the children identical pink dolls or brown dolls (or pictures of the two sets of dolls), Clark asked the children which dolls were "nice," which dolls were "bad," and which doll the child would rather play with. The majority of the African American children preferred the white doll, identifying the white doll as "nice" and the brown doll as "bad." Such research not only was widely publicized but was also used in court cases by the NAACP to demonstrate the negative psychological effects of segregated schooling on African American children.

Finally, the personnel of the Supreme Court itself had begun to change. Five justices were still serving who had been appointed by President Franklin D. Roosevelt between 1937 and 1941, and President Truman had appointed four new justices between 1945 and 1949. After the Court had started to consider the *Brown* case, the relatively conservative chief justice, Fred Vinson, died suddenly from a heart attack at age sixty-three, and President Eisenhower appointed the more liberal Earl Warren, a former governor of California, to replace Vinson as chief justice.

In 1951, Topeka, Kansas, was a pleasant city of approximately 100,000 residents, 7,500 of whom were African American. The state capital, Topeka, had a city college, a good public library, several city parks, a major psychiatric research institute, and more than 100 churches. It was also segregated. Jim Crow laws and local customs prevented blacks from using white hotels, restaurants, movies, or the municipal swimming pool, and the elementary schools were segregated.

Oliver Brown was a thirty-two-year-old World War II veteran, union member, welder, and assistant pastor of his church. Not a militant, he was not even a member of the NAACP. The Browns lived in a racially mixed neighborhood near a railroad yard, and their oldest daughter, Linda, had to walk about six blocks through the tracks to get to her school bus stop. A white elementary school was located only seven blocks in the other direction from her house, but it refused to accept her because she was an African

CHAPTER 9

SEPARATE
BUT EQUAL?
AFRICAN
AMERICAN
EDUCATIONAL
OPPORTUNITIES
AND THE
BROWN DECISION

American. Brown reported this to the local NAACP and became the first plaintiff in the suit against the Board of Education of Topeka.

In spite of assistance from the national NAACP and the presentation of nationally known social science experts who testified about the negative effects of segregated education, Brown and the other plaintiffs lost the case. The school facilities and other measurable educational factors at the white and black elementary schools were roughly equal, the Kansas court said, referring to the precedent set by the *Plessy* case in 1896. Thus, the segregated schools were legal. However, the Kansas District Court also attached several "Findings of Fact" to its opinion, including one that directly reflected the impact of the social science evidence the NAACP had introduced. "Segregation . . . has a detrimental effect upon the colored children," wrote the judge, and he concluded that legal segregation created a sense of inferiority that tended "to retard the educational and mental development of Negro children and to deprive them of some of the benefits they would receive in a racially integrated school system."

By the fall of 1952, five cases challenging the constitutionality of racially segregated schools had been appealed to the U.S. Supreme Court. In addition to Kansas, South Carolina, Virginia, Delaware, and District of Columbia plaintiffs all argued that although the educational facilities for whites and African Americans were equal (or were in the process of being equalized), racial segregation itself was unconstitutional because it violated the equal protection clause of the Fourteenth Amendment.[6] The five cases were argued together late in 1952, and the next spring, the Court asked for a reargument in the fall term of 1953. The first part of the decision was not announced until May 1954. *Brown I,* as it came to be called, declared that racially segregated education was indeed unconstitutional. The Court then called for another reargument, this time to determine how the desegregation decision should be implemented. In May 1955, after unusually long oral arguments, the Court announced in *Brown II* that there would be a flexible timetable for desegregation, which would be overseen by the federal district courts.

What persuaded the U.S. Supreme Court to reverse its thinking after upholding the constitutionality of segregation since *Plessy v. Ferguson* in 1896? What were some of the major arguments that changed the justices' opinions?

✳ THE METHOD ✳

Whenever possible, courts make decisions based on *precedents:* similar cases that other courts have already decided that lay out a direction for new decisions to follow. As we have seen, *Plessy v. Ferguson* (1896), the case that upheld racial segregation if

6. Because Washington, D.C., is not a state, this case was argued on the basis of the Fifth Amendment.

separate but equal facilities were provided, was just such a precedent. For the next sixty years, the courts had simply decided whether the racially segregated facilities were equal and never considered the effects of segregation itself. But in *Brown v. the Board of Education of Topeka, Kansas,* and the four other cases argued at the same time, everyone agreed that the facilities were basically equal or were being equalized. The question now was whether segregation itself violated the Constitution.

Cases are argued before the U.S. Supreme Court in two stages. First, lawyers for both sides submit written arguments called *briefs*. These briefs discuss the factual background of the case and, more important, develop a legal, constitutional argument supporting the decision that they believe the Court should make. In *Brown* and the other cases, the defendants basically argued that segregated education was not unconstitutional because equal facilities had been provided, and the plaintiffs insisted, based on social science research, that racial segregation itself caused inequality in education.

With permission, organizations and individuals who are not directly involved in the case may also file briefs explaining their interest and stating their opinions about the case. Seven of these *amicus curiae* (friend of the court) briefs were filed in the initial phase of the *Brown* school segregation cases, *Brown I,* and they reflect important changes in public opinion about African Americans and equality. Eventually some two dozen *amicus* briefs were filed, including those that the U.S. Supreme Court invited for *Brown*

II from the attorneys general of all the southern states that permitted or required segregated educational facilities.

In the second stage, oral argument, lawyers speak for a limited time to clarify points in their briefs and to answer any questions the justices might have. At the time of the *Brown* case, Robert Carter and Thurgood Marshall were lawyers for the NAACP's Legal Defense and Educational Fund. Carter later became general counsel for the NAACP, and Thurgood Marshall served as a U.S. circuit court judge and then as solicitor general of the United States. He was appointed to the U.S. Supreme Court in 1967. The defense attorneys were either hired by the school system being sued or provided by the attorney general's office of that particular state. In both cases, they were paid by taxpayers' money. John W. Davis represented the defendants in the South Carolina case, *Briggs v. Elliot,* which the U.S. Supreme Court considered along with *Brown* and the three other school cases. Widely admired by other attorneys, Davis had served as a U.S. congressman, U.S. solicitor general, ambassador to Great Britain, and president of the American Bar Association. In 1922, he had declined a nomination to the U.S. Supreme Court and, in 1924, he had run unsuccessfully for president of the United States.

Finally, after considerable discussion among themselves, the justices reached a decision. Since a Supreme Court decision affects so many people's lives either directly or indirectly, it usually contains a carefully worded explanation of the Court's reasoning. Justices who do not agree with the de-

CHAPTER 9

SEPARATE
BUT EQUAL?
AFRICAN
AMERICAN
EDUCATIONAL
OPPORTUNITIES
AND THE
BROWN DECISION

cision may write a dissent, but the decision in the *Brown* case was unanimous. In this chapter, you will read the relevant section of the Fourteenth Amendment, identify the arguments used in the early *amicus curiae* briefs and the oral exchanges between the lawyers and the Court, and study excerpts from the *Brown I* decision to explain why the Supreme Court decided that racially segregated education was unconstitutional.

✳ THE EVIDENCE ✳

Source 1 from United States Constitution, Fourteenth Amendment.

1. First Section of the Fourteenth Amendment to the Constitution.

All persons born or naturalized in the United States, and subject to the jurisdiction thereof, are citizens of the United States and of the State wherein they reside. No State shall make or enforce any law which shall abridge the privileges or immunities of citizens of the United States; nor shall any State deprive any person of life, liberty, or property, without due process of law; nor deny to any person within its jurisdiction the equal protection of the laws.

Source 2 from Justice Henry Brown, writing for the majority, *Plessy v. Ferguson,* 163 U.S. 537 (1896).

2. Excerpts from *Plessy v. Ferguson,* 1896.

[*The opinion begins by reviewing the facts of the case and denying one of Plessy's arguments based on the Thirteenth Amendment, which abolished slavery and involuntary servitude.*]

The object of the [14th] amendment was undoubtedly to enforce the absolute equality of the two races before the law, but in the nature of things it could not have been intended to abolish distinctions based upon color, or to enforce social, as distinguished from political, equality, or a commingling of the two races upon terms unsatisfactory to either. Laws permitting, and even requiring their separation in places where they are liable to be brought into contact do not necessarily imply the inferiority of either race to the other, and have been generally, if not universally, recognized as within the competency of the state legislatures in the exercise of their policy power. . . .

[*Justice Brown then stated that "colored" men were assigned to "colored" railway cars and "whites" to "white" cars, thus neither was being deprived of any property.*]

So far, then, as a conflict with the 14th Amendment is concerned, the case reduces itself to the question of whether the statute of Louisiana is a reasonable regulation, and with respect to this there must necessarily be a large discretion on the part of the legislature. In determining the question of reasonableness it is at liberty to act with reference to the established usages, customs, and traditions of the people, and with a view to the promotion of their comfort, and the preservation of the public peace and good order. . . .

We consider the underlying fallacy of the plaintiff's argument to consist in the assumption that the enforced separation of the two races stamps the colored race with a badge of inferiority. If this be so, it is not by reason of anything found in the act, but solely because the colored race chooses to put that construction upon it. . . .

Legislation is powerless to eradicate racial instincts or to abolish distinctions based upon physical differences, and the attempt to do so can only result in accentuating the difficulties of the present situation. If the civil and political right of both races be equal, one cannot be inferior to the other civilly or politically. If one race be inferior to the other socially, the Constitution of the United States cannot put them upon the same plane.

Source 3 from the *amicus curiae* briefs for *Brown v. Board of Education of Topeka, Kansas,* 347 U.S. 483 (1954).

3. Excerpts from the *Amicus Curiae* Briefs, *Brown v. Board of Education,* 1952.

AMERICAN VETERANS COMMITTEE, INC. (AVC)

The American Veterans Committee (AVC) is a nationwide organization of veterans who served honorably in the Armed Forces of the United States during World Wars I and II, and the Korean conflict. We are associated to promote the democratic principles for which we fought, including the elimination of racial discrimination. Most of us served overseas. There was no "community pattern" of racial discrimination and segregation when the

CHAPTER 9

SEPARATE
BUT EQUAL?
AFRICAN
AMERICAN
EDUCATIONAL
OPPORTUNITIES
AND THE
BROWN DECISION

chips were down and there was only the mud, the foxholes, and the dangers of the ocean and of mortal battle in the fight to preserve our Nation's democratic ideals. We believe that the segregation here involved is of the same cloth as the racism against which we fought in World War II, and that its continuance is detrimental to our national welfare, both at home and abroad.

AMERICAN JEWISH CONGRESS

The American Jewish Congress is an organization committed to the principle that the destinies of all Americans are indissolubly linked and that any act which unjustly injures one group necessarily injures all. . . .

Believing as we do that Jewish interests are inseparable from the interests of justice, the American Jewish Congress cannot remain impassive or disinterested when persecution, discrimination or humiliation is inflicted upon any human being because of his race, religion, color, national origin or ancestry. Through the thousands of years of our tragic history we have learned one lesson well: the persecution at any time of any minority portends the shape and intensity of persecution of all minorities. . . .

CONGRESS OF INDUSTRIAL ORGANIZATIONS (CIO)

. . . The CIO is an organization dedicated to the maintenance and extension of our democratic rights and civil liberties and therefore has a deep interest in the elimination of segregation and discrimination from every phase of American life.

The CIO's interest is also direct and personal. The CIO . . . is endeavoring to practice non-segregation and non-discrimination in the everyday functioning of union affairs. Repeatedly in the past this endeavor has been obstructed by statutes, ordinances, and regulations which require segregation in public dining places, public meeting halls, toilet facilities, etc. These laws attempt to require CIO unions to maintain "equal but separate" facilities in their own semi-public buildings, despite the avowed desire of the membership to avoid segregation in any form. . . .

AMERICAN FEDERATION OF TEACHERS

In a broad sense, the consequence [of segregation] is a denial of the highest ends of education, both to the dominant and minority groups. In an atmosphere of inequality, it is no more feasible to teach the principles of our American way to the white children than to the Negroes. The apparent insincerity of such teaching is as destructive to the moral sense of the majority as to the sense of justice of the minority. . . .

For if justice is relative and depends on race or color how can we teach that ours is a government of laws and not of men? And if justice is relative and considers race and color then a different flag waves over a colored school and the pledge to the flag must mean different things. The one nation is really not one nation but at least two, it is found to be divisible, and liberty, like justice, has two meanings. . . .

FEDERATION OF CITIZENS' ASSOCIATIONS OF [WASHINGTON,] D.C.

The undersigned submit this brief because our organizations represent groups of Americans in the Washington community and throughout the nation of many creeds and many races who are deeply committed to the preservation and extension of the democratic way of life and who reject as inimical to the welfare and progress of our country artificial barriers to the free and natural association of peoples, based on racial or creedal differences. We believe this to be of especial importance in the Nation's capital. We are united in the belief that every step taken to make such differences irrelevant in law, as they are in fact, will tend to cure one of our democracy's conspicuous failures to practice the ideals we proclaim to the world, and to bring us closer to that peace and harmony with other peoples throughout the world for which we all strive.

ATTORNEY GENERAL OF THE UNITED STATES

This contention [about the unconstitutionality of segregation] raises questions of the first importance in our society. For racial discriminations imposed by law, or having the sanction or support of government, inevitably tend to undermine the foundations of a society dedicated to freedom, justice, and equality. The proposition that all men are created equal is not mere rhetoric. It implies a rule of law—an indispensable condition to a civilized society—under which all men stand equal and alike in the rights and opportunities secured to them by their government. . . . The color of a man's skin—like his religious beliefs, or his political attachments, or the

CHAPTER 9

SEPARATE
BUT EQUAL?
AFRICAN
AMERICAN
EDUCATIONAL
OPPORTUNITIES
AND THE
BROWN DECISION

country from which he or his ancestors came to the United States—does not diminish or alter his legal status or constitutional rights. . . .

It is in the context of the present world struggle between freedom and tyranny that the problem of racial discrimination must be viewed. The United States is trying to prove to the people of the world, of every nationality, race, and color, that a free democracy is the most civilized and most secure form of government yet devised by man. We must set an example for others by showing firm determination to remove existing flaws in our democracy.

Source 4 from *Oral Arguments of the Supreme Court of the U.S.* (Frederick, Md.: University Publications, 1984).

4. Excerpts from the Oral Arguments, U.S. Supreme Court.

BROWN, 1952

MR. CARTER. We have one fundamental contention which we will seek to develop in the course of this argument, and that contention is that no state has any authority under the equal protection clause of the Fourteenth Amendment to use race as a factor in affording educational opportunities among its citizens. . . .

JUSTICE MINTON. Mr. Carter, I do not know whether I have followed you on all the facts on this. Was there a finding that the only basis of classification was race or color?

MR. CARTER. It was admitted—the appellees admitted in their answer—that the only reason that they would not permit Negro children to attend the eighteen white schools was because they were Negroes.

JUSTICE MINTON. Then we accept on this record that the only showing is that the classification here was solely on race and color?

MR. CARTER. Yes, sir. I think the state itself concedes this is so in its brief.

BRIGGS v. ELLIOTT, 1952

MR. MARSHALL. I want to point out that our position is not that we are denied equality in these cases [because of inferior physical facilities]. . . . We are saying that there is a denial of equal protection of the laws. . . .

So pursuing that line, we produced expert witnesses. . . .

Witnesses testified that segregation deterred the development of the personalities of these children. Two witnesses testified that it deprives them of equal status in the school community, that it destroys their self-respect. Two other witnesses testified that it denies them full opportunity for democratic social development. Another witness said that it stamps him with a badge of inferiority.

The summation of that testimony is that the Negro children have road blocks put up in their minds as a result of this segregation, so that the amount of education that they take in is much less than other students take in. . . .

MR. DAVIS. If the Court please, when the Court arose on yesterday, I was reciting the progress that had been made in the public school system in South Carolina, and with particular reference to the improvement of the facilities, equipment [curriculum], and opportunities accorded to the colored students. . . .

Now what are we told here that has made all that body of activity and learning [all the state legislatures that passed segregation laws and all the court decisions upholding segregation] of no consequence? Says counsel for the plaintiffs . . . we have the uncontradicted testimony of expert witnesses that segregation is hurtful, and in their opinion hurtful to the children of both races, both colored and white. These witnesses severally described themselves as professors, associate professors, assistant professors, and one describes herself as a lecturer and advisor on [curriculum]. I am not sure exactly what that means.

I did not impugn the sincerity of these learned gentlemen and lady. I am quite sure that they believe that they are expressing valid opinions on their subject. But there are two things notable about them. Not a one of them is under any official duty in the premises whatever; not a one of them has had to consider the welfare of the people for whom they are legislating or whose rights they were called on to adjudicate. And only one of them professes to have the slightest knowledge of conditions in the states where separate schools are now being maintained. Only one of them professes any knowledge of the conditions within the seventeen segregating states.

Rebuttal

MR. MARSHALL. May it please the Court, so far as the appellants are concerned in this case, at this point it seems to me that the significant factor running through all these arguments up to this point is that for some

CHAPTER 9

SEPARATE
BUT EQUAL?
AFRICAN
AMERICAN
EDUCATIONAL
OPPORTUNITIES
AND THE
BROWN DECISION

reason, which is still unexplained, Negroes are taken out of the main-stream of American life in these states.

There is nothing involved in this case other than race and color, and I do not need to go into the background of the statutes or anything else. I just read the statutes, and they say, "White and colored."

While we are talking about the feeling of the people in South Carolina, I think we must once again emphasize that under our form of government, these individual rights of minority people are not to be left to even the most mature judgement of the majority of the people, and that the only testing ground as to whether or not individual rights are concerned is in this Court.

BRIGGS v. ELLIOTT REARGUMENT, 1953

MR. DAVIS. Let me say this for the State of South Carolina. It does not come here as Thad Stevens[7] would have wished in sack cloth and ashes. It believes that its legislation is not offensive to the Constitution of the United States.

It is confident of its good faith and intention to produce equality for all of its children of whatever race or color. It is convinced that the happiness, the progress and the welfare of these children is best promoted in segregated schools. . . .

I am reminded—and I hope it won't be treated as a reflection on anybody—of Aesop's fable of the dog and the meat: The dog, with a fine piece of meat in his mouth, crossed a bridge and saw the shadow in the stream and plunged for it and lost both substance and shadow.

Here is equal education, not promised, not prophesied, but present. Shall it be thrown away on some fancied question of racial prestige?

MR. MARSHALL. It gets me . . . to one of the points that runs throughout the argument . . . on the other side, and that is that they deny that there is any race prejudice involved in these cases. They deny that there is any intention to discriminate.

But throughout the brief and throughout the argument they not only recognize that there is a race problem involved, but they emphasize that that is the whole problem. And for the life of me, you can't read the debates [about the passage of the Fourteenth Amendment], even the sections they rely on, without an understanding that the Fourteenth Amendment took away from the states the power to use race.

7. Thaddeus Stevens (1792–1868) was a lifelong abolitionist and leader of the Radical Republicans.

As I understand their position, their only justification for this [race] being a reasonable classification is, one, that they got together and decided that it is best for the races to be separated and, two, that it has existed for over a century. . . .

Those same kids in Virginia and South Carolina—and I have seen them do it—they play in the streets together, they play on their farms together, they go down the road together, they separate to go to school, they come out of school and play ball together. They have to be separated in school.

There is some magic to it. You can have them voting together, you can have them not restricted because of law in the houses they live in. You can have them going to the same state university and the same college, but if they go to elementary and high school, the world will fall apart. And it is the same argument that has been made to this Court over and over again. . . .

Source 5 from Chief Justice Earl Warren, *Brown v. Board of Education of Topeka, Kansas, et al.*

5. Excerpts from the *Brown I* Decision, 1954.

[Chief Justice Warren began by noting that all the cases had a common argument: that segregated public schools were not "equal," could not be made "equal," and thus denied African Americans the equal protection of the laws. He then briefly reviewed the inconclusive nature of information about the intent of the framers of the Fourteenth Amendment, the separate but equal doctrine established by the Plessy *case, and the subsequent cases involving racially segregated education that had been before the Supreme Court. He concluded that the Court must focus on "the effect of segregation itself on public education."]*

In approaching this problem, we cannot turn the clock back to 1868 when the Amendment was adopted, or even to 1896 when *Plessy v. Ferguson* was written. We must consider public education in the light of its full development and its present place in American life throughout the Nation. Only in this way can it be determined if segregation in public schools deprives these plaintiffs of the equal protection of the laws.

Today, education is perhaps the most important function of state and local governments. Compulsory school attendance laws and the great expenditures for education both demonstrate our recognition of the importance of education to our democratic society. It is required in the performance of our most basic public responsibilities, even service in the

CHAPTER 9

SEPARATE
BUT EQUAL?
AFRICAN
AMERICAN
EDUCATIONAL
OPPORTUNITIES
AND THE
BROWN DECISION

armed forces. It is the very foundation of good citizenship. Today it is a principal instrument in awakening the child to cultural values, in preparing him for later professional training, and in helping him to adjust normally to his environment. In these days, it is doubtful that any child may reasonably be expected to succeed in life if he is denied the opportunity of an education. Such an opportunity, where the state has undertaken to provide it, is a right which must be available to all on equal terms.

We come then to the question presented: Does segregation of children in public schools solely on the basis of race, even though the physical facilities and other "tangible" factors may be equal, deprive the children of the minority group of equal educational opportunities? We believe that it does.

[*Warren reviewed the findings of the Court and social science literature that segregation resulted in feelings of inferiority and hindered the development of African American children.*]

We conclude that in the field of public education the doctrine of "separate but equal" has no place. Separate educational facilities are inherently unequal. . . .

[*Noting the variety of local conditions and wide applicability of the desegregation decision, Warren asked the plaintiffs, their opponents, the attorney general of the United States, and the attorneys general of the states that would be affected to appear again before the Court in reargument, stating how they believed the Court's desegregation decision should be put into effect.*]

❈ QUESTIONS TO CONSIDER ❈

The Fourteenth Amendment was added to the Constitution after the Civil War. The first section (Source 1) was intended to protect the newly freed slaves against the actions of the states, in the same way that the Bill of Rights protects citizens against the actions of the central government. What are some of the "privileges and immunities" of the Bill of Rights? What do you think is meant by "due process of law"? By "equal protection of the laws"?

In many ways, the majority opinion in *Plessy* (Source 2) reflects the American public's attitude of the late nineteenth century. What did Justice Brown say was the intent of the Fourteenth Amendment? Why did the Supreme Court believe that the 1890 Louisiana law requiring separate railway cars for blacks and whites was "reasonable"? What was the Court's response to the argument that enforced segregation made blacks inferior to whites? Read the last two sentences of the *Plessy* excerpt carefully. What did the Supreme Court say about racial equality?

The 1952 *amicus curiae* briefs (Source 3) provide important clues to changing public opinion about racial discrimination. What were the specific, major arguments of the groups representing veterans, American Jews, labor unions of the CIO, unionized teachers, and Washington, D.C., citizens' organizations? Why did the attorney general argue against segregation?

The excerpts from the oral arguments (Source 4) are from the first hearing of *Brown* and the four other cases in 1952, and the reargument ordered by the Court in 1953. Remember that Robert Carter and Thurgood Marshall were the NAACP lawyers for the plaintiffs, and John W. Davis was the primary lawyer for the defense.

What was the fundamental argument Carter established in the *Brown* case? Why was it important? What was

Marshall's major argument about the effects of racially segregated education? How did Davis respond? On what bases did Davis reject the findings of the NAACP's expert witnesses? What are the two major points of Marshall's rebuttal?

In the reargument, Davis used a story about a dog with some meat to make his point. What exactly *was* his point? How did Marshall summarize his opponents' defense of segregation? What was the point of his story about African American and white children?

Finally, analyze the arguments put forth by Chief Justice Earl Warren in *Brown I* (Source 5). What did he mean when he wrote, "We cannot turn the clock back"? Why did the Court hold that education is so important?

Now you are ready to summarize. What major arguments persuaded the Supreme Court to overturn the doctrine of separate but equal that had been established by *Plessy v. Ferguson*?

✳ EPILOGUE ✳

In less controversial cases, once the U.S. Supreme Court has announced a decision, all those affected by it comply voluntarily. Progress in desegregating the school systems, however, was slow and uneven. In some areas of the South that had practiced legal segregation, change came fairly easily and peacefully. In other areas, widespread public hostility escalated into mob violence. Some systems, such as the Prince Edward County, Virginia, school district that was part of the

original Supreme Court suits, simply abolished the public schools rather than desegregate. Ten years after the *Brown* decision, only about 10 percent of African American students in southern states were attending desegregated schools.

By the late 1960s, the federal government and U.S. court system had established new guidelines and timetables that accelerated desegregation in southern schools. Using the *Brown* decision as a precedent, the Supreme

CHAPTER 9

SEPARATE
BUT EQUAL?
AFRICAN
AMERICAN
EDUCATIONAL
OPPORTUNITIES
AND THE
BROWN DECISION

Court had also ordered the desegregation of public beaches, golf courses, and other recreational facilities throughout the South. By the 1970s, African American civil rights groups began to focus their attention on northern cities, where racially separate housing patterns had resulted in all-black and all-white neighborhood schools, but court-ordered busing of students in order to integrate education in these cities created hostility and often accelerated "white flight" to the suburbs. For example, by the early 1970s, after riots, real estate "block busting," and busing, Detroit, Michigan, had so few remaining white residents that *all* its public schools were predominantly African American.

Although the *Brown* decision did not bring about complete and immediate desegregation of all schools, its significance should not be underrated. Segregation laws based on race were struck down, and for the newly expanding African American middle class, *Brown* was a milestone, a case that established new ideals for public education. Looking back, African American leaders have said that they were greatly encouraged in their struggle for further civil rights by the decision.

In 1955, Rosa Parks set off a yearlong boycott by local African Americans after she refused to move from a seat reserved for whites on a Montgomery, Alabama, bus. Two years later, young black students were jeered at and abused when they tried to attend classes at Central High School in Little Rock, Arkansas; the national reaction caused a reluctant President Eisenhower to call out federal troops to escort these students to school.

Clearly, the *Brown* decision divided the nation and created opportunities for organizations based on racial hatred. Violent segregationists, often including law-enforcement personnel, opposed the African American freedom marches in places like Selma, Alabama, and the voter-registration drives in Mississippi during the 1960s. Yet the television and newspaper coverage of such racial confrontations also galvanized public opinion outside the South in support of such far-reaching civil rights legislation as the Civil Rights Act of 1964 and the Voting Rights Act of 1965. Today, in spite of the many accomplishments of the civil rights movement since the 1954 *Brown* decision, Americans are still striving to achieve equal educational opportunities for all.

CHAPTER

10

A Generation in War and Turmoil: The Agony of Vietnam

❀ **THE PROBLEM** ❀

When the middle-class readers of *Time* magazine went to their mailboxes in January 1967, they were eager to find out who the widely read newsmagazine had chosen as "Man of the Year." To their surprise, they discovered that the "Inheritors"—the whole generation of young people under twenty-five years of age—had been selected as the major newsmakers of the previous year. *Time*'s publisher justified the selection of an entire generation by noting that, in contrast to the previous "silent generation," the young people of the late 1960s were dominating history with their distinctive lifestyles, music, and beliefs about the future of the United States.

Those who wrote to the editor about this issue ranged from a writer who thought the selection was a long-overdue honor to one who called it an "outrageous choice," from a correspondent who described contemporary young people as "one of our best generations" to one who believed the choice of a generation was "eloquent nonsense." Furthermore, many writers were frightened or worried about their children, and some middle-aged correspondents insisted that they themselves belonged to the "put-upon" or "beaten" generation.

There is no doubt that there was a generation gap in the late 1960s, a kind of sharp break between the new generation of young people comprising nearly half the population and their parents. The first segment of the so-called baby-boom generation came to adulthood during the mid- to late 1960s,[1] a time marked by the high

1. Although the birthrate began to climb during World War II (from 19.4 births per 1,000 in 1940 to 24.5 in 1945), the term *baby boom* generally is used to describe the increase in

point of the civil rights movement, the rise of a spirit of rebellion on college campuses, and a serious division over the United States' participation in the Vietnam War. For most baby boomers, white and black alike, the war was the issue that concerned them most immediately, for this was the generation that would be called on to fight or to watch as friends, spouses, or lovers were called to military service.

Your tasks in this chapter include identifying and interviewing at least one member of the baby-boom generation (preferably born between 1946 and 1956)[2] about his or her experiences during the Vietnam War era. Then, using your interview, along with those of your classmates and those provided in the Evidence section of this chapter, determine the ways in which the baby-boom generation reacted to the Vietnam War. On what issues did baby boomers agree? On what issues did they disagree? Finally, how can a study of people of the same generation help historians understand a particular era in the past?

BACKGROUND

The year 1945 was the beginning of one of the longest sustained economic booms in American history. Interrupted only a few times by brief recessions, the boom lasted from 1945 to 1973. And although there were still pockets of severe poverty in America's deteriorating inner cities and in some rural areas such as Appalachia, most Americans had good cause to be optimistic about their economic situations.

The pent-up demand of the depression and war years broke like a tidal wave that swept nearly every economic indicator upward. Veterans returning from World War II rapidly made the transition to the civilian work force or used the GI Bill to become better educated and, as a result, secure better jobs than they had held before the war. Between 1950 and 1960, real wages increased by 20 percent, and disposable family income rose by a staggering 49 percent. The number of registered automobiles more than doubled between 1945 and 1955, and the American automobile industry was virtually unchallenged by foreign competition. At the same time, new home construction soared, as thirteen million new homes were built in the 1950s alone—85 percent of them in the new and mushrooming suburbs.[3]

New homes were financed by new types of long-term mortgage loans that required only a small down payment (5 to 10 percent) and low monthly payments (averaging $56 per month for a tract house in the sub-

the birthrate between 1946 and the early 1960s.

2. A person born during the late 1950s to early 1960s would technically be considered a baby boomer but would probably have been too young to remember enough to make an interview useful.

3. There were 114,000 housing starts in 1944. In 1950, housing starts had climbed to nearly 1.7 million.

urbs). And these new homes required furniture and appliances, which led to sharp upturns in these industries. Between 1945 and 1950, the amount spent on household furnishings and appliances increased 240 percent, and most of these items were bought "on time" (that is, on installment plans).[4] Perhaps the most coveted appliance was a television set, a product that had been almost nonexistent before the war. In 1950 alone, 7.4 million television sets were sold in the United States, and architects began designing homes with a "family room," a euphemism for a room where television was watched.

This new postwar lifestyle could best be seen in America's burgeoning suburbs. Populated to a large extent by new members of the nation's mushrooming middle class, suburbanites for the most part were better educated, wealthier, and more optimistic than their parents had been. Most men commuted by train, bus, or automobile back to the center city to work, while their wives remained in the suburbs, having children and raising them. It was in these suburbs that a large percentage of baby boomers were born.

Sociologist William H. Whyte called America's postwar suburbs the "new melting pot," a term that referred to the expectation that new middle-class suburbanites should leave their various class and ethnic characteristics behind in the cities they had abandoned and become homogeneous. Men were expected to work their way up the corporate ladder, tend their carefully manicured lawns, become accomplished barbecue chefs, and serve their suburban communities as Boy Scout leaders or Little League coaches. For their part, women were expected to make favorable impressions on their husband's bosses (to aid their husbands in their climb up the corporate ladder), provide transportation for the children to accepted after-school activities (scouts, athletics, music and dance lessons), and make a happy home for the family's breadwinner. Above all, the goal was to fit in with their suburban neighbors. Thus suburbanites would applaud the 1956 musical *My Fair Lady,* which was based on the premise that working-class flower seller Eliza Doolittle would be accepted by "polite society" as soon as she learned to speak properly.

The desire for homogeneity or conformity would have a less beneficial side as well. The cold war and the McCarthy era meant that the demand for homogeneity could be enforced by the threat of job loss and ostracism. In addition, many suburban women had met their husbands in college and hence had had at least some college education.[5] But the expectation that they be primarily wives and mothers often meant that they were discouraged from using their education in other ways. As a result, one survey of

4. Between 1946 and 1956, short-term consumer credit rose from $8.4 billion to almost $45 billion, most of it to finance automobiles and home furnishings. The boom in credit card purchases ("plastic money") did not occur until the 1960s.

5. One midwestern women's college boasted that "a high proportion of our graduates marry successfully," as if that was the chief reason for women to go to college in the first place. Indeed, in many cases it was. See Elaine Tyler May, *Homeward Bound: American Families in the Cold War Era* (New York: Basic Books, 1988), p. 83.

CHAPTER 10

A GENERATION
IN WAR AND
TURMOIL: THE
AGONY OF
VIETNAM

suburban women revealed that 11 percent of them felt that they experienced a "great deal of emotional disturbance." At the same time, men were expected to be good corporate citizens and good team players at work. It was rumored that IBM employees began each day by gathering together, facing the home office, and singing the praises of IBM and its executive vice president C. A. Kirk (to the tune of "Carry Me Back to Old Virginny"):

Ever we praise our able leaders,
And our progressive C. A. Kirk is one of them,
He is endowed with the will to go forward,
He'll always work in the cause of IBM.

Finally, homogeneity meant that suburbanites would have to purchase new cars, furniture, television sets, and so on to be like their neighbors (it was called "keeping up with the Joneses"), even though monthly payments already were stretching a family's income pretty thin.

There was an underside to the so-called affluent society. Indeed, many Americans did not share in its benefits at all. As middle-class whites fled to the suburbs, conditions in the cities deteriorated. Increasingly populated by the poor—African Americans, Latin American immigrants, the elderly, and unskilled white immigrants—urban areas struggled to finance essential city services such as police and fire protection. Moreover, poverty and its victims could be found in rural areas, as Michael Harrington pointed out in his classic study *The Other America,* published in 1962. Small farmers, tenants, sharecroppers, and migrant

workers not only were poor but often lacked any access to even basic educational opportunities and health care facilities.

Young people who lacked the money or who were not brought up with the expectation of earning a college degree tended to continue in more traditional life patterns. They completed their education with high school or before, although some attended a local vocationally oriented community college or trade school for a year or two. They often married younger than their college counterparts, sought stable jobs, and aspired to own their own homes. In other words, they rarely rejected the values of their parents' generation.

The baby boomers began leaving the suburbs for college in the early 1960s. Once away from home and in a college environment, many of these students began questioning their parents' values, especially those concerned with materialism, conformity, sexual mores and traditional sex roles, corporate structure and power, and the kind of patriotism that could support the growing conflict in Vietnam. In one sense, they were seeking the same thing that their parents had sought: fulfillment. Yet to the baby boomers, their parents had chased false gods and a false kind of fulfillment. Increasingly alienated by impersonal university policies and by the actions of authority figures such as college administrators, political leaders, and police officers, many students turned to new forms of religion, music, and dress and to the use of drugs to set themselves apart from the older generation. The term *generation gap* could be heard across the American landscape as bewildered, hurt, and angry parents confronted their children, who (in the parents' view) had "gotten everything." Nor could the children seem to communicate to their confused parents how bankrupt they believed their parents' lives and values actually were. In the midst of this generational crisis, the Vietnam War was becoming a major conflict.

The Japanese defeat of Western colonial powers, particularly Britain and France, in the early days of World War II had encouraged nationalist movements[6] in both Africa and Asia. The final surrender of Japan in 1945 left an almost total power vacuum in Southeast Asia. As Britain struggled with postwar economic dislocation and, within India, the independence movement, both the United States and the Soviet Union moved into this vacuum, hoping to influence the course of events in Asia.

Vietnam had long been a part of the French colonial empire in Southeast Asia and was known in the West as French Indochina. At the beginning of World War II, the Japanese had driven the French from the area. Under the leadership of Vietnamese nationalist and communist Ho Chi Minh, the Vietnamese had cooperated with American intelligence agents and fought a guerrilla-style war against the Japanese. When the Japanese were finally driven from Vietnam in 1945, Ho Chi Minh declared Vietnam independent.

The Western nations, however, did not recognize this declaration. At the

6. Those in nationalist movements seek independence for their countries.

end of World War II, France wanted to reestablish Vietnam as a French colony. But seriously weakened by war, France could not reassert itself in Vietnam without assistance. At this point, the United States, eager to gain France as a postwar ally and member of the North Atlantic Treaty Organization, and viewing European problems as being more immediate than problems in Asia, chose to help the French reenter Vietnam as colonial masters. From 1945 to 1954, the United States gave more than $2 billion in financial aid to France so that it could regain its former colony. United States aid was contingent upon the eventual development of self-government in French Indochina.

Ho Chi Minh and other Vietnamese felt that they had been betrayed. They believed that in return for fighting against the Japanese in World War II, they would earn their independence. Many Vietnamese viewed the reentry of France, with the United States' assistance, as a broken promise. Almost immediately, war broke out between the French and their westernized Vietnamese allies and the forces of Ho Chi Minh. In the cold war atmosphere of the late 1940s and early 1950s, the United States gave massive aid to the French, who, it was maintained, were fighting against monolithic communism.

The fall of Dien Bien Phu in 1954 spelled the end of French power in Vietnam. The U.S. secretary of state, John Foster Dulles, tried hard to convince Britain and other Western allies of the need for "united action" in Southeast Asia and to avoid any use of American ground troops (as President

CHAPTER 10

A GENERATION
IN WAR AND
TURMOIL: THE
AGONY OF
VIETNAM

Truman had authorized earlier in Korea). The allies were not persuaded, however. Rather than let the area fall to the Communists, President Eisenhower and his secretary of state eventually allowed the temporary division of Vietnam into two sections: South Vietnam, ruled by westernized Vietnamese formerly loyal to the French, and North Vietnam, governed by the Communist Ho Chi Minh.

Free and open elections to unify the country were to be held in 1956. However, the elections were never held because American policymakers feared that Ho Chi Minh would easily defeat the unpopular but pro–United States Ngo Dinh Diem, the United States' choice to lead South Vietnam. From 1955 to 1960, the United States supported Diem with more than $1 billion of aid as civil war between the South Vietnamese and the Northern Vietminh (later called the Vietcong) raged across the countryside and in the villages.

President Kennedy did little to improve the situation. Facing his own cold war problems, among them the building of the Berlin Wall and the Bay of Pigs invasion,[7] Kennedy simply poured more money and more "military advisers" (close to seventeen thousand by 1963) into the troubled country. Finally, in the face of tremendous Vietnamese pressure, the United States turned against Diem, and in 1963 South Vietnamese generals, en-

couraged by the Central Intelligence Agency, overthrew the corrupt and repressive Diem regime. Diem was assassinated in the fall of 1963, shortly before Kennedy's assassination.

Lyndon Johnson, the Texas Democrat who had succeeded Kennedy in 1963 and won election as president in 1964, was an old New Dealer[8] who wished to extend social and economic programs to needy Americans. The "tragedy" of Lyndon Johnson, as the official White House historian, Eric Goldman, saw it, was that the president was increasingly drawn into the Vietnam War. Actually, President Johnson and millions of other Americans still perceived Vietnam as a major test of the United States' willingness to resist the spread of communism.

Under Johnson, the war escalated rapidly. In 1964, the Vietcong controlled almost half of South Vietnam, and Johnson obtained sweeping powers from Congress[9] to conduct the war as he wished. Bombing of North Vietnam and Laos was increased, refugees were moved to "pacification" camps, entire villages believed to be unfriendly were destroyed, chemical defoliants were sprayed on forests to eliminate Vietcong hiding places, and troops increased until by 1968 about 500,000 American men and women were serving in Vietnam.

7. The Berlin Wall was a barricade created to separate East Berlin (Communist) from West Berlin. The Bay of Pigs invasion was a United States-sponsored invasion of Cuba in April 1961 that failed. The American role was widely criticized.

8. Johnson served in Congress during the 1930s and was a strong supporter of New Deal programs.
9. The Tonkin Gulf Resolution gave Johnson the power to "take all necessary measures to repel any armed attack against the forces of the United States and to prevent further aggression."

As the war effort increased, so did the doubts. In the mid-1960s, the chair of the Senate Foreign Relations Committee, J. William Fulbright, raised important questions about whether the Vietnam War was serving our national interest. Several members of the administration and foreign policy experts (including George Kennan, author of the original containment policy) maintained that escalation of the war could not be justified. Television news coverage of the destruction and carnage, along with reports of atrocities such as the My Lai massacre,[10] disillusioned more and more Americans. Yet Johnson continued the bombing, called for more ground troops, and offered peace terms that were completely unacceptable to the North Vietnamese.

Not until the Tet offensive—a coordinated North Vietnamese strike across all of South Vietnam in January 1968, in which the Communists captured every provincial capital and even entered Saigon (the capital of South Vietnam)—did President Johnson change his mind. Two months later, Johnson appeared on national television and announced to a surprised nation that he had ordered an end to most of the bombing, asked North Vietnam to start real peace negotiations, and withdrawn his name from the 1968 presidential race. Although we now know that the Tet offensive was a setback for Ho Chi Minh, in the United States it was seen as a major defeat for the West, evidence that the optimistic press releases about our imminent victory simply were not true.

As the United States' role in the Vietnam War increased, the government turned increasingly to the conscription of men for military service (the draft). Early in the war, all college men up to age twenty-six could get automatic deferments, which allowed them to remain in school while noncollege men (disproportionately poor and black) were drafted and sent to Vietnam. As the demand for men increased, however, such deferments became somewhat more difficult to obtain. College students had to maintain good grades, graduate student deferments were ended, and draft boards increasingly were unsympathetic to pleas for conscientious objector status.[11] Even so, the vast majority of college students who did not want to go to Vietnam were able to avoid doing so, principally by using one of the countless loopholes in the system such as opting for ROTC (Reserve Officers' Training Corps) duty, purposely failing physical examinations, getting family members to pull strings, obtaining conscientious objector status, and so on. Only 12 percent of the college graduates between 1964 and 1973 served in Vietnam. Twenty-one percent of high school graduates and an even higher percentage of high school dropouts served.

As the arbitrary and unfair nature of the draft became increasingly evident, President Richard Nixon finally

10. The My Lai massacre occurred in March 1968, when American soldiers destroyed a Vietnamese village and killed many of the inhabitants, including women and children.

11. Conscientious objectors are those whose religious beliefs are opposed to military service, such as the Society of Friends or the Quakers.

CHAPTER 10

A GENERATION
IN WAR AND
TURMOIL: THE
AGONY OF
VIETNAM

replaced General Lewis Hershey, who had headed the Selective Service System since 1948, and instituted a new system of conscription: a lottery. In this system, draft-age men were assigned numbers and were drafted in order from lowest to highest number until the draft quota was filled. With this action, the very real threat of the draft spread to those who had previously felt relatively safe. Already divided, an entire generation had to come face to face with the Vietnam War.

✳ THE METHOD ✳

Historians often wish they could ask specific questions of the participants in a historical event—questions that are not answered in surviving diaries, letters, and other documents. Furthermore, many people, especially the poor, uneducated, and members of minority groups, did not leave written records and thus often are overlooked by historians.

But when historians are dealing with the comparatively recent past, they do have an opportunity to ask questions by using a technique called *oral history*. Oral history—interviewing famous and not-so-famous people about their lives and the events they observed or participated in—can greatly enrich knowledge of the past. It can help the historian capture the "spirit of an age" as seen through the eyes of average citizens, and it often bridges the gap between impersonal forces (wars, epidemics, depressions) and personal and individual responses to them. Furthermore, oral history allows the unique to emerge from the total picture: the conscientious objector who would not serve in the army, the woman who did not marry and devote herself to raising a family, and so forth.

Oral history is both fascinating and challenging. It seems easy to do, but it is really rather difficult to do well. There is always the danger that the student may "lead" the interview by imposing his or her ideas on the subject. Equally possible is that the student may be led away from the subject by the person being interviewed.

Still other problems sometimes arise. The student may miss the subtleties in what is being said or may assume that an exceptional person is representative of many people. Some older people like to tell only the "smiling side" of their personal history—that is, they prefer to talk about the good things that happened to them, not the bad things. Others actually forget what happened or are influenced by reading or television. Some older people cannot resist sending a message to younger people by recounting how hard it was in the past, how few luxuries they had when they were young, how far they had to walk to school, and so forth. Yet oral history, when used carefully and judiciously along with other sources, is an invaluable tool that helps historians recreate a sense of our past.

Recently, much attention has been paid—and rightly so—to protecting the rights and privacy of human subjects. For this reason, the federal government requires that the interviewee consent to the interview and be fully aware of how the interview is to be used. The interviewer must explain the purpose of the interview, and the person being interviewed must sign a release form (for samples, see Sources 1 through 3). Although these requirements are intended to apply mostly to psychologists and sociologists, historians who use oral history are included as well.

When you identify and interview an individual of the baby-boom generation, you will be speaking with a member of a *birth cohort*. A birth cohort comprises those people born within a few years of one another who form a historical generation. Members of a birth cohort experience the same events—wars, depressions, assassinations, as well as personal experiences such as marriage and childbearing—at approximately the same age and often have similar reactions to them. Sociologist Glen Elder showed that a group of people who were relatively deprived as young children during the Great Depression grew up and later made remarkably similar decisions about marriage, children, and jobs. Others have used this kind of analysis to provide insights into British writers of the post–World War I era and to explain why the Nazi party appealed to a great many young Germans.

Yet even within a birth cohort, people may respond quite differently to the same event or experience. *Frame of reference* refers to an individual's personal background, which may influence that person's beliefs, responses, and actions. For example, interviews conducted with Americans who lived during the Great Depression of the 1930s reveal that men and women often coped differently with unemployment, that blacks and whites differed in their perceptions of how hard the times were, and that those living in rural areas had remarkably different experiences from city dwellers.

In this chapter, all the interviewees belong to the generation that came of age during the Vietnam War. Thus, as you analyze their frames of reference, age will not give you any clues. However, other factors, such as gender, race, socioeconomic class, family background, values, region, and experiences, may be quite important in determining the interviewees' frames of reference and understanding their responses to the Vietnam War. When a group of people share the same general frame of reference, they are a generational subset who tend to respond similarly to events. In other words, it may be possible to form tentative generalizations from the interviewees about how others with the same general frames of reference thought about and responded to the Vietnam War. To assist you in conducting your own interview of a member of the baby-boom generation (or birth cohort), we have included some instructions for interviewers and a suggested interview plan.

Instructions for Interviewers

1. Establish the date, time, and place of the interview well in advance.

CHAPTER 10

A GENERATION
IN WAR AND
TURMOIL: THE
AGONY OF
VIETNAM

You may wish to call and remind the interviewee a few days before your appointment.

2. State clearly the purpose of the interview *at the beginning.* In other words, explain why the class is doing this project.

3. Prepare for the interview by carefully reading background information about the 1960s and by writing down and arranging the questions you will be asking to guide the interview.

4. Keep most of your major questions broad and general so that the interviewee will not simply answer with a word or two ("What was your job in the army?"). Specific questions such as "What did the people in your town think about the war?" are useful for obtaining more details.

5. Avoid "loaded" questions such as "Everyone hated President Lyndon Johnson, didn't they?" Instead, keep your questions neutral: "What did you think about President Lyndon Johnson and his Vietnam strategy?"

6. Save any questions involving controversial matters for last. It is better to ask them toward the end of the interview, when the interviewee is more comfortable with you.

7. Be courteous, and be sure to give the person enough time to think, remember, and answer. Never argue, even if he or she says something with which you strongly disagree. Remember that the purpose of the interview is to find out what *that person* thinks, not what you think.

8. Take notes, even if you are tape-recording the interview (with permission). Notes will help clarify unclear portions of the tape and will be essential if the recorder malfunctions or the tape is accidentally erased.

9. Obtain a signed release form. Many who use oral history believe that the release forms should be signed at the beginning of the interview; others insist that this often inhibits the person who is to be interviewed and therefore should not be done until the end of the session. Although students who are using the material only for a class exercise are not always held strictly to the federal requirements, it is still better to obtain a signed release. Without such a release, the tape cannot be heard and used by anyone else (or deposited in an oral history collection), and the information the tape contains cannot be published or made known outside the classroom.

10. Write up the results of your interview as soon as possible after completing it. Even in rough form, these notes will help you capture the sense of what was said as well as the actual information that was presented.

A Suggested Interview Plan

Remember that your interviewee is a *person* with feelings, sensitivities, and emotions. If you intend to tape-record the interview, ask permission first. If you believe that a tape recorder will inhibit the person you have selected, leave it at home and rely on your ability to take notes.

The following suggestions may help you get started. People usually remember the personal aspects of their lives more vividly than they remember national or international events. That is a great advantage in this exercise because part of what you are attempting to find out is how this person lived during the 1960s. Begin by getting the following important data from the interviewee:

1. Name
2. Age in 1968
3. Race and sex
4. Where the person lived in the 1960s and what the area was like then
5. Family background (what the interviewee's parents did for a living; number of brothers and sisters; whether the interviewee considered himself or herself rich, middle class, or poor)
6. Educational background

Then move on to the aspects of the person's life that will flesh out your picture of the 1960s and early 1970s:

1. Was the person in college at any time? What was college life like during the period?
2. If the person was not in college, what did he or she do for a living? Did he or she live at home or away from home?
3. How did the person spend his or her leisure time? If unmarried, did the person go out on dates? What was dating like? Did he or she go to the movies (and if so, which ones)?

Did he or she watch much television (and if so, which shows)?

These questions should give you a fairly good idea of how the person lived during the period. Now move on to connect the interviewee with the Vietnam War:

1. Did the person know anyone who volunteered or was drafted and sent to Vietnam? How did the interviewee feel about that? Did the person lose any relatives or friends in Vietnam? What was his or her reaction to that?
2. *(Male):* Was the person himself eligible for the draft? Did he volunteer for the service or was he drafted? Was he sent to Vietnam? If so, what were some memorable Vietnam experiences? What did the person's family think of his going to Vietnam? *(Female):* If you intend to interview a female who went to Vietnam as a nurse, alter the preceding questions as needed.
3. Was the person a Vietnam War protester? If so, what was that experience like? If not, did the person know any Vietnam War protesters? What did the person think of them?
4. Did the person know anyone who tried to avoid going to Vietnam? What did the person think of that?

Finally, review the national events and people of the Vietnam era and develop some questions to ask your interviewee about these events and people. As you can see in this plan, you want to guide the interview through three stages, from personal information and background to the interviewee's reactions to a widening sphere of experiences and events.

CHAPTER 10

A GENERATION
IN WAR AND
TURMOIL: THE
AGONY OF
VIETNAM

❋ THE EVIDENCE ❋

Sources 1 and 2 from Collum Davis, Kathryn Back, and Kay MacLean, *Oral History: From Tape to Type* (Chicago: American Library Association, 1977), pp. 14, 15.

1. Sample Unconditional Release for an Oral Interview.

Tri-County Historical Society

For and in consideration of the participation by ___Tri-County Historical Society___ in any programs involving the dissemination of tape-recorded memories and oral history material for publication, copyright, and other uses, I hereby release all right, title, or interest in and to all of my tape-recorded memoirs to ___Tri-County Historical Society___ and declare that they may be used without any restriction whatsoever and may be copyrighted and published by the said ___Society,___ which may also assign said copyright and publication rights to serious research scholars.

In addition to the rights and authority given to you under the preceding paragraph, I hereby authorize you to edit, publish, sell and/or license the use of my oral history memoir in any other manner which the ___Society___ considers to be desirable and I waive any claim to any payments which may be received as a consequence thereof by the ___Society.___

PLACE Indianapolis,
Indiana
DATE July 14, 1975

Harold S. Johnson
(Interviewee)

Jane Rogers
(for ___Tri-County Historical Society___)

2. Sample Conditional Release for an Oral Interview.

<u>Tri-County Historical Society</u>

I hereby release all right, title, or interest in and to all or any part of my tape-recorded memoirs to <u>Tri-County Historical Society,</u> subject to the following stipulations:

That my memoirs are to be *closed* until five years following my death.

PLACE   <u>Indianapolis,</u>
              <u>Indiana</u>
DATE   <u>July 14, 1975</u>

<u>Harold S. Johnson</u>
(Interviewee)

<u>Jane Rogers</u>
(for   Tri-County Historical Society)

Source 3 from the University of Tennessee.

3. Release Form Developed by a Large U.S. History Survey Class at the University of Tennessee, Knoxville, 1984.

This form is to state that I have been interviewed by _____ on
(Interviewer)
_____ on my recollections of the Vietnam War era. I understand that
(date)
this interview will be used in a class project at the University of Tennessee, and that the results will be saved for future historians.

<u>Signature</u>

<u>Date</u>

CHAPTER 10

A GENERATION
IN WAR AND
TURMOIL: THE
AGONY OF
VIETNAM

Sources 4 through 10 are from interviews conducted by the authors. Photographs were supplied by the interviewees.

4. Photograph of John and His Family (*left to right:* John's father, John, John's mother, and John's brother).

John

[*John was born in 1951. His father was a well-to-do and prominent physician, and John grew up in a midwestern town that had a major university. He graduated from high school in 1969 and enrolled in a four-year private college. John dropped out of college in 1971 and returned home to live with his parents. He found work in the community and associated with students at the nearby university.*]

My earliest memory of Vietnam must have been when I was in the seventh grade [1962–1963] and I saw things in print and in *Life* magazine. But I really don't remember much about Vietnam until my senior year in high school [1968–1969].

I came from a repressive private school to college. College was a fun place to hang out, a place where you went after high school. It was just expected of you to go.

At college there was a good deal of apprehension and fear about Vietnam—people were scared of the draft. To keep your college deferments, you had to keep your grades up. But coming from an admittedly well-to-do family, I somehow assumed I didn't have to worry about it too much. I suppose I was outraged to find out that it *could* happen to me.

No, I was outraged that it could happen to *anyone.* I knew who was going to get deferments and who weren't going to get them. And even today my feelings are still ambiguous. On one hand I felt, "You guys were so dumb to get caught in that machine." On the other, and more importantly, it was wrong that *anyone* had to go.

Why? Because Vietnam was a bad war. To me, we were protecting business interests. We were fighting on George III's side, on the wrong side of an anticolonial rebellion. The domino theory didn't impress me at all.[12]

I had decided that I would not go to Vietnam. But I wasn't really worried for myself until Nixon instituted the lottery. I was contemplating going to Canada when my older brother got a CO.[13] I tried the same thing, the old Methodist altar boy gambit, but I was turned down. I was really ticked when I was refused CO status. I thought, "Who are you to tell me who is a pacifist?"

My father was conservative and my mother liberal. Neither one intervened or tried to pressure me. I suppose they thought, "We've done the best we could." By this time I had long hair and a beard. My dad had a hard time.

The antiwar movement was an intellectual awakening of American youth. Young people were concentrated on college campuses, where their maturing intellects had sympathetic sounding boards. Vietnam was part of that awakening. So was drugs. It was part of the protest. You had to be a part of it. Young people were waking up as they got away from home and saw the world around them and were forced to think for themselves.

I remember an argument I had with my father. I told him Ho Chi Minh was a nationalist before he was a Communist, and that this war wasn't really against communism at all. It's true that the Russians were also the bad guys in Vietnam, what with their aid and support of the North Vietnamese, but they had no business there either. When people tried to compare Vietnam to World War II, I just said that no Vietnamese had ever bombed Pearl Harbor.

The draft lottery certainly put me potentially at risk. But I drew a high number, so I knew that it was unlikely that I'd ever be drafted. And yet, I

12. The domino theory, embraced by Presidents Eisenhower, Kennedy, and Johnson, held that if one nation fell to the Communists, the result would be a toppling of other nations, like dominoes.
13. A "CO" is a conscientious objector.

CHAPTER 10

A GENERATION
IN WAR AND
TURMOIL: THE
AGONY OF
VIETNAM

wasn't concerned just for myself. For example, I was aware, at least intellectually, that blacks and poor people were the cannon fodder in Vietnam. But I insisted that *no one,* rich or poor, had to go to fight this war.

Actually I didn't think much about the Vietnamese people themselves. The image was of a kid who could take candy from you one day and hand you a grenade the next. What in hell were we doing in that kind of situation?

Nor did I ever actually know anyone who went to Vietnam. I suppose that, to some extent, I bought the "damn baby napalmers" image. But I never had a confrontation with a veteran of Vietnam. What would I think of him? I don't know. What would he think of me?

Kent State was a real shock to me. I was in college at the time, and I thought, "They were students, just like me." It seemed as if fascism was growing in America.

I was part of the protest movement. After Kent State, we shut down the campus, then marched to a downtown park where we held a rally. In another demonstration, later, I got a good whiff of tear gas. I was dating a girl who collapsed because of the gas. I recall a state policeman coming at us with a club. I yelled at him, telling him what had happened. Suddenly he said, "Here, hold this!" and gave me his club while he helped my date to her feet.

But there were other cops who weren't so nice. I went to the counter-inaugural in Washington in June 1973. You could see the rage on the cops' faces when we were yelling, "One, two, three, four, we don't want your f——ing war!" It was an awakening for me to see that much emotion on the subject coming from the other side. I know that I wasn't very open to other opinions. But the other side *really* was closed.

By '72 their whole machine was falling apart. A guy who gave us a ride to the counter-inaugural was a Vietnam vet. He was going there too, to protest against the war. In fact, he was hiding a friend of his who was AWOL,[14] who simply hid rather than go to Vietnam.

Then Watergate made it all worthwhile—we really had those f——ers scared. I think Watergate showed the rest of the country exactly what kind of "Law and Order" Nixon and his cronies were after!

I have no regrets about what I did. I condemn them all—Kennedy, Johnson, Nixon—for Vietnam. They all had a hand in it. And the war was wrong, in every way imaginable. While I feel some guilt that others went and were killed, and I didn't, in retrospect I feel much guiltier that I wasn't a helluva lot more active. Other than that, I wouldn't change a thing. I can still get angry about it.

---

14. "AWOL" is an acronym for absent without leave.

How will I explain all that to my sons? I have no guilt in terms of "duty towards country." The *real* duty was to fight *against* the whole thing. I'll tell my sons that, and tell them that I did what I did so that no one has to go.

[John chose not to return to college. He learned a craft, which he practices today. He married a woman who shared his views ("I wouldn't have known anyone on the other side, the way the country was divided"), had two children, and shared the responsibilities of child care. John and his wife are now divorced.]

5. Photograph of Mike in Vietnam.

CHAPTER 10

A GENERATION
IN WAR AND
TURMOIL: THE
AGONY OF
VIETNAM

Mike

[*Mike was born in 1948. His family owned a farm in western Tennessee, and Mike grew up in a rural environment. He graduated from high school in 1966 and enrolled in a community college not far from his home. After two quarters of poor grades, Mike left the community college and joined the United States Marine Corps in April 1967. He served two tours in Vietnam, the first in 1967 to 1969 and the second in 1970 to 1971.*]

I flunked out of college my first year. I was away from home and found out a lot about wine, women and song but not about much else. In 1967 the old system of the draft was still in effect, so I knew that eventually I'd be rotated up and drafted—it was only a matter of time before they got me.

My father served with Stilwell in Burma and my uncle was career military. I grew up on a diet of John Wayne flics. I thought serving in the military was what was expected of me. The Marines had some good options—you could go in for two years and take your chances on the *possibility* of not going to Vietnam. I chose the two-year option. I thought what we were doing in Vietnam was a noble cause. My mother was against the war and we argued a lot about it. I told her that if the French hadn't helped us in the American Revolution, then we wouldn't have won. I sincerely believed that.

I took my six weeks of basic training at Parris Island [South Carolina]. It was sheer hell—I've never been treated like that in my life. Our bus arrived at Parris Island around midnight, and we were processed and sent to our barracks. We had just gotten to sleep when a drill instructor threw a thirty-two gallon garbage can down the center of the barracks and started overturning the metal bunks. We were all over the floor and he was screaming at us. It was that way for six weeks—no one ever talked to us, they shouted. And all our drill instructors geared our basic training to Vietnam. They were always screaming at us, "You're going to go to Vietnam and you're gonna f—— up and you're gonna die."

Most of the people in basic training with me were draftees. My recruiter apologized to me for having to go through boot camp with draftees. But most of the guys I was with were pretty much like me. Oh, there were a few s—— birds, but not many. We never talked about Vietnam—there was no opportunity.

There were a lot of blacks in the Corps and I went through basic training with some. But I don't remember any racial tension until later. There were only two colors in the Marine Corps: light green and dark green. My parents drove down to Parris Island to watch me graduate from basic training, and they brought a black woman with them. She was from Memphis and was the wife of one of the men who graduated with me.

After basic training I spent thirteen weeks in basic infantry training at Camp Lejeune [North Carolina]. Lejeune is the armpit of the world. And the harassment didn't let up—we were still called "scumbag" and "hairbag" and "whale——." I made PFC [private first class] at Lejeune. I was an 03-11 [infantry rifleman].

From Lejeune [after twenty days' home leave] I went to Camp Pendleton [California] for four-week staging. It was at Pendleton where we adjusted our training at Parris Island and Lejeune to the situation in Vietnam. I got to Vietnam right after Christmas 1967.

It was about this time that I became aware of antiwar protests. But as far as I was concerned they were a small minority of malcontents. They were the *protected,* were deferred or had a daddy on the draft board. I thought, "These people are disloyal—they're selling us down the drain."

We were not prepared to deal with the Vietnamese people at all. The only two things we were told was don't give kids cigarettes and don't pat 'em on the heads. We had no cultural training, knew nothing of the social structure or anything. For instance, we were never told that the Catholic minority controlled Vietnam and they got out of the whole thing—we did their fighting for them, while they stayed out or went to Paris or something. We had a Catholic chaplain who told us that it was our *duty* to go out and kill the Cong,[15] that they stood against Christianity. Then he probably went and drank sherry with the top cats in Vietnam. As for the majority of Vietnamese, they were as different from us as night and day. To be honest, I still hate the Vietnamese SOBs.

The South Vietnamese Army was a mixed bag. There were some good units and some bad ones. Most of them were bad. If we were fighting alongside South Vietnam units, we had orders that if we were overrun by Charley[16] that we should shoot the South Vietnamese first—otherwise we were told they'd turn on us.

I can't tell you when I began to change my mind about the war. Maybe it was a kind of maturation process—you can only see so much death and suffering until you begin to wonder what in hell is going on. You can only live like a nonhuman so long.

I came out of country[17] in January of 1969 and was discharged not too long after that. I came home and found the country split over the war. I thought, "Maybe there *was* something to this antiwar business after all." Maybe these guys protesting in the streets weren't wrong.

15. "Cong" is short for *Vietcong,* also known as the VC.
16. "Charley" is a euphemism for *Vietcong.*
17. "Country" means Vietnam.

CHAPTER 10

A GENERATION
IN WAR AND
TURMOIL: THE
AGONY OF
VIETNAM

But when I got back home, I was a stranger to my friends. They didn't want to get close to me. I could feel it. It was strange, like the only friends I had were in the Marine Corps. So I re-upped[18] in the Marines and went back to Vietnam with a helicopter squadron.

Kent State happened when I was back in Vietnam. They covered it in *Stars and Stripes*.[19] I guess that was a big turning point for me. Some of the other Marines said, "Hooray! Maybe we should kill more of them!" That was it for me. Those people at Kent State were killed for exercising the same rights we were fighting for for the Vietnamese. But I was in the minority— most of the Marines I knew approved of the shootings at Kent State.

Meanwhile I was flying helicopters into Cambodia every day. I used pot to keep all that stuff out of my mind. Pot grew wild in Vietnam, as wild as the hair on your ass. The Army units would pick it and send it back. The first time I was in Vietnam nobody I knew was using. The second time there was lots of pot. It had a red tinge, so it was easy to spot.

But I couldn't keep the doubts out of my mind. I guess I was terribly angry. I felt betrayed. I would have voted for Lyndon Johnson—when he said we should be there, I believed him. The man could walk on water as far as I was concerned. I would've voted for Nixon in '68, the only time I ever voted Republican in my life. I believed him when he said we'd come home with honor. So I'd been betrayed twice, and Kent State and all that was rattling around in my head.

I couldn't work it out. I was an E5 [sergeant], but got busted for fighting and then again for telling off an officer. I was really angry.

It was worse when I got home. I came back into the Los Angeles airport and was spit on and called a baby killer and a mother raper. I really felt like I was torn between two worlds. I guess I was. I was smoking pot.

I went back to school. I hung around mostly with veterans. We spoke the same language, and there was no danger of being insulted or ridiculed. We'd been damn good, but nobody knew it. I voted for McGovern in '72—he said we'd get out no matter what. Some of us refused to stand up one time when the national anthem was played.

What should we have done? Either not gotten involved at all or go in with the whole machine. With a different attitude and tactics, we could have *won*. But really we were fighting for just a minority of the Vietnamese, the westernized Catholics who controlled the cities but never owned the back-country. No, I take that back. There was no way in hell we could have won that damned war and won anything worth winning.

18. "Re-upped" means reenlisted.
19. *Stars and Stripes* is a newspaper written and published by the armed forces for service personnel.

I went to Washington for the dedication of the Vietnam Veterans Memorial. We never got much of a welcome home or parades. The dedication was a homecoming for me. It was the first time I got the whole thing out of my system. I cried, and I'm not ashamed. And I wasn't alone.

I looked for the names of my friends. I couldn't look at a name without myself reflected back in it [the wall].

One of the reasons I went back to school was to understand that war and myself. I've read a lot about it and watched a lot of TV devoted to it. I was at Khe Sanh and nobody could tell about that who wasn't there. There were six thousand of us. Walter Cronkite said we were there for seventy-two days. I kept a diary—it was longer than that. I'm still reading and studying Vietnam, trying to figure it all out.

[*Mike returned to college, repeated the courses he had failed, and transferred to a four-year institution. By all accounts, he was a fine student. Mike is now employed as a park ranger. He is married, and he and his wife have a child. He is considered a valuable, respected, and popular member of his community. He rarely speaks of his time in the service.*]

CHAPTER 10

A GENERATION
IN WAR AND
TURMOIL: THE
AGONY OF
VIETNAM

6. Photograph of M.M., Boot Camp Graduation.

M.M.[20]

[*M.M. was born in 1947 and grew up in a midsize southern city. He graduated from high school in 1965. A standout in high school football, he could not get an athletic scholarship to college because of low grades. As a result, he joined the United States Army two months after graduating from high school to take advantage of the educational benefits he would get upon his discharge. He began his basic training in early September 1965.*]

I went into the service to be a soldier. I was really gung ho. I did my basic training at Fort Gordon [Georgia], my AIT [advanced infantry training] at

20. Since M.M.'s first name is Mike, his initials are used here to avoid confusion with Mike in Source 5.

Ford Ord [California], and Ranger school and Airborne at Fort Benning [Georgia].

All of this was during the civil rights movement. I was told that, being black, I had a war to fight at home, not in Vietnam. That got me uptight, because that wasn't what I wanted to do—I'd done some of that in high school.[21] I had one mission accomplished, and was looking for another.

A lot of guys I went into the service with didn't want to go to Nam—they were afraid. Some went AWOL. One guy jumped off the ship between Honolulu and Nam and drowned. Another guy shot himself, trying to get a stateside wound. He accidentally hit an artery and died. Most of us thought they were cowards.

I arrived in Nam on January 12, 1966. I was three days shy of being eighteen years old. I was young, gung ho, and mean as a snake. I was with the Twenty-fifth Infantry as a machine gunner and rifleman. We went out on search and destroy missions.

I did two tours in Vietnam, at my own request. You could make rank[22] faster in Nam and the money was better. I won two silver stars and three bronze stars. For my first silver star, I knocked out two enemy machine guns that had two of our platoons pinned down. They were drawing heavy casualties. The event is still in my mind. Two of the bronze stars I put in my best friend's body bag. I told him I did it for him.

I had a friend who died in my arms, and I guess I freaked a little bit. I got busted[23] seven times. They [the army] didn't like the way I started taking enemy scalps and wearing them on my pistol belt. I kept remembering my friend.

I didn't notice much racial conflict in Nam. In combat, everybody seemed to be OK. I fought beside this [white] guy for eleven months; we drank out of the same canteen. When I got home, I called this guy's house. His mother said, "We don't allow our son to associate with niggers." In Vietnam, I didn't run into much of that.

The Vietnamese hated us. My first day in Vietnam, Westmoreland[24] told us that underneath every Vietnamese was an American. I thought, "What drug is he on?" But they hated us. When we weren't on the scene, the enemy would punish them for associating with us. They would call out to us, "G.I. Number Ten."[25] They were caught between a rock and a hard place.

21. M.M. participated in sit-ins to integrate the city's lunch counters and movie theaters.
22. "Make rank" means to earn promotions.
23. "Busted" means demoted.
24. General William Westmoreland was an American commander in Vietnam.
25. "Number Ten" means bad or no good.

CHAPTER 10

A GENERATION
IN WAR AND
TURMOIL: THE
AGONY OF
VIETNAM

We could have won the war several times. The Geneva Convention[26] wouldn't let us, and the enemy had the home court advantage. To win, it would have taken hard soldiering, but we could have done it. America is a weak country because we want to be everybody's friend. We went in there as friends. We gave food and stuff to the Vietnamese and we found it in the hands of the enemy. We just weren't tough enough.

I got out of the Army in 1970. I was thinking about making the Army a career, and was going to re-enlist. But when they wanted me to go back for a third tour in Vietnam, I got out. Hell, everybody told me I was crazy for doing two.

[*M.M. used his GI Bill benefits to obtain three years of higher education: two years at 2 four-year colleges and one year at a business school. According to him, however, jobs were "few and far between." He described himself as "restless" and reported that automobile backfires still frightened him. He was married and divorced twice. In 1999, M.M. died at the age of fifty-two.*]

7. Photograph of Eugene *(second from right)* Marching.

26. "The Geneva Convention" refers to international agreements for the conduct of war and the treatment of prisoners. The agreements began to be drawn up in the 1860s.

Eugene

[Eugene was born in 1948 in a large city on the West Coast. He graduated from high school in June 1967 and was drafted in August. Initially rejected because of a hernia, he had surgery to correct that problem and then enlisted in the Marine Corps.]

It was pretty clear from basic training on, no ifs, ands, or buts, that we were going to Vietnam. The DIs[27] were all Vietnam vets, so we were told what to expect when we got there. They'd tell us what to do and all we had to do was do it.

I got to Vietnam in June of 1968. Over there, the majority of blacks stuck together because they had to. In the field was a different story, but in the rear you really caught it. Blacks would catch hell in the rear—fights and things like that. When we went to the movies with Navy guys, they put us in the worst seats. Sometimes they just wanted to start a fight. My whole time in Vietnam I knew only two black NCOs[28] and none above that.

We were overrun three times. You could tell when we were going to get hit when the Vietnamese in our camp (who cleaned up hooches) disappeared. Usually Charley had informants inside our base, and a lot of info slipped out. They were fully aware of our actions and weapons.

When we were in the rear, we cleaned our equipment, wrote letters home, went to movies, and thought a lot about what we'd do when we got out. I had training in high school as an auto mechanic, and I wanted to start my own business.

You had to watch out for the rookies until they got a feel for what was going on. We told one new L.T.,[29] "Don't polish your brass out here or you'll tip us off for sure." He paid us no mind and Charley knocked out him and our radio man one night.

You could get anything over there you wanted [drugs]. Marijuana grew wild in the bush. Vietnamese kids would come up to you with a plastic sandwich bag of twenty-five [marijuana] cigarettes for five dollars. It was dangerous, but we smoked in the bush as well as out. At the O.P.s,[30] everybody knew when the officer would come around and check. We'd pass the word: "Here comes the Man." That's why a lot of guys who came back were so strung out on drugs. And opium—the mamasans[31] had purple teeth because of it.

27. "DIs" are drill instructors.
28. "NCOs" are noncommissioned officers or sergeants.
29. "L.T." refers to a lieutenant.
30. "O.P.s" are outposts.
31. "Mamasans" refers to elderly Vietnamese women.

CHAPTER 10

A GENERATION
IN WAR AND
TURMOIL: THE
AGONY OF
VIETNAM

We could have won the war anytime we wanted to. We could have wiped that place off the map. There was a lot of talk that that's what we should have done. But we didn't because of American companies who had rubber and oil interests in Vietnam, and no telling what else. To them, Vietnam was a money-making thing. We were fighting over there to protect those businesses.

It was frustrating. The Army and Marines were ordered to take Hill 881 and we did, but it was costly. A couple of weeks later we just up and left and gave it back.

When I got out [in January 1970], I was a E5.[32] I couldn't find a job. So I talked to an Air Force recruiter. I got a release from the Marines[33] and joined the Air Force. I rigged parachutes and came out in 1975.

I stayed in L.A.[34] until 1977. Then I became a long-distance truck driver. I was doing pretty good when I got messed up in an accident. My truck jackknifed on ice in Pennsylvania and I hit the concrete barrier.

[*Eugene has not worked regularly since the accident and he sued the trucking company. He is divorced.*]

32. "E5" means sergeant.
33. Eugene had four years of reserve obligation.
34. Los Angeles, California.

8. Photograph of Helen *(left)* at an Army Hospital in Phu Bai, South Vietnam.

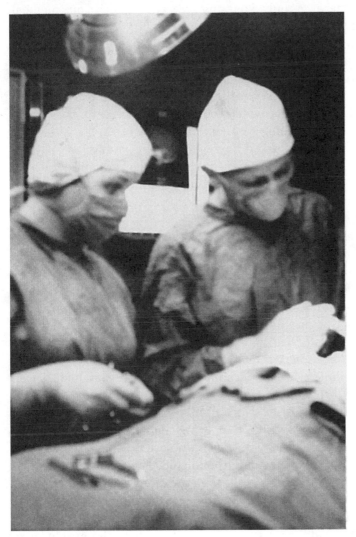

Helen

[Helen was born in 1942 in Cleveland, Ohio, and grew up there. Since grade school, she had wanted to be a nurse. After graduation from high school, she spent three years in nurses' training to become a registered nurse. She worked for three years in the operating rooms of a major medical facility in Cleveland. In 1966, she joined the United States Navy.]

[279]

CHAPTER 10

A GENERATION
IN WAR AND
TURMOIL: THE
AGONY OF
VIETNAM

I joined the Navy in 1966 and reported to Newport, Rhode Island, for basic training. Our classes consisted of military protocol, military history, and physical education. There was only a passing reference made to our medical assignments and what was expected of us.

I was assigned to the Great Lakes Naval Hospital [outside Chicago]. Although I had been trained and had experience as an operating room surgical nurse, at first I was assigned to the orthopedic wards. It was there that I got my first exposure to mass casualties [from Vietnam]. Depending on the extent of their injuries, we would see patients at Great Lakes about seven to ten days after them being wounded in Vietnam.

I became attached to some of the boys—they were young, scared and badly injured. I remember a Negro who in tears asked for his leg to be taken off—he couldn't stand the smell of it anymore and had been to surgery once too often for the removal of dead tissue. He was in constant pain.

On the wards, we always kept nightlights on. If someone darkened a ward by accident, it produced a sense of terror in the patients. Many were disoriented, and a lot had nightmares.

When I made the decision to go to Vietnam, I volunteered in 1968 and requested duty aboard a hospital ship. It was necessary to extend my time on active duty in order to go. I felt I had a skill that was needed and it was something I felt I personally had to do. I didn't necessarily agree with our policy on being there, but that wasn't the point.

The median age of our troops in Vietnam was nineteen years old. It was like treating our kid brothers. I would have done as much for my own brothers. I know this sounds idealistic, but that's the way I felt then.

The troops got six weeks of staging, preparing them for duty in Vietnam. Most of the nurses were given no preparation, no orientation as to what to expect when you go into a war zone. No one said, "These are the things you'll see," or "These are the things you'll be expected to do."

I was assigned to the U.S.S. *Sanctuary,* which was stationed outside of Da Nang harbor. The *Sanctuary* was a front-line treatment facility. Casualties were picked up in the field combat areas and then brought by Medevac choppers to the ship. During our heaviest months, we logged over seven hundred patient admissions per month. That was at the height of the Tet offensive in January through March, 1968. I had just gotten to Vietnam.

It was terribly intense. There was nothing to shelter you, no one to hold your hand when mass casualties came in. If you had time to think, you'd have thought, "My God, how am I to get through this?" We dealt with multiple amputations, head injuries, and total body trauma. Sometimes injuries were received from our own people caught in crossfires. When all hell breaks loose at night in the jungle, a nineteen-year-old boy under ambush will fire at anything that moves.

How do you insulate yourself against all this? We relaxed when we could, and we put a lot of stock in friendships (the corpsmen were like our kid brothers). We played pranks and sometimes took the launch ashore to Da Nang. Occasionally we were invited to a party ashore and a helicopter came out for the nurses. The men wanted American women at their parties.

There were some people who had the idea that the only reason women were in the service was to be prostitutes or to get a man. Coming back from Vietnam, I was seated next to a male officer on the plane who said to me, "Boy, I bet you had a great time in Vietnam." I had my seat changed. When I got home and was still in uniform I was once mistaken for a police officer.

On the *Sanctuary,* we had Vietnamese patients too. But our guys were distrustful of them, especially children who had been observed planting mines (probably in exchange for a handful of rice). The Vietnamese were often placed under armed guard. I have friends who were nurses in country who harbor a real hatred for the Vietnamese.

I heard a story of a Vietnamese child running up to a chopper that was evacuating casualties and tossing a grenade into it. Everyone on board was killed in a split second; both crew and casualties, because they paused to help a child they thought needed them. A soldier I knew said, "If they're in the fire zone, they get killed." War really takes you to the lowest level of human dignity. It makes you barbaric.

After Vietnam, I was stationed at the Naval Academy in Annapolis to finish out my duty. There I dealt basically with college students—measles and sports injuries. It was a hard adjustment to make.

In Vietnam, nurses had a great deal of autonomy, and we often had to do things nurses normally aren't allowed to do. You couldn't do those things stateside. Doctors saw it as an encroachment on their areas of practice. I'd been a year under extreme surgical conditions in Vietnam, and then in Annapolis someone would ask me, "Are you sure you know how to start an IV?"[35] It was hard to tame yourself down. Also, in the civilian setting, mediocrity was tolerated. I heard people say, "That's not my job." Nobody would have said that in Vietnam. There, the rules were put aside and everybody did what they could. When we got back to the states, there was no one to wind us down, deprogram us, tell us that Vietnam was an abnormal situation. . . . It was as if no one cared, we were just expected to cope and go on with our lives. . . .

I guess the hardest thing about nursing in Vietnam was the different priorities. Back home, if we got multiple-trauma cases from, say, an auto-

35. An "IV" is an intravenous mechanism.

CHAPTER 10

A GENERATION
IN WAR AND
TURMOIL: THE
AGONY OF
VIETNAM

mobile accident, we always treated the most seriously injured first. In Vietnam, it was often the reverse. I remember working on one soldier who was not badly wounded, and he kept screaming for us to help his buddy, who was seriously wounded. I couldn't tell him that his buddy didn't have a good chance to survive, and so we were passing him by. That was difficult for a lot of us, went against all we'd been trained to do. It's difficult to support someone in the act of dying when you're trained to do all you can to save a life. Even today, I have trouble with patients who need amputations or who have facial injuries.

It is most important to realize that there is a great cost to waging war. Many men are living out their lives in veterans' hospitals as paraplegics or quadriplegics, who in World War II or Korea would not have survived. Most Americans will never see these people—they are hidden away from us. But they are alive.

Maybe the worst part of the war for many of these boys was coming home. The seriously wounded were sent to a military hospital closest to their own homes. Our orthopedic ward at Great Lakes Naval Hospital had forty beds, and it was like taking care of forty kid brothers. They joked around and were supportive of each other. But quite a few of them got "Dear John"[36] letters while they were there. Young wives and girlfriends sometimes couldn't deal with these injuries, and parents sometimes had trouble coping too. All these people were "casualties of war," but I believe that these men especially need our caring and concern today, just as much as they did twenty years ago.

[*On her discharge from the United States Navy in August 1969, Helen returned to nursing. She married in 1972. She and her husband, an engineering physicist, have two children. Helen returned to school and received her B.S. degree in nursing. She is now a coordinator of cardiac surgery and often speaks and writes of her Vietnam experience. She also actively participates in a local veterans' organization. When her daughter was in high school and offered her mother's services to speak on Vietnam to a history class, she was rebuffed by the teacher, who said, "Who wants to hear about that? We lost that war!" Both Helen and her daughter (who is proud of what her mother did in Vietnam) were offended.*]

36. A "Dear John" letter is one that breaks off a relationship.

9. Photograph of Nick *(right)* with Some Buddies in Vietnam.

Nick

[Nick was born in 1946 in a midsize southern city. Both his parents were skilled factory workers. Nick graduated from high school in 1964 and wanted to work for the fire department, but he was too young for the civil service. He got a job at the local utility company and married in 1966. Nick was drafted in 1967. He served in the United States Army with the First Cavalry Division.]

CHAPTER 10

A GENERATION
IN WAR AND
TURMOIL: THE
AGONY OF
VIETNAM

I suppose I could have gotten a deferment, but I didn't know they were available. My wife was pretty scared when I got drafted, but neither of us ever imagined that I would shirk my duty.

I did my boot camp at Fort Benning [Georgia]. About 80 percent of the people in boot camp with me were draftees. A number of the draftees were black. I had worked with blacks before the Army, had many black friends, and never saw any racial problems. We were then sent to Fort Polk, Louisiana, for advanced infantry training. They had built simulated Vietnamese villages that were very similar to what we later encountered in Vietnam. Overall, we were trained pretty well, but we were still pretty scared.

I arrived in Vietnam on December 12, 1967, and was assigned to go out on "search and destroy" missions. Even though I was prepared mentally, I was still very frightened. I was wounded once when we got ambushed while we were setting up an ambush of our own. Another time I got hit with some shrapnel from a 60 mm mortar. That was at 3:00 A.M. and the medics didn't arrive until 7:30.

I'm not proud of everything I did in Vietnam, but I won't run away from it either. You got so hard at seeing friends killed and things like that. We desecrated their dead, just as they did ours. We used to put our unit's shoulder patches on the VC dead (we nailed 'em on) to get credit for it.

I didn't like the Vietnamese themselves. Most of the civilians were VC sympathizers, and the South Vietnamese army just wouldn't fight. I was in some kind of culture shock. Here we were, trying to help these people, and some of them were living in grass huts. Once I asked myself, "What am I doing here?"

The highest rank I made was sergeant, but I was demoted when I caught a guy in my unit asleep on guard duty and busted him with a shotgun. I was demoted for damaging the shotgun, government property.

I got back to the States in December 1968. There were some protesters at the Seattle airport, but they just marched with signs and didn't harass us at all. Over time, I lost my hostility to the antiwar protesters, although at the time I despised them. Except for Jane Fonda[37] (who went too far), I have no bad feelings for them at all. I have a friend who threatened to run his daughter off because she had a Jane Fonda workout tape.

I'm no hero and didn't do anything special. But college students today need to know that the people who fought in that war are no less important than people who fought in World War I, World War II, or Korea.

37. Movie star and antiwar activist Jane Fonda organized shipments of food and medical supplies to North Vietnam and traveled to Vietnam during the war.

[*Nick returned to his position with the utility company. He and his wife have two sons, born in 1969 and 1972. He never talked about Vietnam and wanted to throw his medals out, but his wife made him keep them. When his sons started asking questions, he told them about Vietnam. They convinced him to bring his medals out and display them. Since returning from Vietnam, he has never voted "and never will. . . . I have no use for politicians at all." He is now enjoying retirement.*]

10. Photograph of Robyn as a College Student.

Robyn

[*Robyn was born in 1955 and raised in a Wisconsin farming town of around fifteen hundred people. Her father owned a small construction business and, like many other men in town, had proudly served in World War II. Her mother was a high school teacher. Robyn has three sisters and three brothers, none of whom served in Vietnam.*]

CHAPTER 10

A GENERATION
IN WAR AND
TURMOIL: THE
AGONY OF
VIETNAM

I remember starting to watch the war on television when I was about ten. I asked my mother, "How come they're killing each other?" She said that America was the land of freedom and that we were in Vietnam to help make the people free. As a teacher, though, she always encouraged us to think for ourselves and find our own answers.

The guys in town started going away [to Vietnam], and, in a town that size, everybody knows. When my ninth-grade algebra teacher suddenly disappeared, no adults would talk about it. Later, we found out that he had received CO status. In my town, that wasn't much different from being a Communist. The peer pressure was tremendous.

I have always believed the United States is the greatest country in the world, but it's not perfect. The more I heard about the war, the more I realized something was wrong. Although only in high school, I felt obligated to let the government know that I thought it was in the wrong. And yet at no time while I was protesting the war was I *ever* against the guys fighting it. My quarrel was with how the government was running the war.

I recall one of my first "protests." I was in the high school band and we were playing "The Star-Spangled Banner" at a basketball game. Although I stood and played with the rest of the band, I turned my back to the flag. When I came home that night, my father hit me for being disrespectful. So much for the right to free speech we were fighting to protect.

When I left for college in 1973, one brother had just gotten a medical deferral, and another would soon be registering for the draft. The war was becoming more and more personal. I skipped classes to attend rallies and antiwar events, and I wrote lots of letters to politicians. When the POW-MIA bracelets[38] came out, I helped sell them. There were quite a few heated discussions with some protesters who thought that wearing a bracelet (my guy is still MIA) was contrary to the cause. In those days, I tended to "discuss" things in decibels.

My second year of college ended with me skipping classes to watch the televised returns of our POWs. I would have loved to hug each one, so this was my way of saying "Welcome home" and to bear witness. I cried the whole time—for them, for their families, and for all the agony we'd all gone through during the war. Then I dropped out of school and just "vegetated" for a year. My idealistic perceptions of humanity had been severely challenged, and I was drained.

After Vietnam, I got involved in some projects that were targets to help Vietnam vets. One of my best and proudest experiences will always be my

38. Bracelets bearing the names of American POWs (prisoners of war) and MIAs (soldiers missing in action) were worn to remember these soldiers left behind in Vietnam and to urge the United States government to act on securing their return home.

work at the Vietnam Veterans Memorial in Washington, D.C. I worked at the wall as a volunteer every week for almost ten years. Unlike past memorials, this one doesn't honor the war. It's the Vietnam *Veterans* Memorial, not War Memorial, and it honors those who fought it.

I have seen firsthand its healing effects on vets and their families. And on me. At the wall, the former protester and the Vietnam veteran share something in common—our great sadness for those who were lost and those who haven't yet returned. Vietnam vets also don't seem to have the glorified view of war that older vets do.

The government's lack of support for Vietnam vets (during and after the war) might be part of the reason. If more people were aware of the other side of war, the side the vets saw, they'd have a lot more incentive to work things out. Instead of seeing war as an alternative solution, people would finally realize that war is simply the result of our failure to find a solution.

[*Robyn returned to college and eventually graduated from law school. She worked in Washington, D.C., for a nonprofit education organization and as a government relations consultant. Robyn now works at a public and government relations firm. She continues to work with Vietnam veterans and, in particular, on the POW-MIA issue.*]

❋ QUESTIONS TO CONSIDER ❋

The interviews in this chapter were conducted between 1985 and 1992. As you read through the seven interviews, try to get a sense of the tone and general meaning of each one. Then try to establish the respective frames of reference for the interviewees by comparing and contrasting their backgrounds. From which socioeconomic class does each person come? From what region of the country? What do you know about the interviewee's parents and friends? What did the person think was expected of him or her? Why?

After high school, all the interviewees' experiences diverged greatly. Eventually, Mike, M.M., Eugene, and Helen enlisted in the armed services. What reason did each of them give (if any) for enlisting? How different were their reasons? For his part, Nick was drafted. What was his reaction to being drafted?

Both John and Robyn became involved in antiwar protests, but for very different reasons. Why did each become involved? Would John and Robyn have agreed on why the war should have been opposed?

Return to the five veterans. What were their feelings about the Vietnamese people? What did they believe were the reasons for American involvement in the war? What were their reactions to events of the time—the draft, antiwar protests, Kent State, and race relations in the armed services? What were their feelings about their respective roles in Vietnam? What did they think about the situation of returning veterans? Some of the interviewees seem to have made the adjustment to civilian life better than others. Can you think of why that might have been so? Finally, what do you think each of the seven veterans or civilians learned from his or her personal experiences during the Vietnam War era?

Now look at the photographs closely. Are they posed or unposed? For whom might they have been intended? What image of each person is projected? How does each person help to create that image?

Now consider carefully the interview that you conducted. You have done some important historical work by creating this piece of oral evidence. Now you must analyze it. What does your interview mean? In other words, how does it fit into or modify what you know about the Vietnam era? Begin by comparing and contrasting your interview with those in this chapter. Do the same with the interviews conducted by other students in your class. What major similarities and differences can you identify in the responses to the Vietnam War among members of this birth cohort? Do you see any patterns based on race, geographic region, socioeconomic class, or other factors? If so, describe and explain these patterns.

The majority of the people we interviewed had never met one another. Do you think they could meet and talk today about the Vietnam era? What might such a conversation be like?

EPILOGUE

In the spring of 1971, fifteen thousand antiwar demonstrators disrupted daily activities in the nation's capital by blocking the streets with trash, automobiles, and their own bodies. Twelve thousand were arrested, but the protest movement across the country continued. In June, the Pentagon Papers, a secret 1967 government study of the Vietnam War, was published in installments by the *New York Times*. The Pentagon Papers revealed that government spokespersons had lied to the American public about several important events, particularly about the Gulf of Tonkin incident.

As part of his reelection campaign in 1972, President Nixon traveled first to China and then to the Soviet Union and accelerated the removal of American troops from Vietnam. "Peace," his adviser Henry Kissinger announced, "is at hand." Withdrawal was slow and painful and created a new group of refugees—those Vietnamese who had supported the Americans in South Vietnam. Nixon became mired in the Watergate scandal and resigned from office in 1974 under the threat of impeachment. The North Vietnamese entered Saigon in the spring of 1975 and began a "pacification" campaign of their own in neighboring Cambodia.

Nixon's successors, Gerald Ford and Jimmy Carter, offered amnesty plans that a relatively small number of draft violators used. Many who were reported missing in action (MIA) in Vietnam were never found, either dead or alive. The draft was replaced by a new concept, the all-volunteer army.

The Vietnam veterans who had no homecoming parades upon their return and who had been alternately ignored and maligned finally got their memorial. A stark, simple, shiny black granite wall engraved with the names of 58,000 war dead, the monument is located on the mall near the Lincoln Memorial in Washington, D.C. The idea came from Jan Scruggs (the son of a milkman), a Vietnam veteran who was wounded and decorated for bravery when he was nineteen years old. The winning design was submitted by twenty-year-old Maya Lin, an undergraduate architecture student at Yale University. A representational statue designed by thirty-eight-year-old Frederick Hart, a former antiwar protester, stands near the wall of names, along with a statue dedicated to the nurses who served in Vietnam. All one hundred U.S. senators cosponsored the gift of public land, and the money to build the memorial was raised entirely through 650,000 individual public contributions. Not everyone was pleased by the memorial, and some old emotional wounds were reopened. Yet more than 150,000 people attended the dedication ceremonies on Veterans Day 1982, and the Vietnam veterans paraded down Constitution Avenue. Millions of Americans have already viewed the monument, now one of Washington's most visited memorials.

As for the baby boomers, many have children old enough to have served in Operation Desert Storm. Many have put their Vietnam-era experiences behind them as they pursue careers, enjoy middle age, and wait for grandchildren (a new birth cohort). For many, however, Vietnam is a chapter in American history that will never be closed.

11

A Nation of Immigrants:
The Fourth Wave in California

❋ THE PROBLEM ❋

In the late nineteenth century, the French contributed a quarter of a million dollars toward the construction of a monument intended to commemorate Franco-American friendship and shared democratic ideals. The rest of the money, nearly a half million dollars, was raised in the United States. The site was on an island in New York Harbor, where sculptor Frederic Auguste Bartholdi created an enormous statue of a woman holding a burning torch in a raised hand. Measuring 305 feet from her pedestal to the top of her head, the Statue of Liberty was dedicated in the fall of 1886 to great public acclaim.

The inscription on the statue's pedestal was taken from a poem written by Emma Lazarus for a literary auction, one of the many fundraising events held to aid the construction of the statue. Lazarus was one of thirteen children born to a prosperous Jewish family, descendants of seventeenth-century Portuguese immigrants. Shy, quiet, and sheltered, she published her first book of poetry at age eighteen. She later wrote and published more poetry, novels, plays, and magazine articles, as well as important English translations of Hebrew literature. In spite of her prolific literary output, however, Lazarus is best remembered for the few lines of her poetry that many generations of school children had to memorize:

> . . . Give me your tired, your poor,
> Your huddled masses yearning to
> breathe free,
> The wretched refuse of your teeming
> shore.

Send these, the homeless, tempest-
  tost to me.
I lift my lamp beside the golden door![1]

The Statue of Liberty immediately became a symbol of hope and of economic, political, and social opportunity for the millions of southern and eastern European immigrants who poured into the United States from the late nineteenth century until the outbreak of World War I. Ironically, however, by the 1920s, the United States had drastically curtailed immigration, a policy that basically continued until the 1960s. As immigration restrictions were eased in the 1960s, it became obvious that the origins of the immigrants had shifted. Of course, some Europeans continued to emigrate, but the so-called fourth-wave of immigrants came primarily from Latin America, Asia, and the Pacific Islands.

In this chapter, you will look at some of these fourth-wave immigrants in California. Why did they come to the United States? What were their lives like once they arrived here? Does the United States still offer the "golden door" of opportunity promised by the verse on the Statue of Liberty's pedestal?

✳ BACKGROUND ✳

The United States has been described as a "nation of immigrants" or a "nation of nations"—and for good reason. The first wave of immigrants included the great voluntary migrations of English and northwestern Europeans as well as the involuntary emigration of enslaved Africans during the seventeenth century. In the second wave, the Protestant Scotch-Irish who came to North America in the early nineteenth century were joined by nearly two million Roman Catholic Irish trying to escape poverty and the potato famine in the 1840s and 1850s. Also included in this second wave of immigration were the Germans, many of whom were fleeing the political revolutions of the 1840s. Somewhat better off financially than the Irish, German immigrants often established small businesses or became independent farmers. Nevertheless, the Irish and Germans of the second wave of immigration tended to cluster in visible communities and display definite ethnic identities and cultural activities. The Irish were further set apart by their extreme poverty and Catholicism. Early nativist movements, such as the Know Nothing Party, were a reaction against the second-wave immigrants.

The rapid industrialization of the post–Civil War era created a nearly insatiable demand for workers at all levels of skills. Many of these jobs were filled by the "new" third wave of immigrants from southern and eastern Europe, many of whom were either Orthodox Catholic or Jewish. Arriving

1. Emma Lazarus, "The New Colossus," *Poems of Emma Lazarus* (Boston: Houghton Mifflin, 1889), Volume I, p. 203.

CHAPTER 11

A NATION OF
IMMIGRANTS:
THE FOURTH
WAVE IN
CALIFORNIA

between 1870 and 1890, with little but the willingness to work hard, more than 7.5 million immigrants moved permanently to the United States. In 1892, Ellis Island was opened to filter out people with contagious diseases, criminals, and other "undesirables," but only about 1 percent of the immigrants were turned back. Most of these new-wave immigrants lived in urban areas, crowded into tenements and slums, and often depended on the work of women and children to supplement the family income. They had a major impact on city politics, which were usually run by urban machines, and were the target of various Progressive reformers, such as social settlement workers, visiting nurses, Americanization advocates, and vice commissions.

In the West, Chinese immigrants who had worked in the mines during the gold rush of the 1850s were joined by newcomers who labored on the construction of the railroads and in small businesses and agriculture. Different from the dominant Anglo pattern in culture, religion, and sometimes race, these third-wave immigrants from southern and eastern Europe and Asia encountered prejudice and often violence in the United States. Anti-Catholic and anti-Semitic organizations were formed in the East and Midwest; by the 1920s, the new Ku Klux Klan was active throughout the country. In the Far West, restrictive laws against the Chinese (and, later, the Japanese) culminated in the Chinese Exclusion Act of 1882. Only the personal intervention of President Theodore Roosevelt in the 1906 Gentlemen's Agreement averted a crisis

with Japan over a California school board's segregation of Japanese children.

When the massive third-wave immigration resumed after World War I in spite of a new literacy test requirement, public pressure forced Congress to limit the total annual immigration. The National Origins Quota Act of 1924 not only greatly reduced European immigration (from 850,000 in 1921 to 150,000 in 1924), but also excluded Asian immigrants totally and gave preference to people from northeastern European countries. Mexicans, who were not included in this legislation, continued to migrate to the western states during the 1920s. This restrictive immigration policy remained basically unchanged for the next forty years, with the exceptions of the occasional admission of a small number of refugees and a quota increase in the 1950s.

In 1965, without much debate, a new Immigration Act removed the quotas for various European countries and allowed family members of U.S. citizens to emigrate without being counted in the annual total. But by the 1980s, immigration was again becoming a hot political issue. About 600,000 legal immigrants, mostly Hispanics and Asians, were coming to the United States each year, while illegal (or undocumented) immigrants were estimated at another 500,000 annually. As had happened before, these fourth-wave immigrants had a visible presence, were often quite poor, and differed culturally and racially from the dominant Anglo pattern. They also had a noticeable impact on local and state politics, and opinion polls reflected the American public's concerns with such issues as crime, education, health care, and other social services.

Today, California is the most populous state in the United States, and it serves as a kind of "mirror" for what is happening in America. As contemporary observer and author Haynes Johnson has noted, California has always been "the pacesetter, the place where national cultural and political trends started."[2] The most ethnically and racially diverse state in the nation, California provides an ideal location in which to study recent immigrants and their experiences.

California's early prosperity was tied to its natural resources, which included gold, lumber, fish, salt, borax, and range land. In the latter half of the nineteenth century, California became a magnet whose population doubled every twenty years until the mid-1920s, with one-third of the increase due to the birthrate and the remainder from immigration and in-migration from states. Ethnic tensions and violence against minority groups were common.

The early twentieth century also witnessed the growth of new sectors of California's economy, such as the birth of the Hollywood film industry, the development of the oil industry, the establishment of wineries, and the rise of the agribusinesses of the Central Valley. At the same time, Progressive reformers moved to restrain the political influence of railroads and big business and began efforts to conserve some of the natural beauty of the

2. Haynes Johnson, *Divided We Fall* (New York: Norton, 1994), p. 98.

state, such as that of the Yosemite area. Ethnic tensions were still evident, however, as Chinese residents were confined to Chinatowns and Japanese residents were denied access to property ownership and education. During the depression of the 1930s, Mexican Americans along with Mexican citizens were forcibly returned to Mexico. Even the displaced "Okies" and other Americans fleeing the Dust Bowl of the Great Plains states were often barred from California's towns and cities.

The two worst outbreaks of prejudiced behavior in California occurred during World War II. The forced relocation and internment of over 100,000 Japanese, two-thirds of whom were U.S. citizens, caused them enormous psychological and financial hardship. Although most returned to California after the war, only about 10 percent of their assets remained; the majority had to start all over again. The other instance, called the "zoot-suit riots" because of the gangster-style clothes worn by some young Mexican Americans, took place in 1943, when about two hundred United States Navy sailors went on a rampage in East Los Angeles, attacking members of the neighborhood Hispanic gangs. The Los Angeles Police Department stood by and watched, maintaining that it was the job of the shore patrol and the military police to control the rioters. Only after a formal protest by the Mexican government did the riots finally end.

The cold war and the increase of defense-related industries such as aircraft and electronics benefited California economically. But the 1960s, a

CHAPTER 11

A NATION OF
IMMIGRANTS:
THE FOURTH
WAVE IN
CALIFORNIA

decade that seemed in some ways to hold out the promise of a better life for all, had a darker side, even in California. Militant Native Americans occupied Alcatraz Island in San Francisco Bay as a symbolic gesture of cultural and economic protest. Cesar Chavez, leader of the United Farm Workers, exposed the terrible living conditions and exploitation of the migrant agricultural workers whom he was trying to organize. The *bracero* (day laborer) program that had permitted "temporary" work by immigrant Mexicans ended in 1964, but illegal workers continued to pour across the border. At the same time, more public concern focused on the young people in the barrios who were deeply involved in gangs.

Preceded by smaller riots in eastern cities and followed by riots in other major cities, the Watts riot of 1965 in Los Angeles shocked many Americans with its violence and revealed poverty and despair in the midst of what had appeared to be prosperity and optimism. After an incident involving a drunk-driving arrest, African American rioters looted and burned buildings in that inner-city ghetto, where the population was ten times greater in 1965 than it had been in 1940. During the six days that the Watts riot lasted, it spread to adjoining areas, and the National Guard was called out to help contain it. Thirty-four people were killed, more than a thousand were injured, and $40 million worth of property was damaged or destroyed. In 1970, and again in 1992, more riots broke out in Los Angeles.

During the 1970s, 1980s, and 1990s, California experienced major changes in its economy, population patterns, and politics. The economy, particularly the large sector dependent on federal defense spending, plunged into a recession as cold war tensions decreased and U.S. foreign policy changed. Blue-collar jobs contracted, low-paying jobs in the service sector expanded only slightly, and, as technical and communications skills became more important for job seekers, access to good education became crucial. Continuing economic instability has contributed to the wide gap between the rich and the poor. Moreover, the uneven recovery experienced by some economic sectors and geographical regions has not spread to other sectors and regions that remain depressed.

Equally striking were changes in the population. After 1965, when the United States began to loosen immigration restrictions, the country experienced another "new" wave of immigration: from Latin America, especially Mexico, and from Asia and the Pacific Islands. For example, between 1970 and 1983, over one million Hispanics, Asians, and other foreign-born people moved to the county of Los Angeles. Because of this wave of immigration, California's population grew so rapidly that Hispanics and Asians often crowded into poorer inner-city areas such as Watts, where African Americans were already living. Conflicts increased between the African Americans and some of the newer immigrants, such as Korean store owners, and even occurred at times between earlier immigrants such as the Chinese and the newer arrivals. Beginning in the late 1960s, politics reflected the new ethnic and racial identities and awareness.

The United States Census taken in 2000 showed that Hispanics numbered 35.3 million, or almost 13 percent of the population; non-Hispanic blacks and African Americans (35.4 million) were also nearly 13 percent. The Asian population was 11.6 million, or approximately 4 percent. In comparison, the Hispanic population was 32.4 percent of the population in California; the non-Hispanic black and African American population was 6.7 percent. Asians accounted for approximately 11.2 percent of California's population. People who identified themselves as Caucasian (white) constituted 75.1 percent of the U.S. population and 59.5 percent of California's population.[3]

These figures make it clear that California has received a disproportionately large number of fourth-wave immigrants. Why do these newcomers continue to settle there? What are their lives like after they arrive? To what degree does California still serve as a land of opportunity for immigrants?

✹ THE METHOD ✹

Most of the evidence in this chapter is in the form of interviews, memoirs, or autobiographies. This kind of evidence is especially useful in giving a historical "voice" to people whose stories or viewpoints are not usually represented. Like all autobiographical material, however, these stories may not always be completely accurate. For example, they may contain exaggerations or create situations that are intended to convey a particular message to the reader or listener. Writer and poet Carlos Bulosan, a Filipino migrant farm worker in the 1930s, described riding a freight train into a little southern California town: "We were told . . . that local whites were hunting Filipinos at night with shotguns."[4] Without corroborating evidence, the historian cannot evaluate the factual accuracy of this statement, but the message—and the perception—of the author are clear.

In using the evidence in this chapter, try to identify first *why* the immigrants came and *what* their experiences were (including the obstacles they encountered). What were their goals? their accomplishments? The central question then asks you to evaluate the degree to which the opportunity to succeed in achieving their goals still exists for this newest wave of immigrants.

3. Hispanics may be of any race. For U.S. Census figures, see http://www.census.gov/index.html. For state figures, choose Quick Facts, select California.
4. Carlos Bulosan, *America Is in the Heart: A Personal History* (Seattle: University of Washington Press, 1973 [originally published 1943]), p. 144.

CHAPTER 11

A NATION OF
IMMIGRANTS:
THE FOURTH
WAVE IN
CALIFORNIA

�֍ THE EVIDENCE �֍

Source 1 from Nathan Caplan et al., *Children of the Boat People* (Ann Arbor: University of Michigan, 1991), p. 5.

1. Two Vietnamese Proverbs.

An uneducated person is like unpolished jade.

A knife gets sharp through honing; a man gets smart through study.

Source 2 from Al Santoli, *New Americans* (New York: Viking, 1988), pp. 209, 232–233.

2. Celia Van Noup, a Cambodian Refugee and Owner of the House of Donuts in Southern California.

I started this business from almost nothing at all. I named it House of Donuts, my own franchise. I spend most of my time in this shop, seven days a week. . . .

I get to the shop at 5:00 in the morning to open for breakfast, and I usually leave around 7:00 P.M. I work behind the counter, serving customers, and do the cleaning and sweeping. I work by myself most of the time. My youngest daughter, Parika, just began college, but she comes with me at 5:00 A.M. to help. At 10:00 A.M., she goes home to study, before she attends afternoon and evening classes. . . .

Another reason that I work and try to save money is to be able to sponsor my cousin and her family from Cambodia. She is just like my sister. . . .

That's one of the main reasons I want to have this donut shop and try to keep it open. There're three reasons: for my children, for my cousin's family, and for the little house that I dream of.

Whenever I can, I drive around and look at "For Sale" signs on houses. When I see a beautiful house on sale, almost new, I write down the phone number. I call up and say, "How much do you want?" They say, "It costs this much. Is this your first house? How much money do you have?" Of course, it's always too much. I don't have the money now. But the dream is always there.

I want the house not only for myself—for everybody to live in. My daughters, my relatives from Phnom Penh—they could live in the garage if we fix it up nice. We wouldn't have to pay rent and be bothered all the time. It's my American dream to have that little house.

Sources 3 and 4 from Joan Morrison and Charlotte F. Zabusky, *American Mosaic* (New York: E. P. Dutton, 1980), pp. 306, 333–334.

3. Betty Chu, a Chinese American Homemaker from San Francisco.

My son is in high school now. With him it was one big adjustment right after the other. He had to learn the different dialect in Hong Kong, and then he had to learn American here. I don't know how the guy went through it, but he never stopped behind in his class. I don't know how he did it. I just don't know how he did it. He's always been a quiet boy. He just doesn't have that many friends. It does still worry me. [*Sighs.*]

One of my son's biggest disappointments is that my daughter doesn't speak Chinese. Well, she was a year and a half when she came over, and she thought she was American all along. Now she wants to grow up to be an Italian.

Last year, December, we became citizens. The doctor at the hospital where I work invited us over for a party. He surprised us by standing up and announcing it. He said, "Something very wonderful happened last week," and told everybody that we were citizens now. He gave us an American flag as a present, and everybody drank to us. It was very heartwarming.

4. Su Chu Hadley, a Chinese American from Taiwan Living in Northern Rural California.

[*At this point in the interview, Su-Chu's two daughters come into the room to say good-bye before going to the beach. They wear bikinis and carry a picnic basket and a transistor radio. After they leave, Su-Chu looks out the window for a moment. Then she speaks softly—*]

You can't know how it makes me feel to see them go off like this. They are ten and twelve, and when I was ten and twelve I was working in the fields all day. . . . Sometimes in the evening I cry, thinking of everything that has happened, and my children say, "Daddy, how come mommy cry?"

CHAPTER 11

A NATION OF
IMMIGRANTS:
THE FOURTH
WAVE IN
CALIFORNIA

"She's remembering bad things from long ago," he tells them.

And then I look at him and at them and at my house here, and I say, "Well, at least I have a happy ending."

Source 5 from Bong-youn Choy, *Koreans in America* (Chicago: Nelson Hall, 1979), p. 333.

5. Bong-youn Choy, a Korean Restaurant Owner from Berkeley.

. . . We soon found that the restaurant business was one of the hardest businesses, but a rewarding one. My wife was the master chef and I was the manager, doing everything from marketing to janitorial work. My two sons, David and Francis, who were still in public school, helped us as dishwashers and waiters. Both of them were very good workers and became valuable assets to the business. My daughter, Cora, also helped whenever she visited us. The restaurant was open six days a week, and every Tuesday night my wife conducted cooking classes.

We worked from fourteen to sixteen hours a day. During the first six months, we lost a little money because we did not know how to run the restaurant and lacked customers.

Source 6 from Mary Paik Lee, *Quiet Odyssey* (Seattle: University of Washington Press, 1990), pp. 4, 129. Courtesy of Washington Press.

6. Photographs of Mary Paik Lee, a Korean American Store Owner, with Her Family in 1905 (Korea) and 1987 (Santa Cruz).

[In this portrait of the Paik family taken in Korea in 1905, Mary (center) is the youngest child in the picture.]

[Here, Mary (center) is shown with her sons, Tony and Allan, and two of her granddaughters, Sarah and Katie, in Santa Cruz in 1987.]

CHAPTER 11

A NATION OF
IMMIGRANTS:
THE FOURTH
WAVE IN
CALIFORNIA

[Mary Paik, her parents, and her ten siblings emigrated to California in the early twentieth century. All eleven children rose to middle-class status through hard work. Most of the next generation, their children, and almost all of the third generation, their grandchildren, attended college and entered the professions.]

Source 7 from June Namia, *First Generation* (Boston: Beacon Press, 1978), p. 179.

7. Graciela Mendoza Pena Valencia, a Mexican Agricultural Worker from Salinas.

. . . The contractor said, "You have never picked strawberries?"

"No."

"Oh! That's easy. Have big trees. You just pick the fruit off the trees."

I come here and I see those strawberries on the floor, oh! It's more hard. I came with my friend. When I come here the first day, I saw the big rooms. I feel like I'm going in jail. Only the little beds, no chair, no nothing, only the bed. For a bedspread you got a gray color. I was in a room with twelve people. . . .

I don't work now. Last year I work at celery, in the shed packing. Now, there's more good places to work. If you come here alone first, it's more complicated. When I know the place and everything, I bring my brothers and my mother and my sister. She marry a good man, they got a big house. My brother's got a new car. I was the first one to do farm work in this country. Second, my sisters; next, my brothers. Because if you here first you don't know nothing. When they come here, my husband have a good job and he help my brothers. It's more good to come like that than alone.

I like it here. I am happy with my kids, my husband, the house. . . .

Source 8 from Paul Ong, Edna Bonacich, and Lucie Chen, *The New Asian Immigration in Los Angeles and Global Restructuring* (Philadelphia: Temple University Press, 1994), p. 104.

8. Ethnic Composition of the Asian American Population, Los Angeles County, 1970–1990.

Ethnic Group	1970	1980	1990	1980–1990	Increase, 1980–1990 (%)
Chinese	40,798	94,521	245,033	150,512	159.2
Filipino	33,459	100,894	219,653	118,759	117.7
Korean	8,650	60,339	145,431	85,092	141.0
Japanese	104,078	117,190	129,736	12,546	10.7
Vietnamese		27,252	62,594	35,342	129.7
Asian Indian		18,770	43,829	25,059	133.5
Thai		9,449[a]	19,016	9,567	101.2
Other Southeast Asian[b]			31,920		
Other Asian	3,300[c]		28,349		

[a]Based on number of immigrants born in Thailand.
[b]Approximately 28,000 Cambodians, 3,700 Laotians, and 300 Hmong.
[c]Estimated from Public Use Micro Dataset.
Sources: U.S. Bureau of the Census, *Census of Population and Housing, 1970, 1980, 1990* (Washington, D.C.: Government Printing Office, 1973, 1983, 1993); and *Census of Population and Housing, 1970, 1980, 1990 Public Use Sample: 5% County Level Sample* [Computer file] (Washington, D.C.: U.S. Bureau of the Census [producer]).

Source 9 from Ivan Light and Edna Bonacich, *Immigrant Entrepreneurs: Koreans in Los Angeles, 1965–1982* (Berkeley: University of California Press, 1988), p. 274.

9. The Brief Life Story of Young Korean Gas Station Owners from Los Angeles.

Dad worked in the gas station 6 am through 12 pm at night. I worked 3 pm to 7 am. Although it was hard and tiring, we thought since we had an opportunity, we ought to work hard. . . . So finally we got the gas station on our own account. We started our own business for the first time. That night my husband and I couldn't sleep. We cried for a long time and promised each other that we would work harder. We didn't even have a bed so we were sleeping on the floor. (Life History)

CHAPTER 11

A NATION OF
IMMIGRANTS:
THE FOURTH
WAVE IN
CALIFORNIA

Source 10 from Victor G. and Brett DeBary Nee, *Longtime Californ'* (Boston: Pantheon, 1973), pp. 165–166.

10. Lisa Mah, a Chinese American Employee of the Chinatown Neighborhood Arts Program in Berkeley.

When my parents would talk about the outside being a bad place, they would refer sort of generally to "the whites out there," they always called them *sai yen*. To me, of course, that meant the whites right around us. It meant the bar downstairs where there was an Irish tavern, Cavanaugh's, that we could hear coming up through the floor every night. We'd hear this crashing, singing, people being thrown around down there, they would have brawls and they would pee on our doorstep. Every other day we would go down there with a bucket to wash it off. But at the same time my parents kept reminding us that "the whites out there," the same people who would vomit and pee on our doorstep, were the people who had the power to take our home away from us. We had to do a little placating of them. Every Easter, every Christmas, every American holiday, I would be sent on a little tour of all the local businesses. I would go to the bakery across the street, the barbershop down the street, the realty company, and the bar. I would deliver a little cake to each one. We wanted to be known as that nice Chinese family upstairs or down the street, you know, whom you wouldn't ever want to hurt in any way.

Source 11 from Ernesto Galarza, *Barrio Boy* (Notre Dame: University of Notre Dame Press, 1971), pp. 203–204.

11. Excerpt from the Autobiography of Ernesto Galarza, a Mexican American Economist and Author.

. . . We cut out the ends of tin cans to make collars and plates for the pipes and floor moldings where the rats had gnawed holes. Stoops and porches that sagged we propped with bricks and fat stones. To plug the drafts around the windows in winter, we cut strips of corrugated cardboard and wedged them into the frames. With squares of cheesecloth neatly cut and sewed to screen doors holes were covered and rents in the wire mesh mended. Such repairs, which landlords never paid any attention to, were made *por mientras,* for the time being or temporarily. It would have been a word equally suitable for the house itself, or for the *barrio*. We lived in run-down places furnished with seconds in a hand-me-down neighborhood all of which were *por mientras*.

Source 12 from Joan Moore, *Going Down to the Barrio* (Philadelphia: Temple University Press, 1991), pp. 76–77.

12. What Gang Membership Meant to Mexican American Teens in East Los Angeles.

[Teenaged boys]

To me it was my life, my one and only way. [What do you mean, "your life"?] My only mission . . . [You were all for your barrio? Could you please tell me how you felt?] Well, I felt that was the only thing going for me. It was my neighborhood. They were like my brothers and sisters. I mean, at that time, that's the only thing I had. It was them and my grandparents.

It was the most important thing in my life at that time. There was nothing that came even close to it except maybe my own personal family. But even then at the time there was no problems at the home, so my gang life was my one love.

[Teenaged girls]

The year that I was there it was like, umm, they were like family, because we would all take care of each other. . . . I think they were like my own family. I think I was more with them than my own family, because I left them for a while.

It was very important. Because that's all I had to look forward to, was my neighborhood, you know. That's all. It was my people—my neighborhood, my homies, my homeboys, my homegirls—that was everything to me. That was everything, you know. It wasn't all about my *familia;* it was all about my homeboys and homegirls.

Sources 13 and 14 from Armando Morales, *Ando Sangrando* (La Puente, Calif.: Perspectiva Publications, 1972), pp. 71, 100ff. Courtesy of Perspectiva Publications.

13. Mrs. Barba, a Mexican American: Testimony Given Before the U.S. Civil Rights Commission.

Saturday, November 9th, at about 1:30 a.m. an officer from Hollenbeck Police Station called me to go pick up my son who had been arrested for burglary. I asked him, "What time did you pick him up?" He said about

CHAPTER 11

A NATION OF
IMMIGRANTS:
THE FOURTH
WAVE IN
CALIFORNIA

10:20. I said, "Why are you letting me know so late?" He said, "Because your son fell down." I started crying. He told me, "Don't worry, it's a small cut." I believed him. The next day I knew he had lied to me. I took my son to the White Memorial Hospital. My son had 40 stitches in his head and two fractures in the vertebrae. Also, the 13th of November, he had surgery for a hernia. I have very much faith in God. I know very well Officer Beckman is lying very much about my son. But I have faith in all the people that are helping me. This, I will never forget. And I hope we can accomplish justice. This *cannot* happen to *any* other boy.

14. Photographs of a Police Recruiting Billboard (*top*) and Child Demonstrators, East Los Angeles.

CHAPTER 11

A NATION OF
IMMIGRANTS:
THE FOURTH
WAVE IN
CALIFORNIA

✳ QUESTIONS TO CONSIDER ✳

California has always been a magnet for Hispanic immigrants, the majority of whom work in the enormously productive and labor-intensive agricultural system of the Central, Imperial, and Salinas Valleys. Other Hispanics, Mexicans and Chicanos, along with Asian immigrants, live and work in cities such as Los Angeles. Although Source 7 provides some insight into the life of a Mexican agricultural worker, most of the sources in this chapter focus on the experiences of the fourth-wave urban immigrants.

First, quickly skim through all of the evidence to get a sense of the diversity among the immigrants and the variety of their experiences. Source 8 further clarifies who is included in the category of Asian immigrants. Use a piece of paper folded in half lengthwise to help organize your notes. Write one question at the top of each side of the paper: Why did they come? What were their experiences? (Be sure to include the obstacles they encountered under the latter heading).

Now go back through the evidence more slowly. What reasons are given for their immigration in the stories told by Sources 2 through 4 and 9? What work experiences are described by Sources 2, 4, 5, 7, and 9? What do the proverbs in Source 1 indirectly advise Vietnamese immigrants to do? According to Source 12, why do Mexican American teens join gangs?

Notice the difficulties encountered by the immigrants in Sources 3, 5, 7, and 9 through 14. Are there any patterns here? How did the immigrants respond to these problems? Consider also the information revealed in the photographs of Mary Paik Lee and her family (Source 6). Finally, after reviewing your notes about the fourth-wave immigrants' experiences, to what degree would you say that opportunity still exists for newcomers to this country?

✳ EPILOGUE ✳

Throughout the late 1980s and 1990s, the national debate about the impact of the fourth wave of immigration continued. Were the new immigrants a drain on our educational institutions and social services, especially our already troubled health care system? Or did the immigrants, as several studies showed, generate more through their productivity and the taxes they paid than they consumed in the form of government services? On a different, much more racist note, some groups began to complain publicly about the "browning" of the United States.

Focusing on some of the problems connected with illegal immigration, Congress has passed four major pieces of legislation in the last fifteen years. The 1986 Immigration Reform and Control Act offered amnesty and legalization to some three million seasonal agricultural and other workers. Special provisions in the Immigration

Act of 1990 facilitated entrance for highly skilled immigrants, while the Illegal Immigration Reform and Immigrant Responsibility Act of 1996 set aside new money for border patrols and made it easier to deport illegal aliens. In 2000, yet another effort was made to encourage illegal aliens to obtain visas or be sponsored for citizenship applications through the Legal Immigration and Family Equity (LIFE) Act.

As certain parts of the California economy weakened during the 1980s and 1990s, and as the racial and ethnic composition of the state's population continued to change, the backlash against the newest immigrants intensified. In 1992, Los Angeles again experienced devastating riots that began in response to the acquittal of white police officers who had beaten a black motorist. The riots expanded, however, into the looting and burning of stores owned by Asians, especially Koreans, in neighborhoods occupied by African, Asian, and Hispanic Americans. Two years later, California voters approved Proposition 187, intended to exclude illegal aliens from public schools and nonemergency medical care. Although a court challenge prevented the proposition from becoming state law, many of its provisions were later put into effect by California's governor. In 1998, Californians voted by a two-to-one margin to replace bilingual teaching with English immersion classes for immigrant children. Nevertheless, as the 2000 census made clear, fourth-wave immigrants have continued to come to California, and they will continue to influence the economic, political, social, and cultural life of the state and of our nation.

TEXT CREDITS

CHAPTER TWO

Source 3: From Edwin S. Redkey, ed., *Respect Black: The Writings and Speeches of Henry McNeal Turner* (New York: Arno Press, 1971), pp. 167–171. Reprinted by permission.

CHAPTER FIVE

Sources 17–19: From Alfred E. Cornbise, *War as Advertised: The Four Minute Men and America's Crusade, 1917–1918,* pp. 72–73, 122, 60. Copyright 1984. Reprinted by permission of American Philosophical Society.

CHAPTER SIX

Sources 1 and 6: From *The Unadjusted Girl* by W. I. Thomas. Copyright © 1923 by William I. Thomas: Copyright © renewed 1951 by William I. Thomas. By permission of Little, Brown, and Company.

Source 2: Reprinted with permission from *Current History* magazine. Copyright © 1923. Current History, Inc.

Sources 3 and 13: Excerpt from *Wholesome Marriage* by Ernest Groves and Gladys Hoagland Groves. Copyright © 1927 by Houghton Mifflin Company; copyright renewed © 1955 by Gladys Hoagland Groves. Reprinted by permission of Houghton Mifflin Company. All rights reserved.

Sources 4 and 12: Reprinted with permission from the July 6, 1927 issue of *The Nation.*

Source 8: Hager, Alice Rogers, "Occupations and Earnings of Women in History," in Annals of the American Academy of Political and Social Science, *Women in the Modern World* (Philadelphia: Sage Publications, 1929). Reprinted by permission of The American Academy of Political and Social Science.

Source 9: Andrews, Benjamin R., "The Home Woman as Buyer and Controller of Consumption," in Annals of the American Academy of Political and Social Science, *Women in the Modern World* (Philadelphia: Sage Publications, 1929). Reprinted by permission of The American Academy of Political and Social Science.

Source 14: Pruette, Lorine, "The Married Woman and the Part-Time Job" in Annals of the American Academy of Political and Social Science, *Women in the Modern World* (Philadelphia: Sage Publications, 1929). Reprinted by permission of the American Academy of Political and Social Science.

Source 16: Mowrer, Ernest, *Domestic Discord.* Copyright © 1928 by University of Chicago Press. Reprinted by permission.

CHAPTER EIGHT

Source 14: News Report of Greer Incident, *New York Times,* September 5, 1941. Copyright 1941 by The New York Times Co. Reprinted by Permission.

Source 15: Additional News Concerning Greer Incident, *New York Times,* September 6, 1941. Copyright 1941 by The New York Times Co. Reprinted by Permission.

Source 18: German Communique, September 6, 1941, *New York Times,* September 7, 1941. Copyright 1941 by The New York Times Co. Reprinted by Permission.

Source 21: Excerpts from Speech by Secretary of the Navy Frank Knox to the American Legion Convention, September 15, 1941. Copyright 1941 by The New York Times Co. Reprinted by Permission.

CHAPTER TEN

Page 256: "Ever we praise . . . " Reprinted by permission from *The IBM Songbook* copyright 1935 by International Business Machines Corporation.